The
BIBLE
for Children

The
BIBLE
for Children

Retold by Philip S. Jennings
Illustrated by Severo Baraldi

AWARD PUBLICATIONS LIMITED

Acknowledgements

Editorial Consultants

Anglican
The Reverend Canon Leonard Cragg
Blackburn Diocese

Roman Catholic
Rita Ferrone
Catechetical Office, Archdiocese of New York

Editor-in-Chief of R.C.S. Libri edition - Anna Maria Mascheroni
Illustrations by Severo Baraldi
Layout by Segni d'Immagine, Bologna
Text composition by Tony Meisel
History sidebars and glossary translated by Dany Bosek

ISBN 0-86163-817-4

Copyright © 1994 R.C.S. Libri & Grandi Opere S.p.A., Milan
English language edition © 1996 Award Publications Limited

This edition first published 1996
Second impression 1997

Published by Award Publications Limited,
27 Longford Street, London NW1 3DZ

Printed in Hong Kong

CONTENTS

INTRODUCTION

The *Bible for Children* is intended to serve as an engaging and stimulating introduction to the World's greatest book. Written especially for children aged nine or older, the splendid artwork that accompanies the over two hundred self-contained stories and prayers also makes this an easy "read-aloud" volume for younger children.

The word "Bible" means The Books. What we know as the Bible is really made up of many books written by different authors over a thousand years. The Bible has two parts: the Old Testament and the New Testament. The word "Testament" is a Latin word which translates a Hebrew term meaning "pact" or "agreement".

The Old Testament contains forty-six books, and they detail the partnership between God and the people of Israel. In the Old Testament, originally written in Hebrew, God creates the world and mankind. The journey of life begins. Adam and Eve are banished from the Garden of Eden; great leaders, like Abraham and Moses, are blessed by God to counsel and lead their people; the Israelites flee from slavery in Egypt and after many wars and hardships find the Promised Land; and David as well as many other kings and prophets struggle to establish a faith and a nation.

The New Testament is made up of twenty-seven books that tell the story of Jesus' life and explain the alliance between Jesus and humanity, as revealed by his words. The New Testament, originally written in Greek, follows the life and teachings of Jesus Christ. The Son of God is a man who lives and suffers with us and for us. He is from a humble background, and yet he is feared by kings. The resurrection shows us there is life after death, and it serves as a message of hope for all people.

The Book, chapter, and often the verse, for every part of *The Bible for Children* is always clearly indicated. And, as the Bible is a book of history as well as faith, special sidebars throughout the book explain the historical background of the events and people described. An encyclopedic glossary of people, places, and terms appears at the end of our volume.

We have attempted to simplify the standard biblical texts, while retaining as much of the essence and rhythm of the originals as possible. These familiar words, combined with Severo Baraldi's dramatic colour illustrations will engage the spirits and stimulate the imaginations of young readers everywhere.

—The Publishers

The Old Testament

The Creation
and the Patriarchs

HOW GOD
MADE THE WORLD

In the beginning God made the heaven and the earth. The earth was dark and empty, and the spirit of God, looking down from above the water, said, "Let there be light." The light appeared, and God saw that it was good. Next He separated the light from the dark, and He called the light day and called the darkness night. There was evening and morning. This was the first day.

On the second day, God said, "I will call the space above the earth heaven. This is a different place from the waters and the land beneath Me." There was evening and morning. This was the second day of creation.

On the third day, God said, "The waters beneath the sky should be in one place and the dry land in another." God called the dry land earth and the waters He called seas. From inside the earth came grass, herbs, flowers, and fruit trees, which bloomed and dropped all kinds of fruit. God saw that everything was good. There was evening and morning. This was the third day.

On the fourth day, God said, "Let there be two sources of light in the sky so that day and night are separated. And let them act as signs for seasons, days, and years. Let there be lights in heaven to shine down on the earth." And so it was. God created two powerful lights: the stronger, the sun, was to light up the day, while the less powerful light, the moon, was to shine at night. He also made the stars and placed them in the heavens to shine upon the earth, divide day from night, and separate light from dark. God saw this was good. There was evening and morning. This was the fourth day.

On the fifth day, God said, "Let the waters overflow with living creatures, and let birds fly above in heaven." God created great whales and all the different fish and birds. He saw this was good. He blessed His creatures and said, "Be fruitful and have many children. Let the fish fill the seas, and the birds fill the earth." There was evening and morning. This was the fifth day.

On the sixth day, God said, "Let the earth be a home for all sorts of animals, like cows, alligators, and tigers." And it was so. God made wild animals, cattle, and reptiles, which crawl on the earth. God saw that this was good. Then He added, "Let Us make man in Our image, and let him have management over all the animals of the sea and the earth." So God created man in His image; in the divine image he created both man and woman. He blessed them, saying, "Be fruitful and multiply, fill the earth and be master of the fish of the sea and the birds of the sky, the cattle and all wild animals that roam the earth. I have given you every plant that carries seed and every tree that bears fruit on the face of the earth. This will be your food. And to all the animals on earth and all the birds in the sky and all the creatures that crawl on their bellies, I have given green plants." And it was so. God saw that it was good. There was evening and morning. This was the sixth day.

By the seventh day, the earth and the sky were complete. On that

Opposite: In the beginning God made the heaven and the earth. The earth was dark and empty, and the spirit of God, looking down from above the water, said, "Let there be light."

God planted a garden in Eden, and there He placed the man, whose name was Adam. In the garden, God made different types of plants for Adam to grow and care for. Everything was beautiful to look at and good to eat. Right in the middle of the garden, God planted the tree of life and the tree of knowledge of good and evil.

Then God added, "It is not good for you to be alone. I will make a partner for you."

Then God dressed Adam and Eve *in animal skins and sent them from the garden of Eden. He placed cherubim and a flaming sword to guard the entrance so that they could never return.*

16

day, God rested and blessed the seventh day, because this was the day He had finished His work.

THE GARDEN OF EDEN

When God made the sky and the earth, there were no plants on the earth. This was because the Lord had not yet created rain. There was also no man to care for the land and to water it. So God made a man from the dust of the earth. He breathed life into his nostrils, and the man became alive.

God planted a garden in Eden, and there He placed the man, whose name was Adam. In the garden, God made different types of plants for Adam to grow and care for. Everything was beautiful to look at and good to eat. Right in the middle of the garden, God planted the tree of life and the tree of knowledge of good and evil.

A river passed through the garden of Eden and then flowed out of it into four smaller rivers. These four rivers were called Pison, Gihon, Hiddekel, and Euphrates.

God placed the man in the garden of Eden so that he could look after it. Then He gave the man an order: "You may eat from all the trees in the garden except the tree of knowledge of good and evil. The day you eat from that tree is the day you will die." Then God added, "It is not good for you to be alone. I will make a partner for you." Before God did this, He brought all the animals and birds of the world to Adam, to see what he would call them. And Adam gave names to all the creatures in the world, but there was still no partner for Adam.

The Lord God made Adam fall into a deep sleep, and while he slept, God took one of his ribs. From Adam's rib God made a woman. God gave her to the man. Adam said, "You are my flesh and blood, and because you were made from me, I will call you woman."

This is why when a man leaves his father and mother, he stays with his wife, because they are one and the same flesh.

The man and the woman were naked, but they were not ashamed of this.

THE SNAKE IN THE GARDEN

The snake was the most crafty of all the creatures that God had made, and he said to the woman, "Did God say you should not eat the fruit from the trees in the garden?"

And the woman answered, "We may eat the fruit from the trees in the garden, but God said, 'You must not eat from the tree of knowledge of good and evil or touch it; if you do, you will die.' "

The snake said, "No, you won't. God only said that because He knows that the day you eat that fruit, your eyes will be opened and, like gods, you will know good and evil."

The woman looked at the tree of knowledge. She saw that it was lovely and full of delicious-looking fruit, which could make a person wise. Unable to resist, she took a fruit from the tree, and she ate it. She gave some to her husband, who also ate it. At once their eyes were opened wide, and they knew they were naked. They were embarrassed and sewed fig leaves together to make clothes for themselves.

The Lord was walking in the cool of the day. They heard the voice of the Lord God in the garden, and Adam and his wife hid from Him behind the trees. Then God called out, "Adam, where are you?"

And Adam said, "I heard Your voice in the garden, but I was afraid because I was naked, so I hid myself."

God said, "Who told you you were naked? Have you eaten from the forbidden tree?"

The man said, "The woman whom You gave to me as a partner gave me some of the fruit, and I ate it."

The Lord God said to the woman, "What have you done?"

And she said, "The snake tricked me, and I ate it."

Then God spoke to the snake: "Because you did this, I will make you the most unhappy of all My creatures. You will crawl on your belly and breathe in dust for as long as you live. Woman will be your enemy, and her children will be the enemies of your children. They will strike you in the head and you will strike them in the heel." He said to the woman, "I will make your life and childbearing miserable. Your happiness will depend upon your husband, who will be your master." To Adam, He said, "Because you listened to your wife and ate from the tree I told you not to, I curse the ground from which you must grow food. Where you look for food, you will find thorns and thistles, and you will be forced to till the soil. You will earn your bread by the sweat of your brow, until at last you return to the dust from which I made you."

Adam named his wife Eve, because she was the mother of all living things. Then God dressed Adam and Eve in animal skins and sent them from the garden of Eden. He placed cherubim and a flaming sword to guard the entrance so that they could never return.

THE STORY OF CAIN AND ABEL

Genesis 4-6

Eve, the wife of Adam, gave birth to a boy, and they called him Cain. And they had a second son, whom they named Abel. Abel looked after flocks of sheep, and Cain tilled the soil. As a young man, Cain grew fruit from the ground, and he made an offering of it to the Lord God. Abel also made an offering to God. He offered the finest of his lambs. And God was pleased with Abel's offering, but He had no respect for Cain's. This made Cain angry, and his face became long. The Lord asked Cain, "Why are you so angry and why the long face?" Then God gave Cain advice: "If you do good, will I not be happy? If you do bad, sin and evil will control you." But Cain was still angry.

Later, when Cain and Abel were walking through a field together, Cain suddenly took hold of Abel and killed him.

The Lord asked Cain, "Where is your brother, Abel?"

And Cain replied, "How should I know? Am I my brother's keeper?"

The voice of the Lord grew angry. "What have you done? Your brother's blood is calling out to Me from the earth. The very ground curses you for shedding your brother's blood. The earth will no longer tolerate you. From now on, you must wander the land like a beggar."

Cain cried, "My punishment is more than I can bear. You have driven me from the face of the earth, and whoever sees me will want to kill me."

God said, "No one will kill you. Whoever kills Cain will suffer a punishment seven times greater than yours."

Then God put a mark on Cain so that anyone finding him would not kill him. And Cain left the Lord's presence and stayed in the land of Nod.

Much later, Cain's wife bore him a son, Enoch. Cain built a city and named it after his son.

Later, when Cain and Abel were walking through a field together, Cain suddenly took hold of Abel and killed him.

The Lord asked Cain, "Where is your brother, Abel?"

And Cain replied, "How should I know? Am I my brother's keeper?"

NOAH'S ARK

As time passed, more and more people were born, and many turned away from the ways of the Lord. God saw the wickedness of man, and He was so upset that He regretted ever having created him. The Lord said, "I will destroy the mankind I made and all the other creatures I made, too. I am sorry I ever made them."

But there was one man whom God saw was good. His name was Noah. Noah was a good and honest man and followed the ways of the Lord. He had three sons: Shem, Ham, and Japheth. God spoke to Noah: "The earth has become a bad place, and I will destroy all those living in it. You must make an ark of cypress wood and divide it into many rooms. Use tar both inside and outside. The ark itself should be three hundred cubits long, fifty cubits broad, and thirty cubits in height. It should have a door, a window, and three floors."

After these instructions, God said, "I will cause a flood to swamp the earth and destroy everything under heaven that has breath. But with you, I will make a promise, a covenant. Take your wife, and sons, and their wives into the ark. Also take a male and female of every creature that flies or walks or creeps on the earth, so that they will survive. Stock up with food for yourselves and the animals."

Noah did as God commanded.

He entered the ark with his family and, two by two, the animals boarded the ark. After seven days, the waters on the earth reached flood level. Then God opened the heavens, and for forty days and forty nights, heavy rain poured down. The waters rose quickly, and the ark floated. The waters rose until they covered the mountains, and everything on the earth died. But Noah and the animals in the ark were safe. This happened when Noah was six hundred years old. And God did not abandon Noah or those with him.

The Lord God caused a wind to rise, pass over the waters, and make them calm. The flood had lasted one hundred and fifty days.

A LITTLE BIT OF HISTORY
According to modern measurements, Noah's ark would be about 150 metres long, 25 metres broad and 15 metres in height.

Genesis 8-9

THE ARK REACHES DRY LAND

The rain from heaven stopped. On the seventeenth day of the seventh month, the ark came to rest on the mountains of Ararat. For three more months, the waters lowered, until the mountaintops were in sight. Forty days more passed before Noah opened the window of the ark and let a raven fly out. This bird flew to and fro over the water until the waters went down. Then Noah sent a dove out, and this bird returned because it could find no resting place save that of the ark. He waited another seven days before he sent the dove out again. In the evening, she returned with an olive leaf in her mouth. When Noah saw this, he knew the waters had started to go down. Then he waited another seven days and sent out the dove once more. She did not return, and this meant she had found dry land.

Noah removed the covering from the ark and looked out. He saw that the ground was dry. He heard the voice of God telling him to leave the ark and to let all the living creatures out so that they could have young and enrich the earth.

Opposite: After these instructions, God said, "I will cause a flood to swamp the earth and destroy everything under heaven that has breath. But with you, I will make a promise, a covenant. Take your wife, and sons, and their wives into the ark. Also take a male and female of every creature that flies or walks or creeps on the earth, so that they will survive. Stock up with food for yourselves and the animals." Noah did as God commanded.

After seven days, the waters on the earth reached flood level. Then God opened the heavens, and for forty days and forty nights, heavy rain poured down. The waters rose quickly, and the ark floated. The waters rose until they covered the mountains, and everything on the earth died.

Noah did this. Then he built an altar for the Lord God, and upon it he made the finest burnt offerings of clean beasts and birds. When the sweet aroma of these sacrifices reached God, He said, "Never again will I curse the earth with floodwaters or destroy living beings as I have done. Day and night will continue for as long as the earth lasts."

God blessed Noah and his sons and told them to fill the earth with children. He told them that the animals and birds and fish and everything that moved on the earth would fear and respect them. These creatures would provide food for people, just as green plants and herbs did.

God said, "This is the covenant I make with you and your children and all the creatures of the world that were in the ark with you. And when you look up into the sky and see a rainbow, you will know that I have not forgotten our agreement and that I will never again cause the floodwaters to rise."

And Noah rejoiced and planted a vineyard and other gardens. He lived for three hundred and fifty years after the flood, and when he finally died, he was nine hundred and fifty years old. His sons grew in strength and founded different nations.

Opposite: God said, "This is the covenant I make with you and your children and all the creatures of the world that were in the ark with you. And when you look up into the sky and see a rainbow, you will know that I have not forgotten our agreement and that I will never again cause the floodwaters to rise."

THE TOWER OF BABEL

At this time the people of the world all spoke the same language. One group of people travelled east to a plain known as Shinar. Here they stopped to build a city and a tower so high it would stretch up to heaven itself. They wanted to make a great name for themselves so they would stay together in their great city. They worked with bricks and mortar, and called their instructions out to one another.

The Lord visited the city and saw the tower that the men had built. He said, "They are one people with one language, but what they are doing is dangerous. If they build this, they will be so proud that they may think that they may do exactly as they please."

So the Lord made their speech and language confused, and they did not understand one another. They stopped their building, and they scattered to different places round the earth.

Thus, Babel has come to mean a confusion of languages, because it was here that the Lord did these things and scattered the people in many different directions.

Opposite: One group of people travelled east to a plain known as Shinar. Here they stopped to build a city and a tower so high it would stretch up to heaven itself. They wanted to make a great name for themselves so they would stay together in their great city. They worked with bricks and mortar, and called their instructions out to one another.

GOD'S PROMISE TO ABRAM

In the land of Haran lived a man called Abram, and the Lord spoke to this man: "Leave this country. Take your family with you, and I will show you another country. I will make your new homeland a great nation. I will bless you, and your name will become great. I will bless those who bless you and curse those who curse you. Through you, all peoples on earth will be blessed."

Abram left the land of his fathers when he was seventy-five years old, and he travelled with his wife, Sarah, and his brother's son, Lot, and other local people. He reached a place called Sichem, near the plains of Moreh, which was where the Canaanites lived, and God said, "I will give this land to your descendants." And Abram built an altar to his God.

He went on to a mountain, with Bethel on the west and Haion on the east, and for some time he pitched his tent there. Then he went south, and to avoid famine, he approached the borders of Egypt. Before he went into that country, he said to his wife, "When we are in Egypt, you must pretend to be my sister or else the Egyptians will kill me in order to marry you, because you are so beautiful."

In Egypt the men saw how beautiful Sarah was, and she was brought to Pharaoh's court. This ruler offered Abram many precious gifts if he would only agree to let Sarah stay there.

Abram left the land of his fathers when he was seventy-five years old, and he travelled with his wife, Sarah, and his brother's son, Lot, and other local people. He reached a place called Sichem, near the plains of Moreh, which was where the Canaanites lived, and God said, "I will give this land to your descendants."

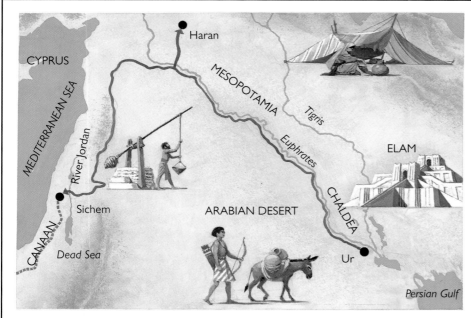

The map shows the route Abram followed at the time of his long journey west. Abram was originally from Mesopotamia and probably lived at the same time as the great king Hammurabi (1792 to 1750 B.C.). This king was responsible for Babylon's code of law.

Abram lived with his father in Ur. He then followed the Euphrates with his family and crossed the river to reach the town of Haran at the foot of the mountains of Anatolia. This was a journey of nearly 621 miles. He settled in an area where the water was plentiful. This area was ideal for a nomadic tribe with flocks of animals. From there Abram went to Sichem and entered the land of Canaan, covering approximately another 373 miles.

When God saw this, He made a plague fall on Pharaoh's court. Pharaoh called Abram to him. "Why didn't you tell me she was your wife? Look what you have done to me! Take your wife and go on your way."

And Abram left Egypt safely, and his wealth and fortune grew. He returned to the place between Bethel and Haion where he had built an altar.

ABRAM AND LOT   *Genesis 13*

Both Abram and Lot became rich, and both had great flocks and herds. Together they crowded the land so much that it could not support them as well as the Canaanites and Perizzites who also lived there. The herdsmen of Abram and Lot quarrelled, and Abram was quick to make peace. He spoke to Lot: "Let there be no trouble between us, for we are related. The land is great. We must share it between us. If you choose the land to the left, I will take the land to the right, and if you choose the land to the right, I will take the land to the left."

Lot surveyed the land of Jordan and saw its beauty and how well watered it was. He chose this land and left Abram.

After Lot had moved away, Abram lived in Canaan. God spoke to Abram: "Look north, south, east, and west, and all the land that you see, I will make yours. In the future your descendants will be as many as there are grains of sand on a beach. Travel through this land now. I give it all to you."

So Abram moved his tent and went to live on the plain of Mamre. He built an altar to his Lord God there.

GOD APPEARS TO ABRAM   *Genesis 17-18, 21*

When Abram was ninety-nine years old, God appeared before him and said, "I am the Almighty God. I will make a covenant between us, and you will become the father of many nations. I will give you and your descendants the land of Canaan, and it will be yours for ever. From now on, you shall be known as Abraham, father of nations."

And God appeared to Abraham in a mysterious way. Abraham was sitting in the entrance to his tent in the heat of the day. Suddenly he looked up and saw three men. He ran to meet them and bowed low before them. He cried, "My Lord, if you look with favour on me, I beg you, rest beneath these trees, drink some water, and wash your feet. I will bring bread to give you strength. Then you may take up your journey again."

And they replied, "Do what you have said."

Abraham ran into his tent and told his wife to make cakes with fine flour. Then he went quickly to his herd and selected a calf for dinner. There was also butter and milk, and Abraham stood by while the men ate beneath the tree. They asked him where his wife, Sarah, was, and he told them she was in the tent. One of the men said, "Your wife will give birth to a son." Sarah, who had come to the entrance of the tent, heard these words and laughed, because, like her husband, she was very old. God said to Abraham, "Why did Sarah laugh? Does she believe she is too old to have a child? With God, everything is possible. The time will come when Sarah will have a baby."

Sarah grew frightened and denied that she had laughed. But God said, "I know that you laughed."

Everything that God had promised happened just as He had said. In her old age, Sarah gave birth to a son, and Abraham called his son Isaac.

Genesis 24

THE STORY OF ISAAC'S WIFE, REBEKAH

Many years passed, and Abraham was very old but blessed by God in every way. One day he called his eldest servant to him and said, "I ask you to give me your hand and swear by God in heaven that you will not choose a wife for my son from the Canaanites. I want you to leave this land and return to my homeland and there choose a wife for Isaac."

The servant took his master's hand and swore to do as he was asked. Then he took ten camels that belonged to his master and loaded them with many precious things.

He went to Mesopotamia, to a city named Nahor. Outside the gates of this city, he bedded down his camels by a well where women came to draw water in the evening. While he waited there, he prayed to God to bring good fortune to his master, Abraham. He said, "I will say to a woman, 'Let me drink from your jug of water,' and she will offer me water and also offer water to the camels. When this happens, I will know that this will be a good wife for Isaac and that You have shown Abraham great kindness."

No sooner had he finished his prayer than a woman named Rebekah appeared. She was young and beautiful. She went down to the well and filled her jug. At once the servant ran to her and said, "May I drink some of your water?"

And she gave him water and said, "I will bring water for your camels." And she went back to the well for more water.

When the camels had finished drinking, the servant gave the young woman an earring and two bracelets of fine gold. He asked her, "Whose daughter are you? Is there room in your father's house for us to spend

Opposite: They asked him where his wife, Sarah, was, and he told them she was in the tent. One of the men said, "Your wife will give birth to a son." Sarah, who had come to the entrance of the tent, heard these words and laughed, because, like her husband, she was very old.

When Rebekah saw Isaac, she recognised him from the servant's description of him. She got off her camel and covered herself with a veil.

The servant told Isaac everything that had happened. Then Isaac led Rebekah to his mother's tent. Later they were married. Isaac loved his wife.

the night?" She replied that she was the daughter of Bethuel and that there was room and food for him and his animals.

Then the servant thanked God, and Rebekah ran home to tell her family what had happened. When Laban, Rebekah's brother, heard her story and saw the earring and bracelets, he ran down to the well to greet Abraham's servant. Laban said, "You are blessed by the Lord. You should not be waiting here. Come into the house. I have prepared a room for you, and there is space and food for your camels."

Abraham's servant was brought to the house, and he and his animals were well looked after. Food was placed before him, but he shook his head and said, "I cannot eat until I tell you why I have come. I am Abraham's servant." Then he told Laban the reason for his visit and how God had led him to Rebekah.

When Laban and Bethuel heard his words, they recognised the ways of the Lord and said, "This is God's will. Rebekah will return with you to be the wife of Isaac." Then they called Rebekah, who said that she was willing to go to Canaan with the servant.

They set out to return to Canaan. In the evening, Isaac saw the camel train and approached it. When Rebekah saw Isaac, she asked the servant, "Who is this man?" The servant said, " It is my master." She got off her camel and covered herself with a veil.

And the servant told Isaac everything that had happened. Then Isaac led Rebekah to his mother's tent. Later they were married. Isaac loved his wife.

ESAU AND JACOB

Genesis 25

Isaac was sixty years old when Rebekah gave birth to twins. The first boy had red hair that covered him all over like a hairy coat. They called him Esau. His brother they named Jacob.

The boys grew up. Esau became a skilful hunter, while Jacob was a peaceful man who liked to stay at home in his tent. Isaac loved Esau the most and liked to eat the meat he brought home from the hunt. But Rebekah preferred Jacob.

One day Esau came back from the fields feeling weak and hungry. He saw that Jacob had prepared a dish of lentils, and he said, "Give me some of your food. I'm dying of hunger."

Jacob replied, "I'll give you my food, if you give me your right as firstborn." This meant that Jacob would inherit his father's wealth instead of Esau.

Esau cared about his hunger more than his birthright, so he agreed to Jacob's offer. Jacob gave him a dish of lentils, and Esau ate them. He didn't think any more about it.

REBEKAH AND JACOB PLOT AGAINST ESAU

Genesis 27

When Isaac was so old that he could hardly see, he called his elder son, Esau, to him and said, "My son, before I die, I want you to go out and bring me some of that meat I love so much. I will bless you for doing this."

Rebekah heard this, and she said to her favourite son, Jacob, "Your father has just asked Esau to go out and bring back some meat. Listen to what I tell you. Bring me two lambs from the flock, and I will cook

34

and spice them in just the way your father likes. Do this, and your father will bless you before he dies."

When Jacob heard this, he said, "Esau is a hairy man, and I am smooth-skinned. No doubt my father will touch me and know that I am not Esau. Then, instead of being blessed, I will be cursed."

His mother shook her head and said, "Just do as I say."

So Jacob did exactly what his mother had told him to do, and he came back with the meat. Rebekah took the lambskins and draped them round Jacob's body. She gave him the cooked meat, and Jacob went to his father.

Isaac said, "Who are you?"

Jacob said, "I am Esau. I have brought you the spiced meat you asked for."

Isaac replied, "You did this very quickly. Let me touch you, so that I know you are really Esau."

Isaac touched him, saying that he had Jacob's voice but Esau's hands. Even so, Isaac didn't guess what was going on. He ate the meat, and he blessed Jacob and kissed him.

No sooner had Jacob left than Esau appeared. He had been out hunting and had finally prepared the meat. Esau said, "I have brought you the spiced meat you desired."

Isaac asked, "Who are you?"

"I am Esau," was the reply.

One day Esau came back from the fields feeling weak and hungry. He saw that Jacob had prepared a dish of lentils, and he said, "Give me some of your food. I'm dying of hunger."

Jacob replied, "I'll give you my food, if you give me your right as first-born."

Rebekah took the lambskins and
draped them round Jacob's body.
She gave him the cooked meat, and
Jacob went to his father.

Isaac trembled in every limb of his body, for he knew he had been tricked. He told Esau he had already given his blessing to Jacob and now he could do nothing about it.

ISAAC AND ESAU UNDERSTAND WHAT HAS HAPPENED

Genesis 27-28

When Esau heard his father's words, he cried out bitterly and begged his father, "You could still bless me!"

But Isaac said, "Your brother came here and stole your blessing."

Esau said, "First he took my birthright, and now he has taken my blessing! Can you not find a blessing for me, Father?"

Isaac said, "I have made him your master, and you will be forced to live by your sword, but a time will come when you will break free from Jacob's grip."

Esau's heart filled with such hatred for his brother that he decided to kill him after his father's death. When Rebekah heard of Esau's plan, she called her younger son, Jacob, to her and told him, "Your brother wants to kill you. Go and stay with my brother, Laban. I will tell you when it is safe to return."

Then Isaac called Jacob to him and said, "Do not marry a woman from Canaan, but go to Bethuel's household and find a wife there. May God Almighty bless you and look after you."

JACOB AND RACHEL

Genesis 29-31

Jacob set off for Haran in Mesopotamia. On his arrival, he stopped near a well where shepherds were watering their flocks of sheep. He called to them, "Brothers, where are you from?"

And they answered, "We are from Haran."

Then Jacob said, "Do you know Laban?"

And they answered, "We do, and here is his daughter, Rachel, with her flock of sheep."

When Jacob saw Rachel, he went to the well and rolled off the big stone that covered it. After giving water to her sheep, Jacob immediately kissed Rachel. He told her that he was the son of Rebekah. Rachel immediately ran home to tell her father.

Laban came to greet Jacob. He embraced Jacob and brought him back to his house.

They had a great deal to talk about. A month went by, and Laban said to Jacob, "Even though you are my nephew, you shouldn't work for nothing. How should I pay you?"

Laban had two daughters. The elder was called Leah; the younger, Rachel. Leah was kind but plain. Rachel, on the other hand, was beautiful and charming. Jacob was in love with Rachel, and he said to Laban, "I will serve you for seven years if you let me marry Rachel."

Laban replied, "I would prefer that she marry you rather than some complete stranger, so stay with us."

Thus, for seven years Jacob worked for Laban. The years went by quickly, because Jacob kept his love for Rachel. When the time was finally up, he said to Laban, "I have served my time. Now give me your daughter for my wife."

Laban prepared a great wedding feast. In the evening, he brought a veiled daughter to Jacob, and the couple were married. Jacob thought he was marrying Rachel. When he discovered he had actually married Leah, he said to Laban, "What have you done? I served you seven years for Rachel. You have tricked me."

Laban said, "In this country the elder daughter must marry first. Stay with Leah, work with me for another seven years, and you may then also marry Rachel."

And Jacob worked another seven years and then married Rachel in accordance with the custom of the time that a man may have more than one wife. He loved Rachel more than Leah, but it was Leah who bore him many sons. Finally, God showed mercy on Rachel, and she gave birth to a son whom she called Joseph.

After many years had passed, God spoke to Jacob: "It is time now to return to the land of your fathers."

So Jacob set out with Leah, Rachel, his sons, and all their possessions. They went back to the land of Canaan.

Jacob opened his eyes and saw Esau and four hundred men in front of him.

Jacob approached his brother, bowing seven times as he did so. But Esau ran to meet him, threw his arms around Jacob's neck, and hugged him. And the brothers wept and were again a family.

On his way back to Canaan, Jacob sent messengers ahead of him to meet his brother, Esau. Their message was this: "Your servant Jacob has been staying with Laban. I have cattle, flocks of sheep, and donkeys with me. I also have menservants and maidservants. I wish to come into the land of Canaan with your blessing."

The messengers soon returned with grave news. They told Jacob, "We found your brother, Esau, but he was already on his way to meet you with an army of four hundred men."

When Jacob heard this, he became very afraid. He prayed to God to deliver him from the anger of his brother. He prayed for his wives and children.

That night Jacob took his two wives and eleven sons and crossed the ford at Jabbok. Ahead of him he had sent many animals as gifts to his brother. Then he left his family so that he could be alone with his thoughts. At last he fell into a deep sleep in which he wrestled with an angel. He would not let the angel go until he received a blessing. Towards dawn, they stopped their struggle, and the angel said, "What is your name?" And the reply was "Jacob." Then the angel said, "In future you will be called Israel for you have contended with both God and men and have prevailed." And at that moment, Jacob opened his eyes and saw Esau and four hundred men in front of him.

Jacob approached his brother, bowing seven times as he did so. But Esau ran to meet him, threw his arms round Jacob's neck, and hugged him. And the brothers wept and were again a family.

JOSEPH AND HIS BROTHERS

JOSEPH AND HIS BROTHERS
In the land of Canaan the tribe of Jacob lived a partly nomadic life. The members of the tribe raised sheep and cultivated land. The area where they had settled was a crossroads for caravans of traders, most of them Ishmaelites and Midianites. These people had made trading their way of life.

They were especially skilled in transporting precious cargo from the East to Egypt, which had been an important kingdom since 3400 B.C.

Egypt was a rich and self-sufficient country. It exported linen, papyrus, agricultural produce, and gold. It imported precious oils to make perfume and incense, which were used in religious ceremonies. The Ishmaelites sold the Egyptians these oils as well as other goods, such as olive oil, wine, precious stones, and wood. The cedar from Lebanon and sandalwood were greatly valued.

Jacob's sons had decided to get rid of their brother, Joseph. They sold him to the Ishmaelites.

Opposite: One brother, Judah, came up with an idea: "We won't make any money by killing Joseph. Let's sell him to these traders."

They sold Joseph for twenty pieces of silver, and he was taken off to Egypt.

Jacob stayed in the land of Canaan. One of his sons was called Joseph. It was clear to everyone that Jacob loved Joseph more than the others, because he was born when Jacob was quite old. The brothers were unhappy about this and often spoke roughly to Joseph.

Jacob made Joseph a coat of many colours. Joseph's brothers saw this as yet another sign of Jacob's special love for his young son.

One day Jacob told Joseph to see what his brothers were doing and how the herds were being looked after. His brothers saw him coming from a distance, and they plotted to kill him.

When Joseph reached his brothers, they took hold of him and tore off his coat of many colours. Then they threw him into a dry pit. Just as they sat down to eat and talk about what they should do next, they caught sight of merchants travelling to Egypt to trade there. One brother, Judah, came up with an idea: "We won't make any money by killing Joseph. Let's sell him to these traders."

They sold Joseph for twenty pieces of silver, and he was taken to Egypt as a slave. Then they dipped his coat in goat's blood and took it to their father. They said, "Doesn't this look like Joseph's coat of many colours?"

"It is my son's coat," Jacob cried. "A wild animal must have eaten him!"

No one could comfort Jacob. It seemed his grief would never end.

JOSEPH IN EGYPT, *Genesis 39*

Potiphar, an officer of the pharaoh of Egypt, bought Joseph from the merchants. God looked after Joseph. Potiphar saw that Joseph was a good person, and he made him the head of his household. Inside the house, all went well. And outside the house, the fields were rich with crops. Joseph was trusted by his master like a son.

After some time had passed, the wife of the master found herself looking more and more at Joseph, who was young and handsome. Finally, she told Joseph of her desire. Joseph refused her, saying, "You are my master's wife. He has trusted me with everything. I cannot betray him. It would be wrong and a sin against God."

This made the woman bitter and angry. She made up stories about Joseph. When Potiphar heard that Joseph had tried to take advantage of his wife, he was full of anger and threw his servant into prison.

But even in prison, God did not abandon Joseph.

THE CUPBEARER'S DREAM AND THE BAKER'S DREAM

It happened that Pharaoh, the king of Egypt, became unhappy with the work of his cupbearer and baker. He threw them into the same prison where Joseph was also being held.

One night, the cupbearer and the baker each had a dream that made them very sad. When Joseph saw this, he asked them why they were upset. They both replied, "We do not know what these dreams mean."

Then Joseph said, "Tell them to me. Perhaps I can help."

The cupbearer said, "In my dream, I saw a grapevine with three branches, and these branches were ripe with fruit. I took these bunches of grapes, and I made wine with them for Pharaoh's cup, and I handed it to him."

Joseph said, "Your dream means that within three days, Pharaoh will return you to your former position as his cupbearer. When this happens, do not forget me."

The baker said, "I saw myself in a dream, and I had three white baskets on my head. The basket on top was full of delicacies for Pharaoh, and birds were eating them."

Joseph said, "Within three days, Pharaoh will hang you from a tree, and birds will come and eat your flesh."

And so it happened. Three days later, Pharaoh gave the cupbearer his old job back. As for the baker, he was taken from prison and hanged, just as Joseph had predicted.

PHARAOH'S DREAMS

Two years later, Pharaoh dreamt that he was standing on the banks of the Nile when seven fat cows came out of the water and grazed in the meadows. After the well-fed cows, there came seven thin and sickly cows, and they ate up the healthy cows. Then Pharaoh awoke.

Later, he fell asleep again and had a second dream. This time he saw seven rich ears of corn on a single stalk. And these were followed by seven thin ears shrivelled by winds from the east. Then Pharaoh awoke again.

In the morning, Pharaoh was troubled by his dreams. He called all the magicians and wise men of Egypt to him and asked them what his dreams meant. But no one could suggest a meaning. Then the cupbearer remembered the man in prison who had interpreted his dream there. He told Pharaoh about Joseph. And Joseph was taken out of prison and presented to Pharaoh, who said, "I have had a dream, but no one can interpret it. I have heard you have this power."

Joseph replied, "It will be God who will interpret and bring you peace of mind."

Pharaoh told Joseph his dreams.

Joseph said, "These two parts form one dream. In this dream, God has shown Pharaoh what He is about to do. The seven fat cows and the seven ears of corn both mean seven years. There will be seven years of plenty in Egypt, but these seven years will be followed by seven years of famine. The sickly cows and corn mean times of hardship. God will soon bring all this to pass. Pharaoh must prepare himself and Egypt for these events. Therefore, I would suggest that Pharaoh hire a wise man to look after the land so that in times of plenty, food may be stored for leaner times. Food will be gathered in the good years that come, and wheat will be stored in the cities so that the people will not starve during the seven years of famine."

Pharaoh saw the wisdom in Joseph's words. He made Joseph overseer of the land. Joseph was the ruler of Egypt, with only one person above him, and that was Pharaoh himself.

In the seven years of plenty, Joseph filled up the barns of Egypt until they could hold no more food. Then came the lean years, just as he had predicted. The people of Egypt cried out to their Pharaoh for bread, and Pharaoh told them to ask Joseph. Joseph opened up the storehouses and sold the corn to the people so that they would not starve. The famine spread, and hungry people from all over the world went to Egypt, where they could buy corn.

JOSEPH'S BROTHERS GO TO EGYPT

Genesis 42

The famine spread into Canaan, where Jacob and his sons lived.

Jacob heard that corn could be bought in Egypt, and he told his sons, "If we are to survive, you must go to Egypt, buy corn, and bring it back here."

The ten brothers agreed to their father's proposal and set off for Egypt with sacks of money to buy corn. The youngest boy, Benjamin, however, stayed at home.

The ten brothers reached the house where Joseph was governor. The brothers bowed low before Joseph, who immediately recognised them but pretended not to. He spoke to them harshly: "What are you doing in this country? I believe that you are spies."

The brothers did not recognise Joseph. They said, "We are from the land of Canaan. We have come only to buy corn."

Joseph repeated, "You are spies who have come here to see how poor our country is."

They shook their heads and said they were his servants. "We are honest men, and we have come here only to buy food. There are twelve of us; one son is missing, and the youngest is at home with our father."

Joseph said, "If what you say is true, you will have to prove it. By the order of Pharaoh, you will not be allowed to leave this country until the youngest brother is brought before me."

Then Joseph put them under arrest for three days. After this time, he called them to him again and said, "Listen to me now, if you are as honest as you say you are, one of you will stay here while the rest of you go back to Canaan with grain supplies in your sacks. Then bring your youngest brother to me, and I shall know that you are not spies but honest men."

The brothers remembered how guilty they had been in the past. Reuben said to his brothers in their native language, which he thought Joseph would not understand, "We have brought this on ourselves by sinning against a child, and now we must pay for it with blood."

When Joseph heard these words, he turned his face away so that his brothers would not see his tears. Then he took Simeon and tied him up. The other brothers set out for Canaan with corn.

When Jacob heard what had happened in Egypt, he cried out in great sorrow, "First it was Joseph, then Simeon, and now you want to take Benjamin!"

Reuben said to Jacob, "All will go well, Father. I will see to it."

"No," said Jacob, "I will not risk losing Benjamin. If anything happened to him, it would be the death of me."

Then they opened their sacks, and each man found not only corn but also his money restored. And all of them were deeply afraid and did not know what this meant.

Following pages: Joseph said, "These two parts form one dream. In this dream, God has shown Pharaoh what He is about to do. The seven fat cows and the seven ears of corn both mean seven years. There will be seven years of plenty in Egypt, but these seven years will be followed by seven years of famine."

BENJAMIN GOES TO EGYPT

The famine continued, and Canaan suffered badly. When the grain supplies brought out of Egypt were used up, Jacob said that they must go back for more. But Judah reminded his father, "The governor there will not even see us unless we bring Benjamin back with us. We will go only if we can take him."

Jacob cried out in despair, "What have you done to me? Why did you tell the governor there was another son at home?"

And they told him how they had been forced to speak about their family, not knowing that the governor would make such a request.

Judah said, "Let me take Benjamin with me. I will look after him and guarantee his life with my own."

Jacob reluctantly agreed and gave them this advice: "Take gifts, and this time take double the money. Perhaps last time it was an oversight. May God have mercy on you. It would break my heart to lose both Benjamin and Simeon."

Soon the brothers reached Joseph's house. And when Joseph heard that they had brought gifts and Benjamin was with them, he told his steward to prepare a feast.

The frightened brothers spoke with the steward and anxiously explained how they had brought back the money that had mysteriously appeared in their sacks. The steward listened and said, "Peace be with you; do not be afraid. God provided the money. And here is Simeon, safe and well." Then the steward made sure that the men were well taken care of and that they had water to wash their feet.

When this was done, Joseph appeared, and they bowed to the ground before him. He asked them how they were. "How is your father? Is he still alive?" They told him that their father was in good health.

Then Joseph saw his younger brother, Benjamin, and said, "Is this the young boy you spoke of? May God bless you!" With these words Joseph left the room, because he did not want his brothers to see his tears. He cried alone in his chamber. Then he washed his face and returned. He ordered food and drink to be served and saw that Benjamin received five times more than the rest.

After the feast, Joseph told his steward to fill the men's sacks with food and to stuff the mouths of the sacks with money. He directed his steward to put his own special silver cup in Benjamin's sack.

As soon as it was daylight, the men were on their way. They were hardly out of the city when Joseph said to his steward, "Ride after them, and when you catch up with them, ask them why they have given evil in return for good."

The steward reached the brothers. He demanded to know where his master's cup was.

The brothers shook their heads. "We do not have it. We returned your money last time. Why would we steal from you? If any man here has your master's cup, he should die, and the rest of us should become your slaves."

The steward agreed to this, and straightaway each man emptied his sack. The steward looked through them all, and when he finally came to Benjamin's sack, he found the silver cup.

Cries of despair rose from the brothers. Returning to the city, they met Joseph in his house, and Judah fell down before him and begged for mercy. Joseph said, "The man who had my silver cup shall be my slave. The rest of you can return in peace to your father."

But Judah pleaded with Joseph: "I beg you to let the boy return home with his brothers. Let me be your slave in his place. I cannot return home without Benjamin and see the sorrow this would bring to my father."

JOSEPH SHOWS HIS BROTHERS WHO HE IS

Genesis 45-46

Then Joseph could hold back no longer. He told his servants and followers to leave him alone with the men from Canaan. Then Joseph wept aloud, and said to his brothers, "Come close to me, and look at me." They did as he said.

Joseph spoke through his tears: "Don't you know who I am? I am Joseph, your brother. Tell me, how is my father?"

The brothers were struck dumb by this news, but Joseph went on: "I am your brother, Joseph, whom you sold into slavery. But that is in the past. I bear no grudge. Do not be angry or sad. God has caused me to prosper. You did not send me to Egypt. It was the hand of God at work."

Then Joseph kissed all his brothers, and all were forgiven.

With Pharaoh's blessing, the brothers returned to Canaan to bring their father back to Egypt.

When Jacob heard the news that his beloved son Joseph was alive, his heart leapt with joy. He shouted, "My son Joseph is alive! I will see him before I die!"

And Jacob, known as Israel, took his family and all his belongings to Egypt, where his son was governor of the land.

THE DEATH OF JACOB

Genesis 47-49

Jacob lived for seventeen years in Egypt. When he felt his death was not far off, he called his son Joseph to him and said, "Do not bury me in Egyptian soil, but carry me back to the land of my fathers. Bury me in the cave in the field that belongs to Ephron the Hittite, because it is there that Abraham and Sarah and Isaac and Rebekah are buried."

Then Jacob brought all the brothers together and blessed them. He spoke of their different characters and how one day the twelve tribes of Israel would descend from them. He spoke of how one day they would all return to their homeland. He advised them all to fear and respect God.

Thus Jacob, known as Israel, died and returned to the land of his ancestors.

THE DEATH OF JOSEPH

Genesis 50

Joseph continued to live in Egypt with his family and his father's family. He was a hundred and ten years old and close to death when he spoke to the descendants of Israel: "After I am dead, God will visit you. And in time you will be led out of this country and into the land of your fathers. When you leave, be sure to take my bones with you."

Shortly afterwards, Joseph died. He was embalmed and put in a coffin in Egypt.

Before long, Pharaoh's daughter came down to bathe in the river. She caught sight of the basket, and she sent her maidservants to bring it to her. They brought it back to Pharaoh's daughter, and she opened it and peered inside. When she saw the baby crying, her heart was touched and she said, "This must be one of the Hebrew children."

THE BIRTH OF MOSES

When Joseph and all the descendants of Jacob had died, all that remained of that generation was a memory. The people of Israel had rapidly multiplied, and they lived across wide areas of Egypt. A new Pharaoh came to the throne, who knew nothing about how Joseph had interpreted dreams and saved the country. He looked round and saw a foreign people growing stronger than his own. This worried him. If there were a war and the Israelites sided with his enemies, he would be likely to lose. Pharaoh decided that the best thing to do was to make this people his servants and slaves.

Then Pharaoh went to the Hebrew midwives and told them, "When a Hebrew woman gives birth to a son, kill him."

But the midwives were God-fearing and could not do such a cruel thing. The population of Israel continued to increase. Pharaoh made new orders: "All Hebrew boys must be thrown into the river; the girls, however, may live."

MOSES IN THE BULRUSHES

At this time there was a man from the Levi family living in Egypt. His wife gave birth to a son. When the woman saw how healthy and strong her son was, she didn't have the heart to kill him. She took some bulrushes from the riverbank and wove them together into a little boat. Then she covered the boat with pitch so that it would not sink. She put the child in the boat and placed it at the river's edge. The baby's sister hid so that she could see what would become of the child.

Before long, Pharaoh's daughter came down to bathe in the river. She caught sight of the basket, and she sent her maidservants to bring it to her. They brought it back to Pharaoh's daughter, and she opened it and peered inside. When she saw the baby crying, her heart was touched and she said, "This must be one of the Hebrew children."

When the baby's sister saw this, she went to Pharaoh's daughter and said, "Would you like me to find a Hebrew nurse to raise the child for you?"

Pharaoh's daughter told her to do that, and the girl came back with her own mother. She was given money to bring up the child for Pharaoh's daughter. Thus, the mother was able to look after her son.

When he had grown into a healthy child, the mother took the boy to Pharaoh's daughter, and he became her son. She called the boy Moses, because this meant he had been taken out of the water.

Opposite: One day while Moses was resting by a well in Midian, seven daughters of a priest came to draw water for their father's sheep. It wasn't long before shepherds arrived and tried to drive the daughters away from the well. When Moses saw what was happening, he stood up for the young women and helped them water their sheep.

MOSES FLEES INTO THE LAND OF MIDIAN

When Moses was fully grown, he became aware of the position of his people in Egypt. He saw how brutal the overseers were. One day he saw an Egyptian giving a Hebrew man a savage beating. Moses could stand it no longer. He looked round him, and seeing no one else about, he killed the Egyptian and buried him in the sand.

The next day Moses saw two Hebrew men fighting, and he told them to stop. But they turned on him and demanded to know who he

Moses looked after the sheep that belonged to his father-in-law, Jethro.

One day, he led them into the desert as far as the mountain of God, known as Horeb. Suddenly the angel of God appeared to him in the middle of a burning bush, and Moses said, "Look at this bush which burns but does not itself get burnt!"

When God saw Moses had stopped to see the burning bush, He called out, "Moses! Moses!"

was to pass judgement on them, when he himself was a killer. Then Moses realised that people knew what he had done.

Eventually the story reached Pharaoh, who became angry and ordered men to kill Moses.

Moses fled into the land of Midian, and there he was safe from Pharaoh.

One day while Moses was resting by a well in Midian, seven daughters of a priest came to draw water for their father's sheep. It wasn't long before shepherds arrived and tried to drive the daughters away from the well. When Moses saw what was happening, he stood up for the young women and helped them water their sheep.

At home, their father was surprised to see them return so early. They told him how an Egyptian had helped them. The father, hearing this, said, "You must bring this man home so that he may eat with us."

Thus, Moses came to live in the priest's house, and he married a daughter named Zipporah. In time she bore him a son, Gershom.

GOD CALLS UPON MOSES

Moses looked after the sheep that belonged to his father-in-law, Jethro.

One day, he led them into the desert as far as the mountain of God, known as Horeb. Suddenly the angel of God appeared to him in the middle of a burning bush, and Moses said, "Look at this bush which burns but does not itself get burnt!"

When God saw Moses had stopped to see the burning bush, He called out, "Moses! Moses!"

And the man replied, "I am here."

And God said, "I am the Lord God, your Father, the God of Abraham, the God of Isaac, and the God of Jacob.

"I have seen the suffering of My people in Egypt. I have heard them cry while being whipped by the overseers. I know their sorrows. I am here to free them from the Egyptians, to bring them out of Egypt and into another land, which is good and large and full of milk and honey. Go back, now, into Pharaoh's land so that you may lead the people out of Egypt."

Moses said to God, "Who am I to tell Pharaoh that I am taking the children of Israel out of his country?"

God said, "I will be with you."

Then Moses asked, "When I speak to the children of Israel and tell them that the God of their fathers has sent me, they will ask me, 'What is His name?' What should I say?"

God told Moses, "You answer them: I AM WHO I AM. Tell them: 'I AM has sent me to you.' You tell the children of Israel that you are sent by the God of their fathers and that this is His name for all eternity."

MAGICAL SIGNS

Moses said to God, "But they won't believe me."

The Lord said, "What do you have in your hand?"

Moses answered, "It is a stick."

"Throw it onto the ground!" ordered the Lord. Moses threw his stick onto the ground, and it turned into a snake. Moses was afraid and

A LITTLE BIT OF HISTORY

Pharaoh Rameses the Second, who reigned from approximately 1301 to 1235 B.C. and belonged to the Nineteenth Dynasty, ordered a great city to be built in the eastern part of the Nile Delta. He named it after himself. At the time that Moses became the leader of the Hebrews, they were performing forced labor on the buildings. Writers of the time described the city as dazzling, with palaces adorned with lapis lazuli and turquoise. This city declined over the centuries. Eventually, peasants began grinding up for fertiliser the bricks that the slaves had made with such care from straw and the mud of the Nile.

A later pharaoh used materials from the buildings of Rameses to construct the city of Tanis in the north. We know that he did so because bricks found in the ruins of Tanis bear Rameses' insignia.

Exodus 5-7

Opposite: Moses and Aaron went back to Pharaoh and did everything the Lord had told them to do. Aaron threw down the rod in front of Pharaoh, and it became a snake. Seeing this, the Egyptian king called his wise men and magicians to him. They all threw down their rods, and all the rods turned into snakes. But Aaron's rod swallowed all the other rods.

Exodus 7

ran away from it. God called him back and said, "Catch it by the tail." Moses did this, and the snake turned back into a stick. Then God said, "Put your hand to your chest." And Moses did this. When he brought his hand away from his chest, it was white as chalk. When he put it back to his chest, it took on its normal colour.

Still Moses was uncertain. He said, "O Lord God, I am not a clever speaker. My speech is slow. My tongue seems to stick in my mouth."

God grew angry and said, "Aaron the Levite is your brother. I know he can speak well. You will put words into his mouth, and he will speak for you. I will be with you and tell you what to say and do. Now take your stick, because it is with this that you will perform miracles: this is the rod of God. You may now safely return to Egypt."

MOSES AND PHARAOH, Exodus 5

Moses and Aaron went to Pharaoh and told him, "The God of Israel speaks and says, 'Let My people go!'"

Pharaoh said, "Who is this God you speak of? Why should I free the people of Israel? I don't know this God, and I'm not going to free these people."

Pharaoh saw that Moses and Aaron were keeping the Hebrews from their work, and he called his overseers to him and said, "Do not give these people straw for their bricks. Let them go and collect it for themselves. And make sure that they make just as many bricks!"

In this way, the suffering of the people of Israel grew worse.

GOD PROMISES MOSES THAT THE HEBREW PEOPLE WILL LEAVE EGYPT

Then Moses returned to the Lord and said, "Why, O Lord, have you brought so much sorrow to the people of Israel? Surely this is not why you brought me here. The people are still not free, but are living like slaves."

God said to Moses, "Soon you will see what will happen to Pharaoh. I will bring great plagues and turn rivers to blood. Only then will Pharaoh know that I am the Lord. And when he asks you to show your powers and perform a miracle, tell Aaron to throw the rod to the ground, and it will turn into a snake."

Moses and Aaron went back to Pharaoh and did everything the Lord had told them to do. Aaron threw down the rod in front of Pharaoh, and it became a snake. Seeing this, the Egyptian king called his wise men and magicians to him. They all threw down their rods, and all the rods turned into snakes. But Aaron's rod swallowed all the other rods. Even with this show of God's power, Pharaoh hardened his heart and would not listen to Moses.

WATER IS TURNED INTO BLOOD

God spoke with Moses again and said, "When Pharaoh goes to bathe in the river Nile, approach him there. Take your rod with you, and tell him that you will change the water into blood."

This they did. Aaron lifted up the rod and brought it down on the river. At once the waters turned to blood before Pharaoh's eyes. Fish

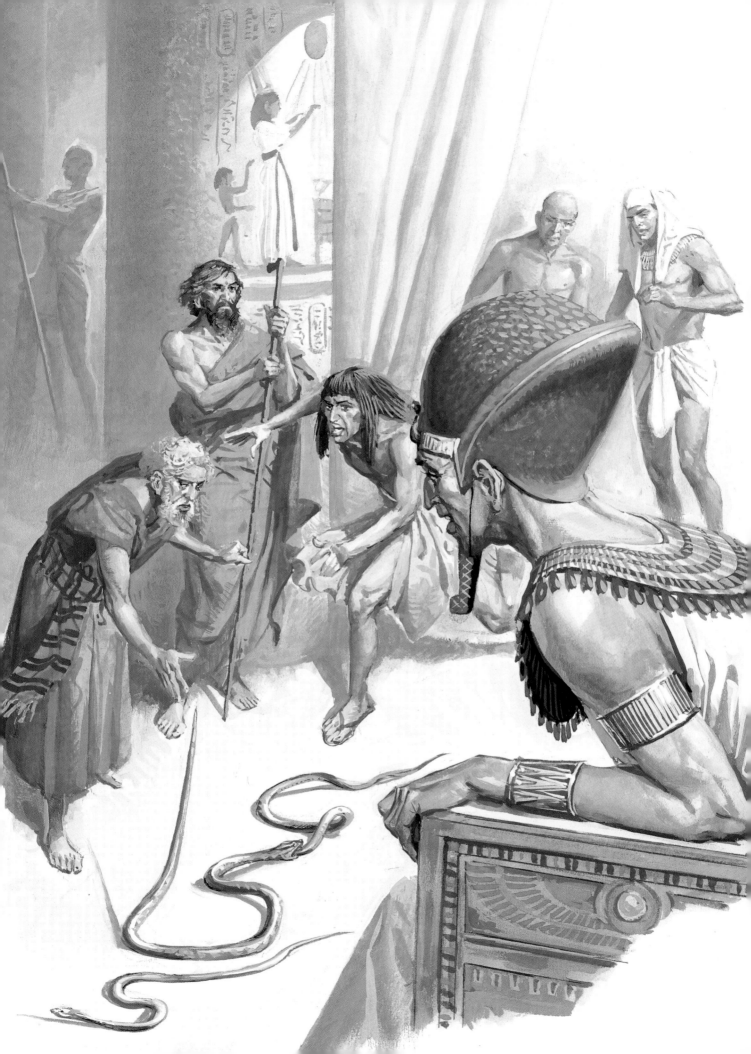

died, and the river stank. There was no drinking water for seven days. But still Pharaoh refused to listen to Moses.

Exodus 8

A PLAGUE OF FROGS

Then God said to Moses, "Go to Pharaoh, and tell him to free My people so that they may serve Me."

Once again Pharaoh would not listen to Moses. So God said, "Tell Aaron to raise the rod above the streams, rivers, and lakes, and I will cause a plague of frogs to invade the country."

Aaron did this. And from every waterway, frogs appeared and covered the land. When Pharaoh saw this, he called Moses to him. "Tell your God to rid my country of these frogs, and I will set your people free so that they can make sacrifices to their God."

The next day all the frogs on land and in the houses died, and a terrible stench filled the country.

But when this was over, Pharaoh went back on his word and would not grant freedom to the people of Israel.

Exodus 8

Exodus 8

Opposite: God said, "Wave your rod across the face of the land, and a plague of locusts will be carried on the wind to Egypt. They will fall like darkness on the earth. There will be so many that the earth itself will not be visible."

A PLAGUE OF LICE

God saw all this and said to Moses, "Tell Aaron to strike the rod into the dust so that it turns into lice throughout the whole land."

Aaron did this, and there was at once a plague of lice. Lice were to be found in all animals and humans. The Egyptian magicians could do nothing about it, and they told Pharaoh, "The finger of God is pointing at us!" But Pharaoh turned away from them all and refused to listen.

A PLAGUE OF FLIES

God told Moses to stand before Pharaoh and say, "The Lord says, 'Let My people go so that they may serve Me.'"

Pharaoh, as usual, refused this request. The rod was raised, and great swarms of flies entered his house and all the houses of Egypt.

Then Pharaoh agreed to free the Hebrew people if Moses would free his country of the plague of flies.

Moses lifted the plague, but Pharaoh went back on his word. He did not free the people of Israel.

Exodus 9

THE DISEASED ANIMALS

Once more God spoke to Moses: "Go to Pharaoh, and tell him to set the people of Israel free so that they may serve their God. If he refuses, warn him that a disease will infect his animals."

Moses did this, but Pharaoh would not free the people.

Then the disease struck hard, and camels, cattle, horses, and donkeys died by the thousands, but not one animal that belonged to the Hebrew people fell sick.

And still Pharaoh resisted.

Exodus 9

A PLAGUE OF BOILS

God said to Moses and Aaron, "Go and stand in front of Pharaoh. Take with you ash from an old furnace fire. Throw this into the air so that

Pharaoh sees what you are doing. After this, a plague of boils will infect the country."

All this happened just as God said it would. Terrible sores and boils broke out on the skin of the Egyptians. Not even the magicians escaped.

Still Pharaoh hardened his heart and resisted.

Exodus 9

HAILSTORMS

God spoke to Moses: "Go to Pharaoh, and tell him to free My people so that they may serve Me. If he does not, I will bring hailstorms to his country."

When he heard once more what Moses had to say, Pharaoh shook his head.

Then Moses stretched out his hand, and the hail roared, and lightning flashed, and thunder exploded. People and animals died, and plant life withered.

Pharaoh summoned Moses and said, "I have sinned against your God. Make these storms stop, and I will do what you ask."

Moses stopped the storms, but as before, the king of Egypt did not keep his word.

A PLAGUE OF LOCUSTS, *Exodus 10*

God said, "Wave your rod across the face of the land, and a plague of locusts will be carried on the wind to Egypt. They will fall like darkness on the earth. There will be so many that the earth itself will not be visible."

Then God said to Moses, "Stretch out your hands over the sea. The waters will return as they were, and the Egyptians will drown with their chariots and horses."

Moses did this. And when Pharaoh and his men saw the water moving, they rode back. But it was too late. The Lord made the Egyptians drown in the middle of the sea. Every chariot was destroyed, and every man and horse died.

When this happened, the fear was so great that Pharaoh's own servants spoke to him and pleaded with him to get rid of the Hebrew slaves.

Pharaoh said to Moses and Aaron, "I have sinned against your God. I pray that He forgives me."

Then the locusts were picked up by the wind and dropped into the Red Sea.

But Pharaoh's heart turned to stone. He changed his mind. He would not free the children of Israel.

DARKNESS

Exodus 10

Then God said to Moses, "Stretch out your hand to heaven, and darkness will fall over the land."

Moses did this, and for three days the darkness was so thick that no one dared move from the spot where he was. Pharaoh told Moses that his people could leave, but their animals could not. Moses told Pharaoh that they must have their flocks for sacrifice, but Pharaoh refused.

THE DEATH OF THE FIRSTBORN

Exodus 11-13

So God spoke to Moses: "Yet will I bring one more plague to Egypt.

"At midnight, I will cause the firstborn of every family to die. The firstborn of Pharaoh in line for the throne will die, as will the firstborn of the humblest servant. Even the firstborn of the animals will die."

God ordered Moses to call all the leaders of Israel together. And

Moses told them what God commanded: "Take a lamb from your flock and kill it. You must use the lamb's blood to mark the sideposts of the doorways of your houses where the meat will be eaten. Do not leave your house until morning.

"Roast the lamb, and eat the meat with unleavened bread and bitter herbs. Eat with your clothes and shoes on, and be ready to leave. Eat quickly, for this is the Passover of the Lord.

"In the night, the Lord will pass through the land of Egypt and kill many people. But where he sees the blood on the sideposts, he will not strike.

"And future generations will remember this day, and it will be celebrated as a feast for all time."

That very night every house in Egypt was touched by the hand of death; even all the firstborn in prisons were killed.

But nothing happened to the children of Israel. This is how the Lord made the difference between the Egyptians and the Israelites clear.

In the darkest hours of the night, Pharaoh summoned Moses and Aaron. He ordered them, "Go and serve your God, and take all your people and sheep and cattle with you. Leave this country!" The Egyptians wanted the children of Israel to leave as soon as possible, before more deaths occurred.

The children of Israel travelled from Rameses to Succoth. There were about six hundred thousand people on foot. In their haste to leave, each one had taken dough for making bread, and they carried it in the folds of their coats.

By day, the Lord showed his people the way with a pillar of cloud; by night, he lit up their path with a pillar of fire. This way they were able to travel both day and night.

Exodus 14

THE WATERS OF THE RED SEA DIVIDE

When Pharaoh heard that all the people of Israel had left, he felt a change of heart. Pharaoh said, "I should not have let them go! Now we have lost our servants! We must hunt them down!"

Pharaoh called all his armies into action. He made six hundred special chariots ready. His people followed him, some on foot and some on horseback.

They raced after the Israelites and found them camping beside the Red Sea. When the Hebrew people saw the Egyptians, they were terrified, and many shouted that they might as well have died in Egypt as here. Others said that they would have been better off serving the Egyptians than dying in the wilderness. There was panic and fear in the Hebrew people.

But Moses said, "Stand firm and do not be afraid. The Lord is with us and will save us. After tonight you will never again see these Egyptians. The Lord will fight for you."

And the Lord said to Moses, "Tell the children of Israel to go forwards. Lift up your rod, stretch out your hands, and the waters of the Red Sea will separate and allow you safe passage through them. The Egyptians who follow after you will learn that I am the Lord."

The angel of the Lord came between the two peoples. The pillar of cloud prevented the Egyptians from seeing the Israelites. But what was

Opposite: In the morning after the dew had disappeared, small round things, white as frost, remained on the ground. The people of Israel did not know what to call this food, so they gave it the name manna. And Moses told them this was the bread that God had promised.

darkness for the Egyptians was light for the Israelites. A strong wind from the east divided the Red Sea and created a passageway with great walls of water on either side.

The children of Israel entered this opening, and the Egyptians began to follow them across the dry seabed.

THE EGYPTIANS ARE DROWNED

Exodus 14

In the morning, the Egyptians grew afraid. Some said, "Let us flee from the Israelites. Their God fights for them against us."

Then God said to Moses, "Stretch out your hands over the sea. The waters will return as they were, and the Egyptians will drown with their chariots and horses."

Moses did this. And when Pharaoh and his men saw the water moving, they rode back. But it was too late. The Lord made the Egyptians drown in the middle of the sea. Every chariot was destroyed, and every man and horse died. Of all the people who had followed Pharaoh, not one remained alive.

This is the way God saved the children of Israel and led them safely out of Egypt. The Hebrew people feared and praised God, and they believed Moses to be His servant.

MANNA FROM HEAVEN

Exodus 15-16

After Moses and his people crossed the Red Sea, they entered a desert. After having marched for three days without any water, they came to a well in a place called Marah. But the water was too bitter to drink, and the people complained to Moses.

The Lord said to Moses, "Go and stand before the people of Israel, and let the elders stand with you. Take your rod that turned the waters of the Nile into blood. Go to the rock of Horeb, and I will be with you. Strike the rock with your rod, and water will gush out of it."

Moses called upon the Lord to help him. The Lord pointed out a piece of wood and told Moses to throw it in the well. He did this, and at once the bitter water became sweet and soothing.

On the fifteenth day of the second month after their flight out of Egypt, the children of Israel reached the wilderness of Sin. It was in this desert that the people lost heart and complained: "It would have been better to die by the Lord's hand in Egypt than to starve to death in this barren place. Does Moses want us all to die here?"

God spoke to Moses and Aaron: "Each day, I will cause bread to fall from heaven like rain, and each day, you will take what you need. On the sixth day, when you prepare your food, you will find it has doubled.

"I have heard the people of Israel complain. Tell them to have faith in God. They will eat meat in the evening and bread in the morning, and no one will go hungry."

In the morning after the dew had disappeared, small round things, white as frost, remained on the ground. The people of Israel did not know what to call this food, so they gave it the name manna. And Moses told them this was the bread that God had promised. He told them how much to gather.

Those who gathered a lot had nothing left over, but those who gathered a little were quite full. Moses grew angry when they kept the bread and it grew old and stank.

On the sixth day when they gathered bread, there was twice as much per person. When they saw this, they rushed to tell Moses, who said, "This is as the Lord has ordered it to be. Tomorrow is the Sabbath, the day of rest. Cook your food this evening and keep it for tomorrow, and it will not spoil."

They did this, and their food stayed fresh.

Moses said, "Eat the food you have cooked today, for this is the Sabbath, the day of our Lord. You will find no food in the fields on this day. For the Lord has said, 'Gather food for six days, but on the seventh day, which is the Sabbath, there will be no food to be found.'"

Despite what Moses said, there were still some people who went out on the Sabbath to gather food, but they found none. When God saw this, He said to Moses, "How long will you refuse to keep My commandments and laws? On the sixth day I give you bread for two days, but on the seventh day nobody should leave the place where he is."

So the people rested on the seventh day.

Moses addressed his people: "I will tell you what the Lord has commanded. You must keep a quantity so that future generations will recognise the bread of the Lord, which you ate when you were led out of the land of Egypt." And Moses told Aaron, "Take a pot and put manna in it. Place this before the Lord so that his name will never be forgotten."

And the children of Israel ate manna for forty years, until they finally reached the borders of the land of Canaan.

A LITTLE BIT OF HISTORY

When did the long journey of the Hebrew people to the Promised Land begin? The flight out of Egypt probably took place about 1250 B.C. There is no record of this event in any Egyptian writings. Perhaps the Egyptians felt that the flight of a group of seminomadic foreigners who had been their slaves was not worth recording. There are, however, carvings on a stone column in the museum in Cairo today that can help. Some carvings on this column that date from around 1220 B.C. record the victories of the reigning pharaoh, Menephtah, a son of Rameses. They also mention the expulsion from the country of a Semitic people called Israel.

The great caravan of people and animals crossed the Red Sea with the help of God. The original Hebrew says that they crossed "Yam-suf", meaning "the sea of reeds and rushes". Probably the writer was referring to a region of swamps where papyrus grew. Perhaps this region was Lake Timsa in the Sukkoth area, or the swamps to the east of the city of Rameses. The Hebrews could cross swamp regions with little danger, while the Egyptian war chariots would get bogged down or sink. Perhaps this is just what happened to them when they pursued the Hebrews, only to "drown in the middle of the sea".

A LITTLE BIT OF HISTORY
Joshua was the son of Nun from the Ephraim tribe. Aided by the supernatural power of Moses, he defeated Amalek and his army, who had attacked the Hebrews. Just before Moses died, he chose Joshua as the Hebrews' next leader. Joshua conquered the Promised Land and is remembered for breaking down the walls of Jericho.

WATER OUT OF A ROCK

The children of Israel left the wilderness of Sin, and following the Lord's commandments, they went to Rephidim, where they pitched their tents. But there was no water in the area. The people complained to Moses: "We must have drinking water!"

Moses replied, "Why do you complain to me when you know it angers your God?"

Things grew worse as the thirst of the people increased. They got angry with Moses and asked themselves questions, such as, "Why were we brought out of Egypt? Was it just to die of thirst?"

Moses spoke to the Lord: "I no longer know what to do with these people. They are nearly ready to stone me."

The Lord said to Moses, "Go and stand before the people of Israel, and let the elders stand with you. Take your rod that turned the waters of the Nile into blood. Go to the rock of Horeb, and I will be with you. Strike the rock with your rod, and water will gush out of it."

Moses did this in front of the elders of Israel, and everything was as the Lord had said it would be.

AMALEK IS DEFEATED

While the Israelites were encamped at Rephidim, they were attacked by Amalek and his army. Moses said to Joshua, "Choose some men, and go out and fight Amalek. I will stand on top of a hill with the rod of God in my hand."

Joshua did as he was ordered and battled against Amalek. Moses, Aaron, and Hur went to the top of a hill, and when Moses held up his hands, the Israelites were victorious. But when he dropped them, the Israelites fell back. When Aaron and Hur saw what was happening, they seated Moses on a stone and held up his hands so that they would not drop with weariness. They held his hands steady until the sun went down.

Joshua defeated Amalek and his people.

And God said to Moses, "Record these events in a book, and let Joshua know all about it. For I will wipe the name of Amalek from the face of the earth."

Moses built an altar, and he gave it the name of Jehovah. And the Lord was his banner, because he had defeated Amalek for ever.

Opposite: When Moses held up his hands, the Israelites were victorious. But when he dropped them, the Israelites fell back. When Aaron and Hur saw what was happening, they seated Moses on a stone and held up his hands so that they would not drop with weariness. They held his hands steady until the sun went down.

THE TEN COMMANDMENTS

In the third month after their exodus from Egypt, the children of Israel came to a mountain called Sinai. This was also the name of that country. It was a wilderness, but it was here that they pitched their tents.

God called to Moses from the mountaintop, and Moses went up to speak to Him. And the Lord said, "You must speak to the people of Israel as I tell you. Say, 'You have seen what I did to the Egyptians and how I carried you here on an eagle's wing.' Tell them that if they listen to My voice and keep My covenant, then they will occupy a special place with Me. They will be a kingdom of priests, and the children of Israel will be a holy nation.

"Tell them, I am the Lord your God, who brought you out of the land of Egypt where you were slaves. You will have no other gods. You must not bow to any image you have made, nor must you serve it in any way. I am a jealous God, and if you serve false gods, you will suffer, as will your children and their children. To the thousands who love Me and follow My commandments, I will show mercy. You must not mock My name, for those who do I will find guilty.

"Remember the Sabbath and keep it as a holy day. You will work for six days, but the seventh day is the day of the Lord. Then you will not work, nor will your sons, daughters, servants, or houseguests. Remember, the Lord made heaven, earth, and the sea and everything that lives there in six days, but on the seventh day, the Lord rested. This day is the Sabbath, and it is a holy day.

"Have respect for your father and mother. In this way you will live good, long lives in the land that the Lord has given you.

"You must not kill.

"You must not commit adultery.

"You must not steal.

"You must not tell lies about your neighbours.

"You must not want your neighbour's wife, or anything that belongs to your neighbours."

The people heard thunder and saw lightning. There was the sound of trumpets, and the mountain was covered in smoke. The Israelites became afraid.

But Moses said, "Do not be afraid! God may test you, but He shows His powers only so that you may know Him and commit no sins."

THE ARK OF THE COVENANT

God spoke to Moses once more on the mountaintop.

"Tell the children of Israel to make an offering for Me. Their offering should be gold, silver, brass, fine-coloured cloths, rams' skins dyed red, badgers' skins, fine woods, oils, incense, and precious stones. Also they should make a wooden ark. The ark should be covered with gold inside and out, and it should have a crown of gold on the top. It should be placed on poles inlaid with gold, so that wherever the people travel they may take their ark with them. On either side of the ark, place a cherub made of gold. They should face one another, because from the

Opposite: God spoke to him: "I am the Lord your God, who brought you out of the land of Egypt where you were slaves. You will have no other gods."

point where their faces meet, I will give My commandments to the children of Israel."

THEY WORSHIP THE GOLDEN CALF

Moses spoke to God for a long time. The people of Israel grew restless, and they went to Aaron and said, "Let us make gods that we can see."

Aaron saw the way things were, and he said, "Tell your sons and daughters and all those who wear gold earrings to bring them to me."

The people did this. Aaron had the gold melted down and made into a statue of a golden calf.

Aaron placed the golden calf before the people, and he said, "Here then, people of Israel, is your god who brought you out of the land of Egypt." Then he built an altar in front of the golden calf and told the people, "Tomorrow is a feast in honour of the Lord."

The next day, the people got up early and brought offerings. They ate and drank and enjoyed themselves.

God knew everything that was going on. He said to Moses, "Go down from the mountain now, for the people you brought out of Egypt are not following My commandments. They have melted down gold and made an image of a calf, and they say it is this which brought them safely out of Egypt. Go immediately, for I am angry and disappointed."

And Moses hung his head and pleaded for his people. He could do no more.

THE ANGER OF MOSES

Moses came down from the mountain. In his hands, he carried two tablets made of stone. On both sides of these tablets, God had written His Ten Commandments.

He approached the camp and heard sounds of dancing and singing. This made him very angry, so he broke the stone tablets. He went up to the golden calf, took hold of it, and threw it in a fire.

The next day Moses said to his people, "You have committed a great sin. I must go back to the Lord and beg Him to forgive you."

Moses went back to the mountaintop and spoke with his God: "Forgive them! I know they have committed a great sin. Punish me, if You must, Lord."

And the Lord replied, "I will blot the sinners out of My book. Go back to your people and lead them in the ways I have shown you. I will send an angel to help you along the way so that you do not get lost. Beware the sins of the people!"

Moses came down from the mountain. In his hands, he carried two tablets made of stone. On both sides of these tablets, God had written His Ten Commandments.

He approached the camp and heard sounds of dancing and singing. This made him very angry, so he broke the stone tablets.

Exodus 33

THE PUNISHMENT OF THE LORD

And the Lord caused diseases to break out among the people, because they had made the golden calf with Aaron.

Moses took the tabernacle with the ark and set it up a long way from the camp, and he called it the Tabernacle of the Congregation. Anyone who wished to speak to God had to go to the tabernacle.

When Moses entered the tent, a cloudy pillar descended and stopped at the entrance to the tent. And all the people left the camp and went to the tabernacle, and they fell on their knees. Then the Lord drew close to Moses and spoke to him face-to-face, as a man would speak to his friend. Moses was blessed by God.

Numbers 13-14

THE ISRAELITES PREPARE TO ENTER THE LAND OF CANAAN

God spoke to Moses when he was in the desert of Paran: "Send some men into the land of Canaan so that they may find out the kind of country it is. This is the land I have promised to the children of Israel. Send a chief from each of the tribes." And Moses chose twelve chiefs from the tribes of Israel and sent them into Canaan.

The twelve men explored the land and reached the brook of Eshcol. Here they cut down a single branch, which contained one bunch of grapes. This fruit was so heavy that two men had to carry it between them on sticks. They also gathered pomegranates and figs.

The twelve men explored the land and reached the brook of Eshcol. Here they cut down a single branch, which contained one bunch of grapes. This fruit was so heavy that two men had to carry it between them on sticks. They also gathered pomegranates and figs.

When forty days had passed, they returned from their investigation of the country. They showed everyone the fruits of the land and made

their report: "We went into the land, as Moses directed us. It really is a country rich in milk and honey. However, the people who live there already are very powerful. Their cities are huge and protected by high walls. And another thing, we saw giants there so big that they made us feel like ants."

When the children of Israel heard this, they cried out in fear and went to their tents and wept.

Once more, they were unhappy with Moses and Aaron. The whole congregation moaned to them: "We might as well have died in Egypt or even in this desert. Has God brought us here to see our families butchered? We may as well return to Egypt! Let's choose a captain who will lead us back to Egypt."

When the Lord heard this kind of talk, He said to Moses, "How long will these people disobey Me? They say those things despite all the signs I have shown to them. I will strike them down with disease."

MOSES PLEADS FOR HIS PEOPLE

But Moses said to the Lord, "I pray that the power of the Lord will be great. You have told me that You are slow to grow angry and full of mercy, that You forgive sin and error. I beg You now to forgive the miserable behaviour of these people as You have forgiven them before, ever since they left the land of Egypt."

Moses made a snake out of brass and placed it on a pole, and whoever looked at this snake was healed of his wound.

72

THE PARDON AND THE PUNISHMENT

God said to Moses, "I will pardon the people because you ask Me to. But as for those who have seen My glory and seen the miracles I performed in Egypt and the desert, and tempted Me ten times and *still* not listened to My voice, they do not deserve to enter the land that I swore to give to their fathers. Those who have said things against Me should wander in this desert for forty years."

WANDERINGS IN THE DESERT

The Israelites left the desert of Paran and reached the desert of Zin. They made camp in Kadesh.

Once more the people found they were without water, and they blamed Moses and Aaron. They said, "It would have been better to have died when our brothers died in view of the Lord! Why have you brought us into this wilderness? What was the point in leaving Egypt to bring us to this barren place? There are no figs, grapes, or pomegranates here, and there is no water!"

Moses and Aaron left the gathering of the people and went into the tabernacle. They knelt in prayer, and the Lord appeared before them.

The Lord said to Moses, "Call the people together. Have Aaron with you, and carry your rod. You will see a rock; speak to it, and it will run with water, which the people and their animals may drink."

Moses did as he was commanded by the Lord. The people gathered round him. He addressed them, "Listen, you rebels. Must we bring water out of this rock for you?"

Moses lifted up his rod and struck the rock twice, and at once it ran with enough water for all the people and their animals.

Then the Lord spoke to Moses and Aaron: "Because you did not believe in Me and glorify My holy name before the people of Israel, you will not enter the land that I have given you."

Then Aaron, the brother of Moses, died in the desert of Moab, and the people of Israel wept for him for thirty days.

The Israelites set out on a long journey. It was not long before they were exhausted and complaining bitterly about God and Moses. "Why were we taken out of the land of Egypt? Was it just to die in this desert, where there is no food and water?"

Then the Lord grew angry and sent poisonous snakes to bite the people. Many died.

The people ran in terror to Moses. "We know we have sinned by talking against you and God. Have mercy. Beg God to send these snakes away."

Moses prayed for the people, and God answered him: "Make a fiery-looking snake and put it on a pole. Whoever has been bitten by a snake, when he looks at this snake, will survive."

Moses made a snake out of brass and placed it on a pole, and whoever looked at this snake was healed of his wound.

BALAAM AND THE KING OF MOAB

At this time a man named Balak, the son of Zippor, was king of the land of Moab. He knew about the number and fierceness of the Israelites, and he was afraid. He sent messengers to Balaam, a seer, saying,

"A people have come out of Egypt. They number in the thousands, and they are coming into my land. Grant me a favour: Curse these people so that if we meet in battle, I will be the victor and will drive them out of my country."

But God said to Balaam, "Do not take your men with you to Moab, and do not curse these people, for they are blessed."

The following morning, Balaam called the messengers from Balak to him. "Go back to your country. The Lord has forbidden me to go with you."

The elders from Moab returned to their leader, Balak, and told him what had happened.

Then Balak sent other messengers to Balaam, and this time they were princes and there were more of them.

Numbers 22

BALAAM AND THE ANGEL

One day Balaam got up, saddled his donkey, and set off with the princes from Moab.

And God grew angry when he saw Balaam leave. He sent his angel and placed him in the road Balaam was traveling.

Balaam's donkey saw in the road the angel of the Lord, with his naked sword in his hand. The donkey turned and went into a nearby field. Balaam slapped his donkey to make it get back on the road. But the angel of the Lord stood on a path in the vineyards where there were walls on either side. The donkey saw the angel again and ran into the wall, so that Balaam's foot was crushed. In anger, Balaam struck the donkey.

Then the angel of the Lord stood on a narrow path, where it was impossible to turn to the left or right. When the donkey saw the angel, it fell down with Balaam on top of it. By this time Balaam was furious, and he struck his beast with a stick.

Then God gave the animal the ability to talk, and it said to Balaam, "What have I done to deserve being hit three times?"

And Balaam said, "You have made fun of me. If I had a sword, I would kill you with it."

The donkey replied, "I am your donkey, and you have always ridden me until now. Did I ever do anything like this to you before?"

Then the Lord opened Balaam's eyes wider so that he saw the angel of the Lord standing in his way, with his sword drawn. Balaam bowed his head and fell down onto his knees.

The angel of the Lord said, "Why did you strike your donkey three times? I am here to fight you, because I do not care for the road you are travelling down. The donkey saw me and turned away from me three times. If the beast had not turned away, I would have killed you and saved the animal's life."

Balaam replied, "I have sinned against you. I did not know you opposed this journey. If I have displeased you, I will return to my home."

The angel of the Lord said to Balaam, "Go on with the princes, but when you stand in front of the king, you must only say what I tell you to say."

A LITTLE BIT OF HISTORY
The Moabites were a people similar to the Hebrews. They were originally nomadic but later settled to the east of the Jordan between the Dead Sea and the Arabian Desert. They were often at war with the Hebrews. They worshipped many gods, but their chief god was called Khemos. Their language was similar to Hebrew.

THE MEETING BETWEEN BALAAM AND BALAK

When Balak saw that Balaam had arrived, he went out to meet him, with promises of honour and promotion. But Balaam said, "I have come here as you requested, but I only have the power to speak the words that God puts into my mouth."

The next day Balak led Balaam to one of Baal's high places so that they could look down and see the tents of the Israelites. Balaam said to Balak, "Build me seven altars here, and prepare seven oxen and seven rams for sacrifice."

Balak did as Balaam had told him, and on every altar there was a bullock and a ram. Then Balaam went off alone, and God met him. Balaam said, "I have prepared seven altars, and there is a bullock and a ram on each one."

God said, "Go back to Balak, and speak as I tell you to."

Balaam went back to Balak, who was standing by his burnt sacrifice with the princes of Moab. When he started speaking, what came out of his mouth was a blessing for the people of Israel, not a curse. Three times they offered sacrifices, and three times the words of God flew from Balaam's lips. Each time, the words blessed the people of Israel.

Balaam's donkey saw in the road the angel of the Lord, with his naked sword in his hand.

And Balaam went into a kind of trance and praised the children of Israel in song:

How fine the tents look, O Jacob!
How fine your tabernacles, O Israel!
They spread like valleys
And look like gardens beside a river.
It was the Lord God who brought you out of Egypt
And He who ate up the nations that were your enemies.
He broke their bones and filled them with arrows.
He lay down like a great lion.
Who would dare to disturb Him?
Those who bless Him will be blessed,
But those who curse Him will be cursed.

When Balak heard all this, he went into a fit of rage and said, "I brought you here to put a curse on my enemies, but you have blessed them three times. Go back to your own country!"

Balaam said, "I told you it would be impossible to go against God's holy commandments. I told you that I would speak with the words of the Lord. Now, before I return to my own people, I will tell you what these people will become."

And Balaam made this prophecy:

"A star will rise out of Jacob, and a sceptre will be in the hand of Israel. They will strike the four corners of Moab and destroy the children of Sheth. Edom will be conquered, and Israel will be victorious. From the offspring of Jacob will come a man who will be triumphant and destroy anything that remains of your cities."

With these words, Balaam left that country and returned to his own.

Deuteronomy 31

THE LAST WORDS OF MOSES TO HIS PEOPLE

It was forty years after their flight from Egypt that God said to Moses, "You are one hundred and twenty years old. The day of your death cannot be far off. Call Joshua, and meet in the Tabernacle of the Congregation."

In the tabernacle, God appeared to Moses and Joshua in a pillar of smoke. The Lord gave Joshua His commandment: "Be strong and brave, because it will be you who will lead the children of Israel into the land that I promised to them. Take heart, for I will be with you!"

Moses spoke to his people: "O Israel, the time is now to follow the laws of God. You must turn neither to the right nor to the left, but you must walk straight ahead as God directs. Do this, and you will be happy and live long lives in the land you occupy. Listen carefully, my people. Practise the commandments of your God, and your numbers will grow, and you will find peace in the land that is rich in milk and honey."

Moses went on: "Hear me, people of Israel. The Lord is our God; the Lord is the one and only God. You will love the Lord God with all your heart, with all your soul, and with all your strength. Keep in your heart what I have said today, and repeat it to your children. You cannot say the words often enough. You should say them when you are sitting at home, when you are about to go on a journey, before you go to bed, and when you get up in the morning.

"These words will be like something firm in your hands; they will be a light to guide you. Write them on the gates and doors of your houses. If you faithfully obey the voice of the Lord, if you faithfully put into practice the commandments I have given you, then the Lord God will make you the strongest nation in the world. Finally, if you listen to the voice of the Lord, He will pour countless blessings on you."

THE DEATH AND THE SONG OF MOSES
Deuteronomy 31-32, 34

Moses recited this song before the whole nation of Israel:

I ask the heavens and the earth
To hear the words that fall from my mouth.
My teachings shall drop like rain;
My speech will be as clear as dew,
And like gentle rain on delicate herbs
And like showers of rain upon the grass.
I will speak the name of the Lord out loud
And give glory to God.
He is the Rock and His work is perfect.
All His ways are fair.
He is the God of truth
And He is without cruelty.
He is just and right.
False generations and unworthy children
Have sinned against Him.
Is this the way to thank God?
My people, you have been foolish and unwise.
God is the Father who created you,
Who shaped your lives and showed you the way.
Look back to the past
And think about the passage of time.
Ask your father, and he will teach you things;
Speak to old people, and they will tell you our history.
Israel is part of the heritage of God.
God found it in a barren country;
He nurtured it, He cared for it,
And it became the apple of His eye.
God was like an eagle,
Which spreads its wings over its young
In order to protect them in the nest.
God alone guided you and led you,
And God was never a stranger to His people.
He caused plants to flourish in the countryside;
He brought honey out of rocks and oil out of flints;
Rich milk came from cows and sheep;
Lambs were plentiful, and the wheat was golden;
And grapes were pressed, and the drink was pure.
In the past, our country grew big and fat;

It was heavy and lazy.
It turned its back on God, its creator;
It forgot the Rock, its salvation.
And when the nation worshipped false gods,
Our own Lord God was angry.
God saw and furiously condemned
Those sons and daughters.
God said,
"This is a lost generation of faithless children."
But even after all their sins,
The Lord showed justice to His people
And had mercy on those who served Him.
And God spoke again, saying,
"I am the God who may give life or bring death;
I may kill, or I may heal wounds.
There are no greater gods, and no one can resist My power.
Now I raise My hands to heaven and tell you,
I am life without end.

Then Moses left the flatlands of Moab. He went up the mountain of Nebo, which overlooked Jericho and the land of Canaan, which God had promised to the children of Israel.

And God said, "This is the land I swore to give to Abraham, to Isaac, to Jacob, and to those who came after them. Look carefully at this land, because you will not live to go there."

Then, as God had said, Moses, His servant, died on that mountain within sight of the Promised Land.

To this day nobody knows exactly where Moses is buried.

Although Moses was a hundred and twenty years old when he died, his eyesight remained good, and he was full of energy.

On the plains of Moab the children of Israel wept for Moses for thirty days. Even after the mourning was over, the people continued to speak of Moses. They said, "In all of Israel there was never a prophet like Moses. He spoke to God face-to-face, just as though he were talking to a friend."

God had commanded Moses to choose a successor, and Moses had chosen Joshua.

As Moses had felt death coming to him, he placed his hands on Joshua's head and in this way passed on to him the spirit of wisdom, which is the spirit of God.

And Israel had a new leader.

Opposite: Then, as God had said, Moses, His servant, died on that mountain within sight of the Promised Land.

To this day nobody knows exactly where Moses is buried.

After their flight from Egypt, the Hebrew people did not take the shortest route to Israel, which would have been along the Mediterranean coast. Instead, they entered the peninsula of Sinai in order to avoid the Egyptians on the border. Their journey took them along some already existing tracks, and they stopped at the oases. The Israelites reached a mountain in the southern part of the peninsula—Mount Sinai. It was there that God gave Moses the Ten Commandments. Then they travelled north toward the land of Canaan. This was the land that God had promised to their ancestors.

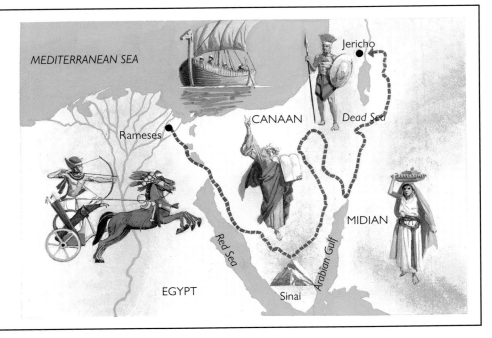

MEDITERRANEAN SEA

Jericho

CANAAN

Dead Sea

Rameses

MIDIAN

Red Sea

Arabian Gulf

EGYPT

Sinai

THE BIRTH OF ISRAEL

THE PROMISED LAND

After the death of Moses, the Lord spoke to Joshua and gave him advice: "Moses, My servant, is dead. It is now up to you to take the people across Jordan and into the Promised Land. For as long as you live, no army will conquer the children of Israel. As I was with Moses, so I will be with you. I will not fail you or abandon you.

"Be brave and strong, and follow the laws which My servant, Moses, passed on to you. Do not stray from the path of righteousness. Do this, and all your efforts will be successful.

"Never be afraid! I will always be with you wherever you go."

Then Joshua went back to the people with God's word. He told his officers to tell the people to prepare food and be ready to move camp, because within three days they would cross the river Jordan and enter the land that God had promised them.

When the people heard this, they knew that Joshua was their new leader and that they should follow him.

JOSHUA'S SPIES IN JERICHO

Joshua chose two men and sent them secretly into Jericho. Here they found a place to stay in a house that belonged to a woman named Rahab.

The men, however, must have been seen, because word soon reached the king of Jericho that men from the children of Israel had entered the city under cover of night and were staying in Rahab's house.

The king of Jericho sent a message to Rahab, saying that she should send the men staying in her house to him, as they were spies. But Rahab hid the two men. When officials from the king arrived, she told them, "It's true there were two men here, but I do not know where they came from. They left when it was dark—just about the time the gates of the city are closed. If you are quick, you may overtake them."

The officials left. Rahab closed her door and went to speak to the men. She had hidden them under stalks of flax on the flat roof.

Meanwhile, the king's men pursued the spies into Jordan, and the gates of the city were closed.

Before the men in Rahab's hiding place went to sleep, she said to them, "I know the Lord has given this land to you. All of us are terrified. We have heard about everything that the Lord has done for you. We know the Lord dried up the waters of the Red Sea when you left Egypt. When we heard all this, we hardly dared breathe, for we were stricken with terror. We knew then that your Lord is God and that He marched before you. He is the God of the heavens above and the earth beneath our feet. This is my request: I beg you to show mercy to me and my family, as I have helped you in your hour of need. Promise me that my father and mother, my sisters and brothers, and all their children will not be killed."

Opposite: The people of Israel broke camp and crossed over the river Jordan. The priests who carried the Ark of the Covenant marched ahead of the people.

This was harvest time, and the waters of the Jordan were swollen from bank to bank. Hardly had the priests who carried the tabernacle put a foot in the water than the waters went down and ran away as though into another place.
The land became dry. The Ark of the Covenant of the Lord stood firm on dry land in the middle of the river Jordan.

RAHAB AND THE SPIES MAKE AN AGREEMENT

The two men quickly replied, "We will let you and all your family live on one condition: that not a word about us reaches the king. Once we have taken this country, we will treat you well and show you mercy."

Preceding pages: On the seventh day, they got up at dawn and marched round the city, but this time they circled the city seven times. Then Joshua gave his command: "Shout your war cry, and the Lord will give you the city!"

The trumpets blasted, and the people shouted. The walls of the city crashed to the ground.

After this agreement, Rahab helped the men to escape. Because her house was built on the city wall, a rope was lowered from a window so that the men could go down the rope. Rahab gave them this advice: "Go into the mountains and hide there for three days. The king's men will have given up the search by then, and you will be able to return to your people."

The men told her, "When the children of Israel enter the country, keep all your family in your house, and make sure you put this scarlet rope used for our escape in your window. If anyone leaves your house and goes into the street, it will be your fault, but if anyone inside your house is hurt, it will be our fault. We must keep the promises we have made."

And Rahab replied, "It will be exactly as you say."

With this exchange, the men left, and the scarlet rope was bound in Rahab's window.

They hid in the mountains for three days. It was then safe to return to Joshua and tell him everything that had happened. They said, "The Lord has really given us this country. The inhabitants tremble at our very name!"

Then Joshua knew it was time to act.

Joshua 3-4

CROSSING THE JORDAN

The people of Israel broke camp and crossed over the river Jordan. The priests who carried the Ark of the Covenant marched ahead of the people.

This was harvest time, and the waters of the Jordan were swollen from bank to bank. Hardly had the priests who carried the tabernacle put a foot in the water than the waters went down and ran away as though into another place. The land became dry. The Ark of the Covenant of the Lord stood firm on dry land in the middle of the river Jordan.

This is how the whole nation of Israel crossed the river, from bank to bank, without getting wet.

Joshua gave the order that the Lord had given him: "Take stones from where the Ark of the Covenant of the Lord dried the waters of the river. Let twelve men, one from each tribe, go and carry a stone on his back. These stones must be placed in your houses. Remember, in the future, when your children ask you, 'What is the meaning of these stones?' you will then be able to reply, 'They remind us of the day the ark of the Lord's covenant swept back the waters of the Jordan.'"

Joshua 6

THE FALL OF JERICHO

Jericho was a walled city. Its gates were closed. Nobody dared enter or leave, for fear of the children of Israel.

And God said to Joshua, "You see, I have given you the city of Jericho, and its king and its bravest warriors.

"Surround the city with your soldiers and walk round it once. Do this for six days. Seven priests will walk in front of the ark with seven trumpets made from rams' horns. On the seventh day, circle the city seven times, and the priests must blow their trumpets.

"When the people hear the long blast of the trumpet, they must give a great shout. Then the walls of the city will fall down flat."

Joshua ordered the Ark of the Covenant to be taken round the city for the first time, and then the people went back to their camp for the night.

The next day Joshua got up early. Seven priests with seven trumpets of rams' horns marched in front of the ark, sounding their instruments. The soldiers marched in front of the priests, and the crowd followed the ark. They did this and then went back to camp. This was done for six days.

On the seventh day, they got up at dawn and marched round the city, but this time they circled the city seven times. Then Joshua gave his command: "Shout your war cry, and the Lord will give you the city!"

The trumpets blasted, and the people shouted. The walls of the city crashed to the ground. The soldiers of Israel charged into Jericho, and the city was theirs.

Joshua did not forget Rahab. He sent the two spies who had stayed with her to her house. They brought out Rahab and her family, gave them safe escort, and looked after them. Everything had gone according to their agreement.

JOSHUA AND THE INHABITANTS OF GIBEON

Joshua 8-9

The Lord said to Joshua, "Do not be afraid or alarmed. Take your best warriors and go to the city of Ai. As I gave you the city of Jericho, so will you take this one also."

Joshua chose thirty thousand of his most valiant warriors and attacked the city of Ai, and it fell as Jericho had. The goods and cattle of Ai became the property of the children of Israel.

When the kings of the countries on this side of the Jordan and the kings in the hills and valleys heard what had happened to Jericho and Ai, they were very frightened of Joshua and his men. They decided to unite as one army and attack Israel.

The people of Gibeon also heard what Joshua had done to Jericho and Ai, but they made their own secret plan. They sent messengers to Joshua. These messengers were dressed in filthy old rags, and their shoes were falling apart. They carried old bottles of wine and dry, mouldy bread with them.

They met Joshua at his camp in Gilgal, not far from Jericho. They said, "We have come from a distant land and wish to make a pact with you. We will gladly serve you."

Joshua said, "Who are you? Which country do you come from?"

And they repeated, "Our country is far away, but we have heard of your Lord and what He did in Egypt. The elders of our country instructed us to make this journey. Our bread had scarcely cooled from the oven when we set off, and now it is old and mouldy. It's the same with our wine; even that has spoiled. The journey was so long, our clothes have fallen to pieces and our shoes have come apart."

The men of Israel looked at the food and drink and clothing of these strangers, and without seeking advice from the oracle of the Lord, Joshua made peace with them and swore that they should live.

Three days went by before Joshua discovered the truth. These so-called strangers from a distant land were really the natives of that same territory. The children of Israel reached the wealthy city of Gibeon, but

A LITTLE BIT OF HISTORY
Before the Hebrew people left Egypt, the Canaanites and the Amorites, both Semitic peoples, occupied the land next to the Promised Land and the Jordan valley. They were trading nations that exported wood and purple cloth to Syria, Egypt, and the islands in the Aegean Sea. Their culture is primarily remembered for the invention of a written alphabet. Before the end of the third millennium B.C., the Canaanites of Byblos had developed a syllabic writing that drew its inspiration from Egyptian hieroglyphics. In the fourteenth century B.C., the writers of Canaan were using a linear alphabet that had been perfected by the Phoenicians, who lived in the same region. The Greeks based their alphabet on that of the Phoenicians, the Romans based theirs on the Greeks', and ours is based on the Romans'. Toward the end of the thirteenth century B.C., the Hebrew people came into possession of the Promised Land.

they did not dare go into battle, because they had given promises of peace. Joshua decided that the inhabitants of Gibeon should become woodcutters and drawers of water for the altar of the Lord. And this should be their situation wherever the people were and for all time.

Joshua 10-11

SUN, DO NOT SET! MOON, DO NOT RISE!

When Adoni-zedec, the king of Jerusalem, learnt that Joshua had taken Ai and Jericho and completely destroyed them, and that he had made a pact of peace with the inhabitants of Gibeon, he was struck with terror. Gibeon was a great and royal city, full of mighty warriors. He knew he had to act at once.

He joined forces with four other kings, and together they made ready for war. They attacked the city of Gibeon to punish it for making a pact with the children of Israel.

The people of Gibeon did not lose a moment in sending word to Joshua's camp in Gilgal. They pleaded, "Come quickly and save your servants! We are surrounded by Amorite kings!"

Joshua made his army ready, and it was full of brave and strong men. And the Lord spoke to Joshua and told him not to be afraid: "I will bring you victory. Your enemy will fall beneath your swords and spears."

Then Joshua left his camp, and with his army he took the Amorites by surprise. Vast numbers died by the sword, and the rest were put to flight. The Lord poured heavy hailstones on those who ran from battle,

The sun and the moon did not move until the armies of Israel had killed all their enemies.

Never before had such a thing happened! The Lord heard the words of His subject and fought with the children of Israel!

and more died from the hailstones of the Lord than died in battle.

Joshua's voice rose with these words: "Sun, do not set! Moon, do not rise until I have conquered my enemies!"

The sun and the moon did not move until the armies of Israel had killed all their enemies.

Never before had such a thing happened! The Lord heard the words of His subject and fought with the children of Israel!

Joshua conquered all the kings in that area. He was victorious in the hills and in the valleys. Gradually he conquered the whole country. This was what the Lord had promised to Moses, and this was what He had promised to the people of Israel. All the land was divided among the twelve tribes of Israel.

JOSHUA IN HIS OLD AGE
SPEAKS TO HIS PEOPLE, *Joshua 23-24*

Time passed, and the Lord brought peace to the people of Israel. Their enemies were dead, and Joshua had grown old. Joshua knew that he would soon die, so he called a meeting. The elders, the leaders, and the judges were all present.

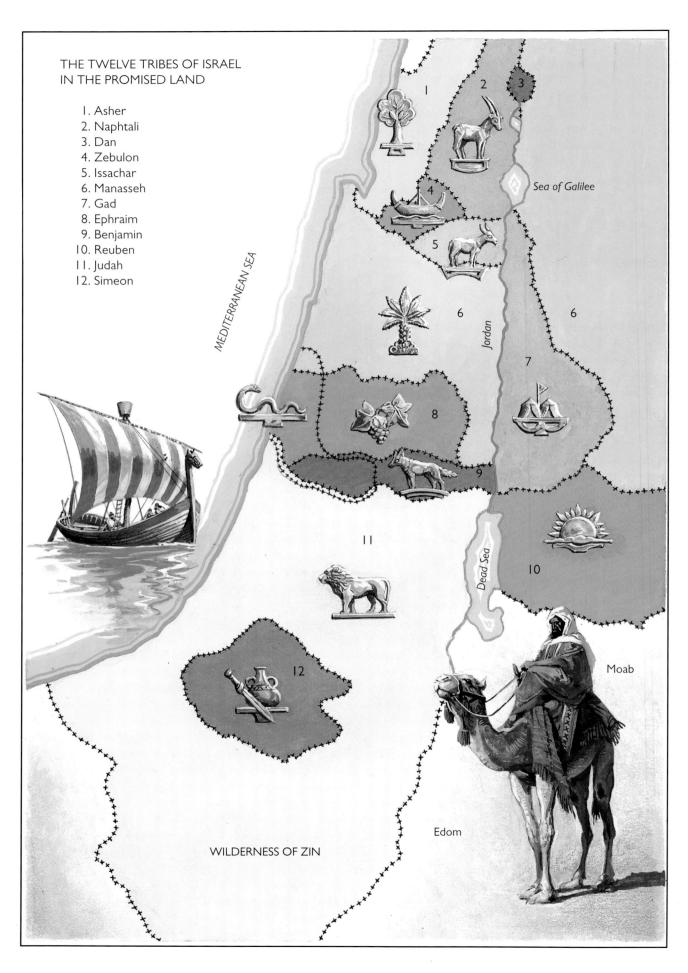

THE TWELVE TRIBES OF ISRAEL
IN THE PROMISED LAND

1. Asher
2. Naphtali
3. Dan
4. Zebulon
5. Issachar
6. Manasseh
7. Gad
8. Ephraim
9. Benjamin
10. Reuben
11. Judah
12. Simeon

MEDITERRANEAN SEA

Sea of Galilee

Jordan

Dead Sea

Moab

Edom

WILDERNESS OF ZIN

Joshua addressed the gathering: "I am an old man now. You have seen what the Lord has done for you. He has fought on your side and made victory possible. I have divided the land as God directed. It is now up to you to remain faithful to God and follow the laws that Moses brought from God. Remember, you must turn neither to the left nor to the right, but always follow His laws. If there are any among you who still follow false gods, turn away from them and worship the one true God! Stay with the Lord! If you do not do this, God will not help you. Your enemies will not fall and die by your sword. You will lose the land that the Lord your God has given you. You see, I have grown old, and I am fast approaching the end of my life on earth. It is for this reason that I have called this meeting. I am here to tell you to follow the ways of the Lord and to remember the covenant He made with you. Always remember it, and remember His mercy and His love. Never stray from the commandments of the Lord; if you do, the Lord will grow angry, and you will disappear from the land that God has given you."

With these words Joshua left his people, and they returned to their lands.

Joshua died at the age of one hundred and ten years.

He was buried at Timnath-serah in the mountains of Ephraim on the north side of the hill of Gaash.

And while Joshua was their leader, the children of Israel had served him and the Lord faithfully.

A LITTLE BIT OF HISTORY
Joshua distributed the conquered land as an inheritance to the people of Israel. He divided it among the twelve tribes according to their size. On the map we can see which areas were allotted to which tribes. One tribe stayed at least temporarily beyond the river Jordan. Another, the Manasseh, was divided into two groups. One group stayed beyond the river Jordan, while the other entered the Promised Land. Each tribe is shown on the map opposite by its number. The tribes had carried standards with these symbols on them throughout their long exodus. Edom and Moab to the south were the enemies of the people of Israel.

When Samson was alone and walking by a vineyard, a young lion, roaring ferociously, sprang at him. Samson had no weapon, but the spirit of God was in him. He took hold of the lion and pulled it apart, as though it were nothing more than a baby goat.

SAMSON AND THE PHILISTINES

Many years after the death of Joshua, the children of Israel once again turned to evil, so God punished them by making the Philistines conquer them. This period of hardship lasted forty years.

At this time there was a man of the Danites whose name was Manoah. The angel of the Lord appeared to Manoah's wife and said, "You have no child, but a child will be born. You will have a son. You must take care that his head is never shaved. This boy will be blessed at birth by God, and your son will free the children of Israel from the hand of the Philistines."

In due course a son was born, and he was named Samson. The child grew strong, and God watched over him and blessed him.

One day when Samson was a young man, he was in Timnath, where he saw a young woman who was a Philistine. He wanted her to be his wife, and he told his mother and father about her.

They shook their heads and said, "Surely there must be a woman from our own people you could marry without looking among the Philistines?" They did not know that God had planned these things.

Samson said, "This is the woman I wish to marry. I ask you to come with me and help me in this matter."

Samson and his parents went to Timnath. When Samson was alone and walking by a vineyard, a young lion, roaring ferociously, sprang at him. Samson had no weapon, but the spirit of God was in him. He took hold of the lion and pulled it apart, as though it were nothing more than a baby goat. He did not tell his parents what had happened.

Some time later he returned to Timnath to marry the young Philistine woman. He went a little out of his way to see the body of the lion. In it he saw a swarm of bees and fresh honey. He ate some honey and took some for his parents.

Samson's father stayed with the Philistine woman and made arrangements for the wedding. The feast would last seven days, as was the custom then.

Thirty young Philistines joined Samson. He gave them a riddle, saying, "If you can solve this within the seven days of the wedding feast, I will give you thirty sheets and thirty changes of clothing. If you cannot solve the riddle, you must give me the sheets and clothing."

They replied, "Let us hear the riddle!"

Samson said, "Out of the eater came meat, and out of the strong came sweetness."

For three days, the Philistines struggled to find the meaning of the riddle, but without success. On the fourth day, they said to Samson's new wife, "Find out the meaning of this riddle from your husband. He will tell you. If you do not do this, we will burn you alive—not only you, but your father and his household also!"

Samson's wife pleaded with him: "You do not love me! You must hate me! You have given my people a riddle, but you have not told your own wife what it means."

A LITTLE BIT OF HISTORY

During the period described in the Book of Judges, a radical evolution had taken place in the way the twelve tribes of Israel lived. They were no longer a nomadic people but had settled on the land.

Although they were surrounded by enemies and had no single government, the twelve tribes nevertheless survived.

The judges were men inspired by the spirit of God. They led the people to victory in war. Their military power, which lasted from 1200 to 1030 B.C., became in times of peace a civic authority. They were the arbitrators in matters of dispute. The Book of Judges is best known for the story of the judge Samson, who fought against the might of the Philistines.

About 1200 B.C. the Philistines were mentioned in Egyptian documents. They were referred to as seagoing people, originally from the island of Crete. They had settled in the area later called Palestine, whose name comes from the Hebrew word for Philistine. For a long time they imposed their will on the Israelites. Samson tried in vain to oppose them. They remained the dominant power until the beginning of the reign of David.

Samson said, "I have not even told my father and mother the answer. Why should I tell you?"

While the wedding feast went on, Samson's wife moaned and wept until at last, on the seventh day, Samson gave in and told her what the riddle meant. She at once told her people.

On the seventh day, in the evening before the sun had set, Samson was seated with the Philistines, and they gave him the answer to the riddle: "What is sweeter than honey? What is stronger than a lion?"

Samson replied, "You would have no answer if my wife hadn't told you."

And the spirit of the Lord rose up in Samson. He went to a place called Ashkelon and killed thirty Philistines. He took their clothes and brought them to the men who had solved the riddle.

Then he returned to his mother and father's home, still in great anger. The father of Samson's wife thought his daughter had been abandoned, so he made another marriage for her with a friend of Samson's.

THE DEEDS OF SAMSON

Judges 15

It was some time after these events that Samson went back to Timnath with a gift of a baby goat for his wife. It was harvest time when Samson reached the house. He told his father-in-law that he had come to see his wife. The man explained that he had thought Samson had abandoned her. He offered Samson his other daughter in marriage.

Samson flew into a great rage. He went out into the fields and trapped three hundred foxes and tied them tail to tail. He put flaming torches between their tails and set the animals free. The foxes ran through the Philistines' corn, and through their vineyards and olive plantations, and all the crops were set on fire and reduced to piles of smouldering ash.

The Philistines shouted, "Who has done this?" But they knew the answer. It was Samson.

The Philistines went to the house of Samson's wife, and they burnt her to death and her father with her.

When Samson learnt what had happened, he took a terrible revenge. He killed many Philistines. And when his rage was over, he went to a cave in a rock at Etam, which is in Judah.

The Philistines made camp in Judah, and the Israelites said, "Why have you come here now?"

The Philistines replied, "We have come here to take Samson and to do to him what he has done to us."

The three thousand men of Judah went to the rock at Etam and said to Samson, "You know the Philistines rule us. What have you done? We will suffer for this."

Samson replied, "I did to them what they did to me."

The men of Judah said, "We have to tie you up and take you to the Philistines."

Samson made the men of Judah swear that they would not kill him, and they agreed.

They tied up Samson with two pieces of new rope, and led him out of the cave and brought him to Lehi, where the Philistines were camped. The Philistines greeted him with cries of anger and triumph.

The spirit of the Lord entered Samson, and an enormous energy

Opposite: That evening she cradled Samson like a baby until he fell asleep. Then she called softly to the Philistines, and they entered the house with their gifts of money. One of the men stepped forward and cut off the seven great locks of Samson's hair.

swept through his body. He tore the rope apart as though it were nothing more than strands of cotton. He picked up the jawbone of an ass which was lying at his feet, and using only this as a weapon, he attacked and killed a thousand Philistines.

THE GREAT STRENGTH OF SAMSON

Judges 16

The Philistines were always looking for ways to capture and kill Samson, but his enormous strength saved him time and time again. Then something happened.

Samson fell in love with a woman named Delilah. When the Philistine leaders heard about Samson's new love, they went to her secretly and said, "He will do anything for you. Find out the source of his strength. Once we know that, we can capture him. Do this, and each of us will give you eleven hundred pieces of silver."

Delilah agreed. Later, when she was with Samson, she said, "Tell me where your great strength comes from. How can you be tied up?"

Samson said, "If I am tied up with seven green ropes that have never been dried, I will be as weak as any ordinary man."

Delilah told the Philistine leaders what Samson had said, and they gave her the ropes.

That night while the Philistines were waiting in ambush at her home, Delilah tied up Samson. When she had finished, she called out, "The Philistines are in the house, Samson!" Then Samson snapped the ropes like little twigs, and the Philistines fled.

Delilah tried again. She said, "Samson, you have lied to me and made fun of me, but tell me now where your strength comes from. How is it possible to tie you up?"

Samson said, "If you tie me up with new ropes that have never been used before, I will be as weak as any ordinary man."

That night she tied him up with the new ropes, and once more the Philistines were waiting in ambush. Delilah shouted, "Samson, the Philistines are here!"

Then Samson broke the ropes as easily as if they had been strands of wool.

Delilah did not stop there. She asked him again. This time he said that if she wove the seven locks of his hair into a web, his strength would vanish. Delilah did this, fastening his hair with a pin, and Samson fell asleep like this. He was awakened by Delilah's cry: "The Philistines are here!" But Samson sprang to his feet and was as strong as ever.

Every day Delilah begged him to tell her. Again and again, she asked the same question: "Where does your mighty strength come from?"

SAMSON REVEALS HIS SECRET

Judges 16

Samson grew tired of Delilah's question. Every day he heard it. Every day she demanded an answer. Finally, he weakened and told her the truth: "From birth I have been a Nazarite from God. My head has never been shaved. My strength is in my hair. If I lost my hair, I would lose my strength. Then I would be like any other man, and just as weak."

Delilah realised that Samson had at last told her the truth. She went straight to the Philistine leaders and told them to come in the evening, because now she knew where his strength lay.

That evening she cradled Samson like a baby until he fell asleep. Then she called softly to the Philistines, and they entered the house with their gifts of money. One of the men stepped forwards and cut off the seven great locks of Samson's hair. Delilah called out as before, "The Philistines are here, Samson!"

Samson immediately woke up and went to chase them from the house. But his strength had left him. The spirit of the Lord did not move inside him. And when the Philistines saw this, they grabbed hold of him and blinded him. They took him to a place called Gaza. They put brass chains on his body and forced him to work in a prison.

However, as the days went by, his hair began to grow back.

REVENGE AND THE DEATH OF SAMSON

Judges 16

The Philistines were overjoyed to have taken Samson prisoner at last. They decided after some time to offer a sacrifice to their god, Dagon. "Our god gave us Samson!" they cried. "He destroyed our crops and killed so many of our people!"

The Philistines drank wine and grew merry. They shouted out that the people should see Samson so that everyone could make fun of this man who was once so strong.

Men were sent to the prison to pull Samson out of that dreary place and bring him to a great building supported by two vast pillars. They made him stand there for all the world to see.

A boy led him to the spot, because Samson was blind. Samson said to the boy, "Lad, direct my hands to the two pillars so I can support myself." The boy did this for Samson, and he stretched out his hands and felt how big round the pillars were.

The building was packed with men and women. All kinds of officials and leaders stood there, mocking Samson. There were three thousand men and women on the roof. The place echoed with jeers for the man who was at their mercy.

Samson turned his unseeing eyes to heaven and spoke to the Lord: "O God, be with me now. Let me for the last time take my revenge on the Philistines for blinding me. Give me back my strength!"

After this prayer, Samson felt in his hands the two pillars that supported the building. He held one pillar in his right hand and the other in his left.

"Lord," he cried, "let me die with the Philistines! I ask no more!"

The spirit of the Lord came into Samson's body, and his strength grew. He pressed his hands on the pillars. His body strained. The pillars trembled, and the building tottered. Then the building gave way and came crashing down on all the people who had gathered there to make fun of Samson.

On that day, Samson killed more Philistines than he had ever killed in his life. And Samson died with the Philistines.

The body of Samson was taken by his family and buried next to his father, Manoah.

Samson turned his unseeing eyes to heaven and spoke to the Lord: "O God, be with me now. Let me for the last time take my revenge on the Philistines for blinding me. Give me back my strength!"

After this prayer, Samson felt in his hands the two pillars that supported the building. He held one pillar in his right hand and the other in his left.

"Lord," he cried, "let me die with the Philistines! I ask no more!"

The spirit of the Lord came into Samson's body, and his strength grew. He pressed his hands on the pillars. His body strained. The pillars trembled, and the building tottered. Then the building gave way and came crashing down on all the people who had gathered there to make fun of Samson.

SAMUEL, THE CHILD OF THE LORD

At Ramathaim-zophim, in the mountains of Ephraim, there lived a man named Elkanah. This man had two wives. One was called Hannah and the other, Peninnah. Peninnah had children, but Hannah did not.

Every year, Elkanah left his city and went to Shiloh to offer sacrifices to his Lord. The two sons of Eli, whose names were Hophni and Phinehas, were there. They were priests.

Elkanah made his sacrifices as usual. He offered up a good sacrifice for Peninnah, who had given him sons and daughters. He made a good sacrifice for Hannah, too, for even though she had given him no children, he loved her dearly.

When Peninnah saw the sacrifices, she mocked Hannah for being childless.

Hannah cried so much that she could not eat or drink. When her husband saw this, he said, "Hannah, why are you crying and not eating? I am your husband, and surely I am worth more than ten sons."

Then Hannah ate a little and went to the temple of the Lord, where Eli was a priest. She wept bitterly in the temple and prayed to the Lord.

HANNAH'S PRAYER

Hannah praised God and prayed to Him: "O Lord of all life, I beg You to look down on me, Your humble servant. Grant me one wish: Let me have a son. I will dedicate the child to the Lord, and he will serve Him every day of his life. A razor will never cut his hair, and this will be a sign of my holy intention."

The priest, Eli, who was seated by the door of the temple, understood Hannah's sadness and said, "Go in peace. God will hear your prayer."

Hannah left the temple. She ate, and her face no longer looked sad.

The following day, Elkanah and his wives got up, said their prayers, and returned home. Elkanah embraced Hannah, and the Lord did not forget her.

Towards the end of the year, Hannah gave birth to a son, whom she named Samuel, because this meant he had come from the Lord. And the time came when her husband, Elkanah, was to go again to offer his yearly sacrifice to the Lord. But Hannah did not accompany her husband, because she would not go until the child was fully weaned. After that, she said, she would bring him to appear before the Lord, and Samuel would serve Him for ever.

"Do what you think is for the best," Elkanah said. "Stay at home, and God's will be done."

Later, when the child was weaned, she took him to Shiloh. She had three bullocks with her, and she carried a bottle of wine and a bag of flour.

A bullock was sacrificed in Shiloh, and the child was taken to the priest, Eli. Hannah said, "I am the woman who stood next to you,

Opposite: One night, when the priest was sleeping in his bed in the house of God, the Lord called Samuel. Samuel thought Eli was calling him, and he ran to him and answered, "Here I am!"

Eli said, "I did not call you. Go back to bed."

praying for a son. The Lord answered my prayer, and the boy is with me. He will always work now in the service of God."

Hannah left Samuel in the protection of Eli, but each year she went to see him with her husband when they made their yearly sacrifices in Shiloh. And each time she saw Samuel, she brought him new clothing. The child grew up healthy and with a good character. He worked for God in the house of the Lord.

I Samuel 3

GOD CALLS SAMUEL

Years passed. Eli was now an old man with poor eyesight. One night, when the priest was sleeping in his bed in the house of God, the Lord called Samuel. Samuel thought Eli was calling him, and he ran to him and answered, "Here I am!"

Eli said, "I did not call you. Go back to bed."

Samuel went back to his bed, and once again the Lord called, "Samuel!"

Samuel got up and ran to Eli, who once again assured him that he had not called him and that he should go back to bed. Samuel returned to his bed, still unaware that God was calling him.

Then the voice called him for the third time, and as before, Samuel ran immediately to Eli and asked him how he could be of service.

Then Eli understood that God was calling the child. He said to Samuel, "Go back to your bed, and if the voice calls you again, say, 'Speak, Lord, for I am listening.'"

Samuel went back to bed. God visited him and stood before him, calling, "Samuel! Samuel!"

This time Samuel replied, "Speak, Lord, for I am listening!"

And the Lord said to Samuel, "I have a task to perform that will shock the people. I am going to punish Eli's family and Eli himself, because he did not control the evil ways of his sons. Sacrifice or offering cannot help in this case."

Samuel fell into a deep sleep which lasted until morning. Then he opened the gates of the house of the Lord, but he did not have the courage to tell Eli about the vision he had had.

Eventually Eli called Samuel to him, saying, "Samuel, my son!"

And Samuel replied, "I am here."

Eli said, "What has the Lord told you? Hide nothing from me, and may God punish you if you do not tell me every single word He told you!"

When Samuel heard this, he told Eli everything.

Eli said, "The Lord must do what He judges to be good."

Samuel was only a boy when these things happened. He continued to grow under God's guidance. All Israel, from Dan to Beersheba, knew that Samuel was the prophet of the Lord.

THE PHILISTINES SEIZE THE ARK

At this time the Philistines were gathering forces to do battle with Israel. When the two armies met in the field, Israel was badly beaten and lost four thousand men. The elders then spoke to their people: "Why has the Lord deserted us today? Let us bring the ark of the Lord's covenant from Shiloh. We will be strong and kill our enemies if we keep the ark with us."

At once people were sent to Shiloh to bring back the ark. When at last the Ark of the Covenant of the Lord reached the camp of the Israelites, a great shout went up that was so powerful the earth shook.

In their own camp, the Philistines heard the shouting and wondered what it was all about. Then it dawned on them that the ark of the Lord was in the camp. They grew afraid and said, "They have God on their side now. Nothing like this has happened before. Who will save us? This is the ark of the God who brought Egypt to its knees."

But other voices cried, "You Philistines, behave like men or else we will end up becoming servants of the Hebrews! Take your weapons! Get ready to fight!"

A terrible battle was fought between the Israelites and the Philistines. When the day was over, the Israelites fled into their tents. They were badly defeated and lost thirty thousand of their foot soldiers. The Philistines had captured the ark of God. And two of Eli's sons, Hophni and Phinehas, who were with the ark, had been killed. When Eli, an old man now, heard about the death of his sons and the loss of the ark, he was stricken with grief and died shortly afterwards.

The Philistines carried the ark back to the house of Dagon, their god. The next day, however, Dagon was found lying flat on his face on the ground. After this incident and a number of other misfortunes that the Philistines believed came from their being in possession of the ark, they returned it to Israel. The Philistine priests also advised that sacrifices be made and gifts sent back with the ark. All this was done. And seven months after its capture, the ark came back to Israel.

The ark was brought into the house of Abinadab. The son of that household was blessed, and he became keeper of the ark for the Lord.

A LITTLE BIT OF HISTORY
Samuel, the last of the judges, lived in the eleventh century B.C. This was a period when no one could stop the might of the Philistines. This people wanted to be like the Egyptians, who had ruled for so long over the land of Canaan. The Philistines had reached the Promised Land a short time after the Israelites fled Egypt. Their intention was to conquer all the land that belonged to the twelve tribes. Their military supremacy was clear. They had mines that gave them iron from which they made weapons. The warriors of Israel, on the other hand, were poorly armed and had no means of fighting back against the Philistines' massive onslaughts. The defeat of Israel took place about 1050 B.C. There is little information about the time of Samuel. It is clear, however, that the Israelites were determined to preserve their lands from the Philistine menace. They formed a political union to make themselves stronger. This was how their kingdom came into being. Saul, king of Israel, reigned from about 1020 to 1000 B.C.

After this incident and a number of other misfortunes that the Philistines believed came from their being in possession of the ark, they returned it to Israel. The Philistine priests also advised that sacrifices be made and gifts sent back with the ark. All this was done. And seven months after its capture, the ark came back to Israel.

Samuel took out a small bottle of oil
and poured it on Saul's head. He
kissed him and said, "Have you not
been anointed to be the prince of
Israel and the leader of its people?"

SAMUEL AND SAUL

Samuel was judge over Israel throughout his life. He lived in Ramah, and it was here that he built an altar to the Lord. He was an old man and had two sons, named Joel and Abiah. They also were judges, but they were nothing like their father. They accepted bribes, loved money, and gave false judgements when it suited them.

THE PEOPLE ASK FOR A KING

The elders of Israel went to see Samuel at his house in Ramah. They said to him, "You are old now, and your sons are dishonest. Should we not have a king to rule us, as other countries do?"

These words made Samuel very unhappy. He prayed and looked for guidance from God. And the Lord said to Samuel, "Listen to the voice of the people. They are not rejecting you; it is I they have rejected, for I no longer reign over them. Accept their wishes, and advise them on the rights a king will have over them."

Samuel took the words of the Lord back to the people. He said, "Listen carefully to me now. I will tell you what a king does. He will take your sons to drive his chariots, to be his horsemen, and to run in front of his chariots. Some will be captains over thousands of people, others over fifty. Many of you will sow crops and bring in the harvest; others will make his weapons of war. As for your daughters, he will turn them into cooks and bakers. And as for your fields, your olive groves, and your vineyards, a king will have the best of them and give them to his faithful servants. He will take a tenth of all your crops and give them to his officers and servants. The best menservants and maidservants that you have will go to his household. You will also lose the best of your animals; a tenth of all sheep will belong to the king. You will be his servants! When you fully understand what has happened, you will cry to heaven for mercy and regret the day that you ever chose a king. But on that day, the Lord will not hear you!"

Despite Samuel's harsh words, the people of Israel still wanted a king.

Samuel listened to the words of the people and repeated them to the Lord. And the Lord said to Samuel, "Listen to the voice of the people; let them have a king!"

Samuel then told the men of Israel to return to their cities.

In the tribe of Benjamin there was a strong, brave man whose name was Kish. Kish had a son named Saul, who was not only young, handsome, and good but also taller than most men by a head.

One day, Saul's father, Kish, lost his donkeys. He called to his son: "Saul, take a servant with you, and see if you can find where they have wandered off."

Saul and the servant looked for the donkeys. Their journey took them past Mount Ephraim, through Shalisha, through Shalim, and through the land of the Benjamites, but nowhere were the donkeys to be found.

When they reached the land of Zuph without success, Saul said to his servant, "By this time my father will be more concerned about us than about his donkeys. I think it is time to turn back."

The servant said, "But there is in this city an honourable man of God. He is a seer: Everything he says comes true. Let us go and see him now. Perhaps he can point us in the right direction."

Saul was worried because they had no gift to take to the man of God. Their bread was old, and their wine used up. The servant held up the fourth part of a shekel of silver. "I have this," he said.

Saul agreed, and the two men set off for the city where the man of God lived.

I Samuel 9-10

SAUL MEETS SAMUEL

As they went up the hill that led to the city, they met some girls taking water from the well. Saul asked, "Will we find the seer here?"

And they replied, "He passed this way a short time ago. He is in the city today, because people are making a sacrifice in a high place. He is the one who blesses the sacrifice."

As Saul and his servant entered the city, they came face-to-face with Samuel, who was on his way to the high place.

The day before this meeting, God had told Samuel, "I will send you a man from the land of Benjamin. Anoint him with oil, because he is the one I have chosen to be king over the people of Israel. I have seen the suffering of My people, and he will save them from the Philistines."

When Samuel saw Saul, he heard God's voice inside him, saying, "This is the man I spoke of."

Saul approached Samuel near the city's gate and asked, "Can you tell me where I may find the house of the seer?"

Samuel answered, "I am the seer. Come with me now to the high place. Eat with me today, and tomorrow I will tell you everything that is in your heart. As for your donkeys that were lost three days ago, they have been found."

Later Samuel said to Saul, "You are the chosen one for the people of Israel."

Saul was mystified and wondered, "How can that be? I am a Benjamite. We are the smallest of the tribes of Israel, and my family is humble and has no rank."

There were about thirty people eating dinner that day, and Samuel led Saul and his servant to the place of honour. He instructed the cook to serve Saul the choicest cut of meat, saying it had long been prepared for him. Afterwards, they left the high place and went back to the city.

It was warm that night, and Saul slept on the roof of the house. At dawn, Samuel called to Saul, "Get up now, for I must send you away."

Saul got up and went out of the house with Samuel. They walked together to the end of the city. Then Samuel told Saul to send his servant on ahead. When this was done, Samuel said, "Stand still, and I will tell you what God has said."

Samuel took out a small bottle of oil and poured it on Saul's head. He kissed him and said, "Have you not been anointed to be the prince of Israel and the leader of its people?"

Then Saul returned to his family, and the spirit of God lived inside him. He told his family what Samuel had told him about the donkeys, but he told no one about the other things that Samuel had said.

SAUL IS MADE KING

Samuel called together the people of Israel and said, "I am here to tell you the words of the God of Israel. He is the God who brought you out of Egypt. He is the God who saved you from your enemies, from the Egyptians, and from all the kings of enemies who wanted to make you slaves. Now you have turned your back on God, who saved you from all this suffering and hardship, and you say, 'Give us a king!' Step forwards before God, and let Him see your tribes and families."

And all the tribes and families of Israel drew closer to Samuel. Then the tribe of Benjamin was singled out. Among the members of this tribe was a family to which Saul, son of Kish, belonged. And Saul was head and shoulders taller than anyone in his family or tribe. Samuel pointed to him, saying, "He is the one chosen from all the people present. Nobody can compare with him. He will be your king!"

Then the Hebrew people were happy and shouted, "Long live the king!"

After this outcry, Samuel explained the rights of royalty. He wrote them in a book, and he laid the book up before the Lord. Having done this, he sent the people away.

In this way, Saul became king of Israel. And he was a great and valiant king. Time and time again, he led the children of Israel against their enemies, the Philistines, and he was always victorious.

But Saul did not always obey the laws of God. When Samuel saw this, he told Saul, "Because you have strayed from God's laws—and remember, He is the God who chose you to be king—God will reject you. Your reign as king will not be remembered as noble."

JONATHAN DOES NOT OBEY SAUL, I Samuel 14

Saul had a son whose name was Jonathan. One day, when the Israelites had fought hard against the Philistines, Saul gave an order: "I curse any man who eats before evening and before I have taken revenge on the Philistines!"

The warriors heard Saul's words, and nobody dared eat. The army passed through a forest where there was honey shining in the sunlight. Still nobody dared taste it. But Jonathan had not heard his father's words, and when he saw the honey, he pushed a stick into it and brought the stick up to his mouth so that his eyes grew big with pleasure.

Then one of his group said, "Your father said that anybody who ate today before the enemy was beaten would be cursed."

Jonathan replied, "My father is going to ruin his people! Just look how happy I am to have tasted a little honey! If we had eaten, we might have done much better in battle."

Then the people fought the Philistines from Michmash to Aijalon. They fought until they were tired and starved and could no longer control themselves. They took their reward, and they ate the sheep and oxen and calves they had captured.

When Saul heard about this, he said, "These men have done wrong to eat in this way. I call upon your leaders to bring forth those men who have sinned."

A LITTLE BIT OF HISTORY

Saul, the first king of Israel, governed in much the same way the judges had. Above all, he was a military leader, not concerned with royal palaces and capital cities. What distinguishes him from the judges is that he was chosen by God and elected by the people. The Bible does not make clear the extent of his kingdom. It is certain that the territories in the centre of the Promised Land, those belonging to the tribes of Benjamin and Ephraim, and Gad beyond the Jordan, were under his control. Perhaps he also controlled certain lands in the north, but it does not seem that the tribe of Judah, in the south, obeyed him. Certainly the inshore strip under Philistine domination was not part of his kingdom. Within his realm, there were Canaanite zones of influence such as Jerusalem. There was also a cone-shaped territory that separated the central and northern regions and was dominated by the Canaanites. This was the valley of Jezreel. Saul needed to take this valley in order to unite the two regions. It was in this area that the decisive battle took place. The Philistines conquered the Israelites on Mount Gilboa.

But there was no reply. Then Saul said, "Stand on one side, and I will stand with my son Jonathan on the other side."

The people did as they were ordered. Saul prayed to the Lord to reveal the innocent. It was clear then that the people were innocent and that Saul and Jonathan were guilty.

Saul said, "Choose now who is more guilty, my son or myself."

Jonathan was chosen, and Saul said to him, "Tell me what you have done."

Jonathan replied, "I was hungry. I put a little honey on the end of my stick and tasted it. That is why I will die."

Saul said, "You should die!"

Then the people shouted, "He cannot die! He led us to a great victory!"

When Saul heard this, he spared his son. They left the Philistines and returned to their camp.

I Samuel 15

SAUL DISOBEYS THE LORD

Samuel spoke to Saul again: "God sent me to anoint you king of Israel. Now you must listen to my words, because these are the words of God: 'I remember what Amalek did to Israel when he lay in wait for you when you left Egypt. This must not happen again. Go now and destroy his army and all his animals. Spare nothing.'"

Saul assembled his army of two hundred thousand footmen and ten thousand men from Judah. He led his army to the city of Amalek, and there he ambushed the Amalekites and captured Agag, their king.

Saul did not destroy all the animals as he had been told to do. He only killed the weak and sick animals.

Then the Lord said to Samuel, "I am sorry I ever made Saul king of Israel. He has turned his back on Me and not followed My commandments."

When Samuel heard these words, he cried all night to the Lord. In the morning he went to Saul, who greeted him with these words: "Blessings to the servant of the Lord! I have done as I was told."

Samuel said, "But I hear the bleating of sheep and the lowing of oxen! How is that possible?"

Saul replied, "We saved the best of the animals to make sacrifices to God. The rest we destroyed."

Then Samuel said, "The Lord sent you to destroy the Amalekites and all their property. Why did you not obey His word? The Lord was looking for obedience. Obedience is better than any plump sacrifices you might make. Disobedience is itself a sin. You have turned your back on the Lord, and He will turn His back on you as king!"

Saul said, "I see that I have sinned in disobeying God. I was afraid of upsetting the people, and I listened to what they wanted. But now, I beg you, forgive me my sins, and lead me to a place where I may worship God with you."

Samuel could not do that. He said, "That is no longer possible, because you did not listen to the word of the Lord. For this sin, you will no longer remain king."

Samuel turned to go, but Saul seized his robe to stop him, and it tore. Samuel said, "You have torn my robe, but God has torn the kingdom of Israel out of your hands. A greater king than yourself will soon replace you."

Saul said, "It is true that I have sinned, but at least show respect for me in front of the elders of Israel. Come with me so that I may worship the Lord your God."

Samuel did as Saul asked, and afterwards he went back to Ramah. Saul went quietly back to his own home.

Samuel never saw Saul again after this. But often, when he thought about this disobedient king, his eyes filled with tears and he wept.

Samuel turned to go, but Saul seized his robe to stop him, and it tore. Samuel said, "You have torn my robe, but God has torn the kingdom of Israel out of your hands. A greater king than yourself will soon replace you."

DAVID IS CHOSEN BY GOD

When God saw Samuel weeping for Saul, he said, "How long will you mourn for him? You know that I have rejected him, and he is not to reign over Israel. Fill your horn with oil. I am sending you to Jesse, the Bethlehemite. He has a son who will be the new king."

Samuel did as the Lord commanded and went to Bethlehem. And the people of the town were fearful that such a seer should visit them. But Samuel put their minds at rest and said he was in Bethlehem only to make sacrifices.

He blessed Jesse, and Jesse introduced his seven sons. Then the Lord made it clear to Samuel that none of the seven were to be king. So Samuel said to Jesse, "Are all your sons here?"

Jesse shook his head and said, "My youngest boy is not here. He is looking after our sheep."

Samuel said, "Send for him. We cannot sit at the table without him."

The boy was sent for, and shortly afterwards he appeared. He had an open face and was handsome. God whispered to Samuel, "He is the one! Anoint him!"

Samuel brought out his horn of oil, and in front of all the brothers, he anointed the youngest.

From that day on, the spirit of the Lord burnt in David.

And Samuel, who had done his duty, returned to Ramah.

DAVID MEETS KING SAUL

The spirit of the Lord had long ago left Saul. An evil spirit now troubled him. He was moody and bad-tempered.

The servants made the following suggestion to him: "An evil spirit has been sent by the Lord to trouble you. Order us to find someone who plays the harp so beautifully that when you hear it, all evil spirits will fly away and you will feel well."

Saul waved his hand and said, "Very well! Find a man who plays like that and bring him here."

Then one of the servants answered, "I have heard such a man play! He is a son of Jesse, the Bethlehemite. He is a skilful player and is brave, handsome, and trustworthy. He is blessed by the Lord."

When Saul heard this, he sent messengers to Jesse, saying his son should visit him.

Jesse got a donkey ready for the journey, and he put bread, wine, and a baby goat on its back. And his youngest son, David, set off on the donkey.

When Saul saw David, he was immediately struck by his good qualities. He made David his armour-bearer and sent word to Jesse that his son was in his service.

When Saul went into a dark mood, he called for David to play to him on the harp. And David played so beautifully that Saul felt refreshed and his spirits rose. All evil spirits left him.

Opposite: When Saul went into a dark mood, he called for David to play to him on the harp. And David played so beautifully that Saul felt refreshed and his spirits rose. All evil spirits left him.

DAVID AND GOLIATH

Once again the Philistines declared war on Israel. Both armies were ready for battle. Saul and the Israelites were camped on one side of a valley, the Philistines on the opposite side.

In front of the Philistine army stood their champion. His name was Goliath. He was a giant of a man, his height being six cubits and a span. He wore a great brass helmet, and his armour, a coat of mail, was so big it weighed five thousand shekels of brass. The spear he carried was huge, and its head alone weighed six hundred shekels of iron. A man at his side carried his shield.

The roar of Goliath's voice sounded across the valley: "I am Goliath! I am a Philistine! Choose any man from your army to fight me. If your man kills me, we Philistines will become your servants. If I kill your champion, then the Philistines will rule over you. Today I defy the armies of Israel! I challenge you to find a man who dares fight me!"

Saul and the whole army heard the giant's words and were terrified. There was no one in Israel who could match Goliath in strength and size.

But when David heard Goliath's challenge, he went to Saul and said, "We need not be afraid of this Philistine. I am your servant; I will fight this man."

Saul replied, "You cannot fight this giant of a man. All his life he has been a soldier. He knows all there is to know about weapons. In comparison, you are just a baby!"

But David meant what he said. He told Saul, "It is true that your servant has been a shepherd boy. I looked after my father's sheep, and sometimes a lion or a bear came to steal an animal. But I killed the lion or the bear, and I took the sheep out of the jaws of the thief. If a wild animal turned on me and attacked, I always killed it. Your servant has killed ferocious beasts; I will do the same with this Philistine. He will die like an animal, because he dares defy the armies of the living God. The Lord has saved me from lions and bears; He will save me from this Philistine!"

Then Saul said to David, "So be it. Fight him, and may God be with you!"

He wanted David to wear armour and carry a sword, but David said he was not used to fighting like that.

He left Saul and the army of the Israelites, and with a stick in his hand he went down to a stream. There he paused and selected five smooth stones from the water. These he put into a shepherd's bag that hung from his shoulder. Then he took out his slingshot and put a stone in it. With this in his hand, he went forwards to fight the giant Philistine who was waiting for him.

A STONE BRINGS VICTORY

Gradually the two men drew closer and the man who carried Goliath's shield ran slightly ahead of his champion. Goliath stopped when he saw David, because David was young and handsome and did not look like a warrior.

A LITTLE BIT OF HISTORY
According to modern measurements, Goliath was approximately three metres tall, his armour weighed about 70 kilos and the head of his spear eight kilos.

Goliath shouted, "Do you think I am a dog? Are you going to chase me away with a stick?" He cursed David and said, "If this is the way it is going to be, so be it. The birds will peck at your flesh, and the wild animals will finish up your body."

But David was not afraid. He shouted back, "You have a sword, a spear, and a shield. For me, that is nothing. I fight for the Lord God. I fight for the armies of Israel whom you have defied. Today you will die. The Lord is with me. I will strike you down and cut off your head. I will feed your body to the animals. Then the world will know that there is a God and that He is with Israel. A sword and a spear are nothing against the spirit of God!"

Having said that, David ran towards the giant Philistine. As he ran, he made sure that the stone was firmly in its sling. He whirled the sling-shot above his head and released the stone. His aim was good. The stone flew and sank into the forehead of Goliath. The huge Philistine tumbled over, with his face to the ground.

Yet David had carried no sword.

He ran up to Goliath, pulled the Philistine's sword out of its sheath, and cut off Goliath's head.

A great moan went up from the Philistines' camp when they saw that their champion was dead. They picked up their weapons and ran. The men of Israel shouted in triumph and chased the Philistines along the valley and into the country beyond. Then they returned to their camp and packed up their tents.

David took the head of the Philistine and carried it with him to Jerusalem.

SAUL GROWS JEALOUS   *I Samuel 18*

After this victory, Saul kept David close to him and would not let him return home to his old way of life. He made him captain of all his warriors, and all the people rejoiced in this. Saul's son, Jonathan, loved David as though he were his own brother, and the two young men became great friends. Jonathan gave David many fine gifts, including some of his own clothes, a sword, and a bow.

When David returned from killing Goliath, women poured out of the cities of Israel to dance and sing praises. They struck their tambourines and musical instruments with great joy. They made up songs, one of which ran: "Saul has killed thousands, but David, tens of thousands!"

When Saul heard this song, he flew into a rage. He said to himself, "The women say David has slain tens of thousands and myself mere thousands. The only thing he does not have now is my kingdom!"

From that day onward, Saul grew jealous of David.

The next day the evil spirit from God filled Saul, and David was called to play for him. As usual on these occasions, Saul toyed with a spear in his hand. This time, however, his jealousy reached a fever pitch, and he threw the spear at David, hoping to pin him against the wall. But David ducked, and the spear fell uselessly away.

In his heart of hearts, Saul was afraid of David. He knew the spirit of the Lord was with David and that the Lord had deserted Saul.

David behaved wisely, and the people loved and trusted him.

David ran toward the giant Philistine. As he ran, he made sure that the stone was firmly in its sling. He whirled the slingshot above his head and released the stone. His aim was good. The stone flew and sank into the forehead of Goliath. The huge Philistine tumbled over, with his face to the ground.

Michal, Saul's daughter, fell in love with David. It was not long before Saul's servants brought word of this to the king. Saul was not displeased with this match, because he thought it would give him a chance to trap David and feed him to the Philistines. With this in mind, Saul sent for David and said, "Today you will marry my daughter and become my son-in-law!"

I Samuel 18-19

DAVID MARRIES MICHAL

But when David heard these words, he said, "I am too poor and too unworthy to marry the daughter of a king."

But Saul was full of cunning and replied, "I do not demand a dowry or wealth. I wish instead that you bring me a hundred dead Philistines."

Saul hoped that David would be killed by the Philistines in this way. But David liked the idea, and wishing to become the son-in-law of the king, he took some men and went off to do battle with the Philistines. And although David killed two hundred Philistines, he himself was not hurt. Then Saul had no choice but to offer his daughter, Michal, as a wife for David. He knew the Lord was with David, and he saw that his daughter loved this man. But he still planned to get rid of him, for he was mad with jealousy.

Then Saul approached his son and his servants and gave them the order to put David to death. When Jonathan heard this, he ran to his friend and said, "My father wants to have you killed. Be on your guard! Tomorrow at dawn, hide in a secret place. I will meanwhile join my father out in the fields, near where you will be hidden. I will talk to him and find out more about his plans."

The following day Jonathan spoke to his father about David. He reminded him of how David had fought against the Philistines for the people of Israel. He pointed out how brave David had been in battle. He asked his father, "How can you spill the blood of an innocent man? He has not sinned against you. How can you kill a man for no reason?"

Then Saul swore that he would not kill David. He made this a promise.

Jonathan called out to David, who came out of his secret hiding place and stood before Saul. Then all bad things were forgotten, and the relationship was as friendly as it had been in earlier times.

But this time of peace was short-lived. The evil spirit sent from the Lord again entered Saul. His mood darkened. In front of him he saw the handsome David playing his harp. As before, he brought back his spear and hurled it at David. But David dodged, and the spear stuck in the wall. David then quickly made his escape.

Then Saul sent men to David's house so that they could see when he came out and then kill him. Michal, David's wife, understood what was going on. She said to her husband, "You must escape tonight, or else they will kill you in the morning."

She dropped a rope out of a window, and her husband ran far away from the house. Then she went into David's room and put a dummy in his bed. She put the bedclothes over the dummy so that it looked as though her husband were asleep.

In the morning, Saul's men knocked on Michal's door and demanded to see David. She said, "He is sick."

When Saul's men told him what had happened, he ordered them back to the house. "If necessary," Saul said, "bring him back in his bed, and I will kill him."

The men returned to Michal's house and soon discovered that they had been fooled. Saul raged at his daughter, saying, "Why did you trick me? Why did you let my enemy escape?"

And Michal, afraid for her own life, gave a crafty answer: "He told me he would kill me if I didn't help him!"

Meanwhile, David made his way to Ramah, where Samuel lived.

DAVID AND JONATHAN

I Samuel 20

Some time later, David came out of hiding and arranged to meet his friend Jonathan. He asked him, "What have I done to your father? Why does he hate me?"

Jonathan replied, "I will do all I can to save you. I know everything my father does. It may be a big thing or a small thing, but he will always tell me about it. If he intends to harm you, he will tell me. If he has started to think well of you again, I will let you know. Whatever happens, you and I will remain friends for ever."

The bond of friendship was strong between David and Jonathan. Jonathan loved David as much as he loved his own life. He said to David, "Wait three days, then go, and wait by the stone known as Ezel. I will fire three arrows on one side of it, as though I were aiming at a target. Then I will send a young man to bring back the arrows. If I shout to him, 'The arrows are on your side,' you will be safe and can come out of hiding, because everything will be well. But if I tell the young man, 'The arrows have gone past you,' then make your escape, and may God be with you."

David hid himself in the field and waited.

The moon was new when King Saul sat down to eat his dinner. Suddenly his temper exploded, and he shouted at his son, Jonathan, "You are a worthless son! You make friends with this son of Jesse and bring shame on us! Do you not realise that as long as that man is alive you have no kingdom? Bring him here, and I will cut his throat!"

Jonathan said to his father, "Why must he die? What has he done?"

Then Saul picked up a spear and flung it across the room. There was no mistaking what Saul planned to do with David. He was determined to kill him.

The following morning Jonathan went out into the fields with a young manservant. He was able to pass on information to David in the way they had planned. Jonathan fired his arrows and shouted instructions to the servant as to where they had landed. And David understood the secret message.

Then Jonathan sent the servant back to town with his weapons. When the young man was out of sight, David came out from behind the stone. The two friends wept together. Jonathan said, "Go in peace; the Lord has made us friends."

They were forced to separate because of Saul's hatred. David went his own way, and Jonathan returned to the city.

SAUL AND THE SPIRIT OF SAMUEL

David travelled to Nob, where a priest named Ahimelech lived. David asked for food, and the priest gave him holy bread. David had no weapons, and thinking he might need to defend himself, he asked the priest for a sword or spear.

The priest said, "I have the sword of Goliath the Philistine." And he unwrapped a piece of cloth and gave David the sword.

Then David left that place quickly, because he feared the anger of Saul and did not know if he was being pursued. He took refuge in a cave known as Adullam.

When David's brothers and all the members of his father's household learnt where he was staying, they went at once to see him. And everyone who was in distress, in debt, unhappy, or poor visited David. It was not long before David had four hundred men at his command, because these people had made him their captain.

When David had visited the priest in Nob, it happened that he was spotted by one of Saul's men, called Doeg the Edomite. This man lost no time in running to Saul and telling him that the priest Ahimelech had given bread and Goliath's sword to David.

When Saul heard this piece of news, he immediately ordered Ahimelech and all the priests of his household to appear before him. They could not refuse, and they all soon stood before Saul, who said, "Why have you plotted against me, you and that son of Jesse? Why did you give him bread and a sword? Do you want him to lead a revolt against me?"

Ahimelech replied, "Surely there is no one more faithful and loyal to his king than David. He is your son-in-law; he is your captain. He is respected wherever he goes in your house. I saw no harm in what I did, nor did my servants, nor my fellow priests, nor any member of my father's household. We are all innocent."

But the king's voice rang out in rage, "For what you have done, Ahimelech, you will die."

But Saul's guards dared not lift a finger against the priests of the Lord. Then Saul turned to Doeg the Edomite and shouted, "These men are your enemies. Cut them down!"

And on that terrible day, Doeg the Edomite murdered eighty-five men. And the violence did not stop.

Saul went with armed men to the holy city of Nob. He destroyed it completely and massacred the entire population, except for one man. Abiathar, one of Ahimelech's sons, managed to escape. He fled to tell David what Saul had done.

DAVID ESCAPES FROM SAUL

Later, David and his men wandered into a desert of Judah, and Saul sent out his men to track them down. Saul soon realised where David

Opposite: Later, David and his men wandered into a desert of Judah, and Saul sent out his men to track them down. Saul soon realised where David was, and he gave chase. He had nearly surrounded David's forces, when a messenger rushed up to him, saying, "We must go! The Philistines are invading our land!"

was, and he gave chase. He had nearly surrounded David's forces, when a messenger rushed up to him, saying, "We must go! The Philistines are invading our land!"

So Saul was forced to call off his attack, and he went to do battle against the Philistines.

While all these things were happening, all Israel was in tears. Samuel had died. He was mourned in every corner of the country. His body was buried near his house in Ramah. He was one of the great servants of God.

I Samuel 26

DAVID SPARES SAUL'S LIFE

One night when David could not sleep, he got up and went to the spot where Saul was camped. He stood in the dark and observed where Saul was sleeping, close to his army chief, Abner, the son of Ner. Saul was in fact sleeping in the middle of his camp, with all his men round him. But no one noticed David. Then David went forwards and took Saul's spear and his container of water. And no one woke up, no one saw anything, because the Lord had plunged them into a deep sleep.

David left the camp and went off to a hill, quite a long way off. He shouted out, "Can you hear me, Abner?"

Abner woke up and called out, "I hear you. What business do you have with the king?"

Then David shouted, "I hear you are a brave man. Why have you not looked after your master? Just tonight an assassin stood over him and took his spear and his water."

With this exchange of words, Saul woke up. At once he recognised David's voice.

"Is that really the voice of David I hear?" Saul cried.

And David replied, "It *is* my voice, my king." He said, "Why do you chase your servant? What have I done? Why am I guilty?"

Then Saul replied, "I have sinned. That is clear. Come back to me, my son, and I will no longer think of harming you. Today you have shown me the value of my life. You could have killed me, but you did not. I have been a fool and committed many sins."

Then Saul and David met, and Saul blessed David.

I Samuel 28

SAUL AND THE WITCH FROM EN-DOR

Once again the Philistines brought their armies together to make war on Israel. When Saul saw the size and strength of the Philistine armies, he was overcome with dread. In desperation he prayed to the Lord for help, but the Lord made no reply and offered no guidance. Saul said to his servants, "I need to consult a fortune-teller; find one for me."

His servants replied, "There is a witch living in En-dor."

That night Saul disguised himself and went to the woman's house. He told her, "I wish to see into the future. I want you to bring someone's spirit into the room."

The woman asked, "Whom do you want me to call from the dead?"

He replied, "Samuel!"

And the witch of En-dor called for Samuel. When he appeared, she shouted in alarm and asked Saul, "Why did you not tell me you were Saul? Why did you trick me?"

The king answered, "There is nothing to be afraid of. Now tell me what you are able to see."

She said, "I see an old man. He is covered in a cloak."

Then Saul himself recognised Samuel, and he bowed to the ground.

Samuel demanded, "Why have you disturbed my peace and brought me up here?"

Saul said, "The Philistines are about to make war on me. I felt afraid and looked to the Lord for help, but He was silent and would not show Himself in a dream or through the voice of a prophet. I have come to you for advice."

Then Samuel asked Saul, "Why is it that you come to me, when the Lord has rejected you and you are His enemy? The Lord has only done what He said He would do. I told you the kingdom would be taken from you, and that is what is happening. The kingdom must go to David. You did not obey the Lord. You wish to see the future? Then be warned: tomorrow you will live with me, you and your sons. As for Israel, the Philistines will take it."

When Saul heard this, he fainted. His body was weak, and fear ate away the little strength he had left. Saul left the witch of En-dor and went to meet his fate with the Philistines.

THE DEATH OF SAUL

I Samuel 31
II Samuel 1

The Philistines fought hard against Israel, and at last they won. Jonathan was killed, and so were his brothers. Saul was wounded by Philistine archers. When he saw that the battle had gone against him and that his sons had died, Saul called to his armour-bearer, saying, "Take out your sword and kill me with it. I would rather be killed by you than by a Philistine."

The armour-bearer was afraid and could not do it. When Saul saw this, he unsheathed his own sword and, pressing it against himself, fell on it. Then Saul's armour-bearer did the same.

And worse was to come! When the men of Israel who were on the other side of the valley saw this defeat, they, too, ran and left their cities behind them. At once the Philistines moved upon the cities and took possession of them without any struggle.

Meanwhile, David returned from the slaughter of the Amalekites and was staying in Ziklag. It was here that a man who was covered in dirt and wearing torn clothes fell at David's feet. David looked at the wretched state of the man and asked, "Where have you come from?"

The man answered, "I escaped from the camp of Israel."

Then David demanded, "What has happened there?"

And the man told David the terrible news: "Saul is dead and so are his sons. We fled the battlefield. The Philistines chased after us and cut us down."

David cried out and tore his clothes to shreds in a show of misery, and all those round him did the same. They wept and mourned and could not eat. They cried out in sorrow for Saul, Jonathan, the people of the Lord, and all those who had been killed.

Then David sang a lamentation for Saul and Jonathan. He told the children of Judah never to forget these events.

The beauty of Israel
Lies dead in the hills!
The mighty have fallen!
Do not mention it in Gath,
Do not whisper it in the streets of Askelon,
Unless you wish the daughters of the Philistines to rejoice
And the uncircumcised to triumph.
Mountains of Gilboa!
Let there be no dew or rain,
Or fields of offerings,
For there lies the shield of the brave,
The shield of Saul thrown to one side
As though the man were never anointed king!
The land is stained with the blood of the brave;
There lies the great bow of Jonathan
And the sword of Saul which drank its fill.
Saul and Jonathan were lovely in their lives;
Death did not divide them.
They were swifter than eagles;
They were stronger than lions.
Daughters of Israel, weep for Saul.
He clothed you in scarlet and found ornaments
Of gold to make you shine.
The mighty have fallen in battle!
Jonathan, my friend, my brother,
Sorrow for your death penetrates me like a knife!
Jonathan, you were dear to me.
Your friendship was a precious thing,
More precious than the love of women.
The mighty have fallen!
The weapons of war have perished!

After a time of mourning, the Lord came to David and said, "Go now to the place called Hebron."

David led his family and his people to Hebron, and they lived in the cities there. The men of Judah anointed David king of Judah, and he blessed them for their kindness.

Opposite: Saul called to his armour-bearer, saying, "Take out your sword and kill me with it. I would rather be killed by you than by a Philistine."

The armour-bearer was afraid and could not do it. When Saul saw this, he unsheathed his own sword and, pressing it against himself, fell on it.

DAVID, KING OF JUDAH AND OF ISRAEL

Then all the tribes of Israel went to Hebron and told David, "We are the same flesh and blood as you. In the past Saul led us. He was our king. The Lord instructed him to feed the people of Israel and be its captain. Now he is gone."

The elders of the tribes of Israel gathered round David at Hebron. David made friends with them, and they anointed David king of Israel.

David was thirty years old when he became king, and he reigned for forty years. He was king in Judah for seven years and six months. In Jerusalem he reigned for thirty-three years over Judah and Israel.

DAVID CONQUERS JERUSALEM

King David and his men marched towards Jerusalem and the country where the Jebusites lived. When he was in earshot, the Jebusites called out to him, "We are blind and lame. You will not want to come in here!"

David thought nothing of these words, which were intended to make him retreat. He stormed the fort of Zion and captured it. From then on, the place was known as the City of David. Round the city he built fortifications.

David and his army grew stronger, and the spirit of the Lord lived inside him.

But when the Philistines learnt that David had been anointed king of Israel, they reached for their weapons and marched against him. David looked to God for guidance. The Lord said, "I am with you; you will be victorious."

David led his armies against the Philistines and all the other people who were opposed to Israel. Wherever David and his men were engaged in battle, he was victorious, because the Lord God was with him.

DAVID LOOKS FOR THE SONS OF JONATHAN, II Samuel 9

After his many victories against the Philistines, David's thoughts turned to Jonathan. He wondered if any of Saul's family were alive. If there were relatives still living, David wanted to help them in memory of Jonathan.

In Saul's old house there lived a servant named Ziba. David sent for him.

"Tell me, Ziba," David said, "I would like to do something good in memory of my friend Jonathan. Do you know if any of his family are still alive?"

At once Ziba replied, "Jonathan has a son who is a cripple."

David asked, "Where is he now?"

Ziba told David that he was living in the Machir household in Lodebar. When David heard this news, he sent for him.

At last Mephibosheth, the son of Jonathan, reached David's court and was brought to King David. The young man threw himself at David's feet and hid his face in the ground. David exclaimed, "Mephibosheth!"

A LITTLE BIT OF HISTORY
David became king of Judah after the Philistines defeated Saul. Then Ishbosheth, one of Saul's sons, became king of Israel. The division between the kingdoms did not last long. Ishbosheth was murdered, and David became the monarch of the united kingdom.

The reign of David lasted from about 1000 to 960 B.C. The union of the tribes became a union of state and army and made the Promised Land effective politically. The kingdom of Israel was in a position to impose its force, and the Philistines could easily lose theirs. David expanded the frontiers of his kingdom by getting rid of the Canaanites in his territory and conquering the Ammonites and the Moabites. On the other hand, he established friendly relations with the Phoenician kingdom. During the first years of his reign, David lived in Hebron in the territory of Judah. But when he became king of all Israel, he felt the need to give his country a capital city. He chose Jerusalem, a walled city built at an altitude of 800 metres in a central part of the country. It was easy to defend and at a strategic point on the road that linked the north and south of the country. Jerusalem became the site of the royal palace and the seat of government. After the Ark of the Covenant had been moved there, Jerusalem was established as the centre of national culture.

And Mephibosheth looked up and said, "I am your servant."

David told him, "Do not be afraid. I can only treat you with the love I bore your father, Jonathan. Remember all the land you lost after the death of Saul? I will see that it is returned to you. You will share food with me and eat at my table whenever you wish."

Mephibosheth bowed and said, "Why should you bother with a dead dog like me?"

Then David asked for Saul's servant, Ziba, to appear before him. He told Ziba, "I have given your master's son all the land that once belonged to Saul's family. I want you, your sons, and your servants to work that land for him. Harvest the crops so that there is food on the table. As for Mephibosheth, he will stay with me and eat at my table."

Ziba said, "I will do as my king commands."

Ziba had fifteen sons and twenty servants.

Mephibosheth stayed with David in Jerusalem, where he was treated like one of the king's sons.

Then all the tribes of Israel went to Hebron and told David, "We are the same flesh and blood as you. In the past Saul led us. He was our king. The Lord instructed him to feed the people of Israel and be its captain. Now he is gone."

The elders of the tribes of Israel gathered around David at Hebron. David made friends with them, and they anointed David king of Israel.

On the day of the battle,
Absalom was riding a
mule through the forest.
Suddenly his great head
of hair became entangled
in the branches of a huge
oak tree. He was swept
off the beast and
suspended from the
branches while the mule
ran off.

128

DAVID AND ABSALOM

In all of Israel there was no one more famous for his good looks than Absalom, the son of David. From head to toe there was not a fault or mark to be seen on his person. At the end of every year his hair was cut short, because it weighed so much. The hair on his head weighed as much as two hundred shekels (which is nearly three kilos). King David loved this son with all his heart.

ABSALOM PLOTS AGAINST DAVID

But Absalom plotted against his father, the king. One morning he got up very early and stood by the side of the road that led to the city gate. Every time a man came along who had a legal dispute to be settled by the king, Absalom would stop him and ask what his dispute was about. After hearing the man, Absalom would say, "You have good cause to seek help, but there is no one who will listen to your problem." He added, "Now if I were appointed judge of these affairs, I would always be available and ready to give a just decision to any man who needed help."

And whenever anyone saw Absalom and fell on his knees before him, Absalom offered his hand, and hugged and kissed the person. In this way Absalom drew attention to himself and won the affection of all the people of Israel.

Four years passed, and Absalom said to the king, "Grant me permission to go to Hebron, for I have made a certain vow to the Lord."

King David replied, "Of course, my son, go in peace!"

ABSALOM'S REVOLT

Absalom set out for Hebron, and he sent messengers to all the tribes of Israel, saying, "When you hear the sound of trumpets, shout out that Absalom has been made king of Hebron."

Absalom had left Jerusalem with two hundred men at his service. These men followed him without knowing what Absalom had plotted against his father.

Gradually, the plot against David grew. More and more Hebrews flocked to Absalom.

Finally, a messenger told King David what was happening. When David heard this news, he said to his ministers and servants who were with him in Jerusalem, "We must leave the city at once. We do not know what Absalom intends. He may storm the city and put us all to the sword."

David and all his family and servants fled from Jerusalem. A priest named Zadok remained alone in the city to look after the ark of God.

A terrible battle took place in a forest. David had given strict instructions to his men that his son Absalom should not be killed. The battle was fierce, but David's army beat back the rebels, and twenty thousand men were killed. The battle spread beyond the forest, but on that day, the forest was filled with men who had met their death by the edge of a sword.

A LITTLE BIT OF HISTORY
The last years of the reign of King David were troubled by the problem of who should succeed him on the throne. The revolt of his son Absalom was particularly serious. It expressed the dissatisfaction of one section of the population with the king, who was forced to abandon Jerusalem. It was his other son, Solomon, who finally emerged as the victor in the power struggle after the death of David.

THE DEATH OF ABSALOM AND THE END OF THE REVOLT

On the day of the battle, Absalom was riding a mule through the forest. Suddenly his great head of hair became entangled in the branches of a huge oak tree. He was swept off the beast and suspended from the branches while the mule ran off. A man saw this happen, and he ran to David's manservant Joab and shouted, "Absalom is caught by his hair in an oak!"

Then Joab said, "You saw him like that, and you did not kill him! I would have given you ten shekels of silver and a good belt if you had!"

The man replied, "I would not have raised a hand against the son of the king, even for a thousand shekels of silver. King David stated that his son Absalom was not to be killed. David would have learnt what had happened if I had killed his son. I could not do it!"

Joab said, "I cannot waste my time with people like you."

He left the man and hurried to the tree where Absalom was hanging. He carried three short spears in his hand, and ten young men went with him.

Absalom struggled to free himself, but Joab went up to him and speared him through the heart. Then the ten armour-bearers encircled Absalom and plunged their knives into him.

Joab blew on a trumpet and called back his men from pursuing the rebels. Absalom was thrown into a pit in the forest, and stones were placed on top of him. The revolt was over.

DAVID LEARNS OF THE DEATH OF HIS SON

While all this was happening, David was seated between two gates. The lookout went up to the roof, above the gates, and onto the city wall. He spotted a man running and cried out, "One man running!"

David remarked, "If he is alone, he will have news."

Then the lookout shouted, "Another man running!"

The king said, "He will also have news."

The lookout said, "I think the first man is Ahimaaz, the son of Zadok."

David said thoughtfully, "He is a good man and will have good news."

Ahimaaz fell down gasping in front of the king. "All is well," he said, panting. "The Lord has given you a victory!"

King David said, "Is my young son, Absalom, safe?"

And Ahimaaz replied, "When Joab sent me and the other messenger, something was going on, but I do not know what it was all about."

"Wait here next to me," David said as the next messenger, Cushi, came running up. He bowed low before the king and said, "Good news! The Lord has given you a victory, and all the rebels have been crushed!"

King David asked, "What about my son Absalom? How is he?"

And Cushi replied, "All the enemies of the king, all those who rose up against you, have suffered the same fate as Absalom."

King David was overcome with grief. He climbed the steps to his room above the gate. His voice was thick with sorrow, and tears streamed down his face. "My son, my son Absalom! God, You could have taken my life instead! Oh, my son!"

THE DEATH OF DAVID

King David had grown old. His body felt the cold, so his servants covered him with blankets and massaged his limbs. But David felt that his death was near. He told his son Solomon, "I am dying as all men do. Be brave; be a man. Do not stray from the path of the Lord. Follow His commandments as they are written in the law of Moses. Do this, and you will lead a good life no matter what you do. God made a promise that if you follow Him with all your heart, with all your faith, and with all your soul, one of your descendants will always have the throne of Israel.

"You know the men that I have supported in the past. Use your wisdom to deal with them now."

Then David spoke these last words to his people, to show how a good king should reign:

He who rules his people with justice
And reigns with the fear of God
Is like the first light of the day
On a morning without clouds,
When, after the rain,
The seeds of the earth sprout.
He who looks after his family and home
Is blessed by God, with whom I have agreement for ever.
In this way, the king and nation are safe always.

David made a census of the people in his country. He learnt that in Israel he had eight hundred thousand soldiers armed with swords. In Judah he had five hundred thousand men. When David heard these figures, his heart swelled with pride. But pride did not please the Lord, and He punished Israel with a plague that lasted three days. During that time, seventy thousand people died.

Then David knew he had sinned. He asked the Lord what he could do to save his people. And the Lord told him to leave Jerusalem and go to Araunah. David did this, and there he built an altar to the Lord and offered sacrifices.

And the Lord was merciful. He put an end to the plague, and the people were saved.

Finally, David died and was buried in the city of David. He had reigned over all Israel for forty years: seven years in Hebron and thirty-three years in Jerusalem.

David's son Solomon came to the throne. And the kingdom was strong and safe.

THE TIME OF
THE PROPHETS

THE WISDOM OF SOLOMON

Solomon inherited from his father, King David, a vast kingdom that stretched from Mount Hermon in the north as far as Egypt in the south. He reigned over his country from about 960 to 930 B.C. He did not devote himself to war but to building towns and developing administrative, commercial, and cultural activities. Under Solomon the administration of the country became more complex. The country was divided into twelve districts, each having its own prefect, who answered to a chief prefect. The old tribal boundaries were done away with. In order to build great public works, the king obliged young people to work for him one month in every three.

Solomon loved the Lord and followed his father's advice. He made sacrifices in high places and burnt incense. He made a journey to Gibeon, where he made a thousand sacrifices. Then the Lord appeared to Solomon in a dream and asked, "What shall I give you?"

Solomon replied, "O Lord God, I come after my father, David, Your servant. You showed him great mercy when he followed Your ways. You have brought me to the throne. But I am not more than a child. I do not always know which path to follow. And I am king over a mighty nation! Therefore, I ask this: give me a heart that understands the difference between right and wrong, so that I may be a good judge over my people."

This request pleased the Lord, and He said, "You have not asked for long life, wealth, or the death of your enemies. You have asked for understanding and the ability to judge fairly. This pleases Me. I give you a heart that is wise and understanding. You will be unique. There has never been anyone like you before, and there will never be anyone like you after your death. Because you have asked for wisdom, I also give you riches and honour for as long as you live. And if you follow My commandments, your life will be long."

Then Solomon awoke and knew that he had spoken with the Lord in a dream.

He went back to Jerusalem and, in front of the Ark of the Covenant of the Lord, he made sacrifices for peace and a feast for all his servants.

SOLOMON SHOWS HIS WISDOM

One day, two women were shown into the presence of the king. Solomon told them to speak and explain their problem.

One woman said, "My king, we live in the same house. I had a baby there. Three days after I had given birth, this other woman also had a child. We were alone in the house together; nobody else was there. Then a dreadful thing happened: this other woman's baby died, because she had put too many covers over it. Midnight came, and she got up and took my baby son, while your handmaid slept, and left me with her dead child!

"In the morning I went to feed my baby and found it was dead. Then I looked at it and saw that it was not the son I had given birth to!"

The other woman said, "She is wrong. The dead boy belongs to her; the one who is alive is mine."

The two women argued in front of Solomon. Each claimed that the living child belonged to her. Their quarrelling went on for some time.

At last King Solomon called to his servants, "Bring me a sword!"

A servant left the room and came back a moment later with a sword. Then Solomon said, "I must judge this case fairly. The child shall be cut into two pieces. Each woman then shall have a fair share."

The servant heard the words of his king and raised the sword up above the child.

Opposite: When Solomon heard these words, he knew who was speaking the truth. He said, "Put away the sword! The woman who shows mercy for the child is its mother."

The woman to whom the child really belonged was overcome with terror. She cried out to Solomon, "The baby is mine, but that is not important now. I beg you to give the living child to the other woman. I beg you not to kill him!"

The other woman said, "The king's decision is fair. Cut the baby in two."

When Solomon heard these words, he knew who was speaking the truth. He said, "Put away the sword! The woman who shows mercy for the child is its mother."

The baby was saved and stayed with its true mother.

This story spread throughout Israel, and the people knew that Solomon was a wise king and that the spirit of God lived inside him.

In his wisdom and largeness of heart, Solomon appointed twelve thousand officers to provide food and drink for his household, so that no one went hungry.

Solomon was wiser than all the people who lived in the East and all the people of Egypt. There was no one wiser, and his fame spread from nation to nation. Solomon wrote three thousand proverbs and more than a thousand songs.

His knowledge of nature was great. He could talk about the cedars of Lebanon or the common hyssop that grows along a wall. He knew about all the animals, birds, reptiles, and fish that lived on earth.

People came from far and wide to hear his wisdom.

One day, Hiram, the king of Tyre, sent his servants to see Solomon. Hiram had always considered Solomon's father, David, a good and great king. When Solomon saw Hiram's servants, he sent word back to the king: "You well know that my father, David, could not build a temple to the Lord, because he was busy with war. Now I intend to build a temple to God. I ask you, therefore, to send me cedar trees from Lebanon. My men will work with your men. I need your skills. I know that no one can carve timber the way you Sidonians can."

When Hiram received this message, he became very happy. He sent word to Solomon that the cedar would be floated by sea to him.

In return, Solomon gave Hiram wheat and oil.

The arrangement was good, and the kings became great friends.

THE BUILDING OF THE TEMPLE

Four hundred and eighty years after the children of Israel had left Egypt, Solomon began to build the house of the Lord.

The temple Solomon was building for the Lord was to be sixty cubits long, twenty cubits wide, and thirty cubits tall. The porch in front of the temple would be twenty cubits long, in keeping with the length of the frontage, and ten cubits wide.

The windows of the building were tall and narrow.

Against the wall of the temple, he built little circular rooms. These rooms went round the temple and the oracle.

The lowest floor was five cubits wide, the middle six, and the third seven. On the outsides of the walls, he constructed narrow shelves, so that beams would not have to go through into the temple.

Stones were carved and then brought to the construction site, so that the temple could be built in silence. There was no sound of hammers, axes, or any iron tool.

The door of the middle room was on the right-hand side of the house and was reached by winding stairs, which went through it and up to the third room.

Solomon finished the temple with wooden beams and cedar planks. He panelled the interior walls and the ceiling with cedar, and the floor of the temple with fir. He made a space of twenty cubits from the base of the temple. This enclosure was made of cedarwood, which rose from the ground to the ceiling, and it was the sanctuary of the oracle and the most holy place. It was decorated with pure gold, as was the altar, which was made of cedar. And there were golden chains in front of the oracle.

Solomon furnished the entire inside of the temple with pure gold, and the altar next to the oracle was covered with gold.

Inside the oracle, two identical cherubim were carved out of olive wood. Each cherub was ten cubits high, and their stretched wings touched in the middle and reached both walls. The cherubim were covered with gold. The walls of the temple were carved with palm trees, flowers in bloom, and more cherubim.

Inside and outside, the floor of the temple was covered with gold.

To enter the oracle, one passed through doors made of olive wood. Carved cherubim were reproduced and worked with gold.

There was also an inner court with three rows of hewed stones and a row of cedar beams.

In the eleventh year of its construction, the temple of the Lord was finally finished and furnished with many holy objects. Solomon brought into the temple things that his father, David, had blessed. There were silver, and gold, and precious cups. All these became the treasures of the house of the Lord.

Then Solomon called together the elders of Israel and the heads of the tribes. He sent them to the city of David, known as Zion, to bring back the ark of the Lord's covenant.

The priests brought the ark of the Lord's covenant into the oracle of the temple. They placed it in the most holy place, beneath the

A LITTLE BIT OF HISTORY
The temple was built with blocks of white stone. It measured about 30 metres long, 10 metres wide, and 15 metres high.

Opposite: Then Solomon called together the elders of Israel and the heads of the tribes. He sent them to the city of David, known as Zion, to bring back the ark of the Lord's covenant.

The priests brought the ark of the Lord's covenant into the oracle of the temple. They placed it in the most holy place, beneath the outstretched wings of the cherubim.

I Kings 10

outstretched wings of the cherubim. The ark contained the two tablets made of stone, which Moses had put there in Horeb.

As the priests left the holy sanctuary, a cloud filled the temple of God. The cloud became so thick that the priests could not stay to perform their duties. The glory of God was so great!

Then Solomon spoke to his people, saying, "The Lord said He would live in a thick darkness, and now we see it is true. The Lord is here with us in the temple. This is a house where He may live for ever."

Solomon blessed the children of Israel. He blessed the Lord God of Israel who had brought them out of the land of Egypt. And they rejoiced that, after so many years, promises had come true.

SOLOMON AND THE QUEEN OF SHEBA

Solomon's fame for showing wisdom and following the ways of the Lord spread through the world. When the queen of Sheba heard of this king, she decided to journey to his country and test him with some hard questions.

She reached Jerusalem safely with all her followers. Her camels carried spices, gold, and precious stones. She was shown into Solomon's court, and they sat down together and spoke. The queen of Sheba asked the king many questions, and he answered her truthfully and revealed his wisdom. Then she saw the temple he had built and studied the ways of his kingdom. She saw how good the food was, and how well dressed and polite his servants, cupbearers, and ministers were. When finally she watched him enter the temple to give thanks to God, she was convinced.

She said to Solomon, "Everything I heard about you in my own country is true! But I had to come here and see it for myself. In fact, your wisdom and wealth are even greater than what I had heard. Your men and your servants must be happy to serve you and hear your words of wisdom every day. I bless the Lord your God who blessed you and made you king of Israel."

The queen of Sheba gave Solomon many gifts. There was much gold, a huge supply of spices, and many precious stones. The navy from Hiram also brought gold, sandalwood trees, and precious stones from Ophir. The trees were especially marvelous, and Solomon used them to make pillars for the house of the Lord, as well as harps for his singers.

King Solomon gave the queen of Sheba everything she desired. Nothing was too much trouble for him.

Finally, the queen of Sheba returned to her own country with her servants.

I Kings 10-11

THE DEATH OF SOLOMON, AND A DIVIDED KINGDOM

King Solomon was richer than any king ever had been. Yearly he received an income of six hundred and sixty-six talents of gold. Besides this he had spice merchants and traders at his command. And Solomon used this great wealth to make shields of gold, solid gold drinking cups, and a great throne of ivory overlaid with the best gold. Exotic animals and birds were to be found in court, and every man there received gifts. Solomon's army expanded until he had fourteeen hundred chariots and

twelve thousand horsemen. Everything was luxurious, and the best produce of the world was imported to the king's court.

But then Solomon strayed from the path of God. He took wives from other nations. He burnt incense and offered sacrifices to other gods.

The Lord became angry with Solomon, because the king had turned his back on the Lord God of Israel. He told Solomon that He would eventually divide his kingdom for what he had done. Then He caused various individuals to turn against Solomon in whatever way they could. One of these opponents was a very brave man named Jeroboam, the son of one of Solomon's servants.

One day as Jeroboam was leaving the city of Jerusalem, he met the prophet Ahijah, who stood in his way. As Jeroboam passed, Ahijah tore his new robe off his back and ripped it into twelve pieces. Then the prophet said, "You see how I have torn up your nice new robe. So God will tear up the kingdom of Israel for what Solomon has done. The

Lord will give you ten tribes. In time you will become king over Israel. Solomon's son Rehoboam will be king of one tribe in Jerusalem, which is the city where I have chosen to leave my name."

When word reached Solomon of this meeting between Ahijah and Jeroboam, the king sent men to kill Jeroboam, who was forced to hide in Egypt until Solomon died.

God kept His promise in all things. Solomon reigned over Israel in Jerusalem for forty years. When he died, he was buried in the city of David. Rehoboam became king after his father's death. But Israel revolted against him. Then Jeroboam was made king over Israel, and he reigned for twenty-two years.

Rehoboam reigned in Jerusalem for seventeen years, over the one tribe of Judah. These two kings, Rehoboam and Jeroboam, were at war throughout their lives. After their deaths, their sons became kings.

The queen of Sheba asked the king many questions, and he answered her truthfully and revealed his wisdom.

ELIJAH, A PROPHET OF ISRAEL

Elijah the Tishbite, who came from Gilead, approached King Ahab with these words: "The God of Israel has made me His servant, and I am here to say that no rain or dew will fall unless I say so."

In the third year of the drought, God had said to Elijah, "It is time for you to visit Ahab. I will make the rain fall."

King Ahab was vexed when he saw Elijah. He said, "It is you who have brought this misery to Israel."

And Elijah replied, "I am not destroying Israel. This is what *you* have done. You have broken God's holy commandments and followed the false gods of Baal. Listen closely to what I have to tell you. Bring all Israel to Mount Carmel. Make sure the four hundred and fifty prophets of Baal are there, all those who eat food with your queen, the evil Jezebel."

King Ahab did this, and a huge crowd gathered at Mount Carmel. Elijah addressed the people: "How much longer will you go back and forth between two opinions? Either you worship God, or you worship Baal! Make your choice! Who is it to be?"

The people said nothing.

Elijah spoke to them again: "I am the one prophet of the Lord. Baal has four hundred and fifty prophets. I propose this: Bring two bullocks here. Choose one of the bullocks, cut it in pieces, and put the pieces on wood, but do not set fire to it. I will take the other bullock and do the same. When we are both ready, you will call on your god, and I will call on mine. The god who answers by setting fire to the sacrifice will be the true God."

Then the people found their tongues and said, "This is a good idea! That seems fair!"

When the prophets of Baal had prepared their bullock, they began their prayers. And they prayed and called and cried from morning until noon. They danced and even jumped upon their little altar, but nothing happened. Then Elijah could hold back no longer, and he poked fun at these priests. He said, "Perhaps your god is on holiday or talking to someone else. Perhaps he is away visiting, but then again, he could be asleep. Shout louder and try to wake him up!"

These priests were so angry and frustrated that they took daggers and, in a rage, cut themselves with them. But still nothing happened! It was evening. The shadows grew. Then Elijah raised his hand and beckoned the people to come closer to him. They stood round him and watched as he built an altar with twelve stones. He used twelve stones because there were twelve tribes of Israel. He prepared his bullock and put it on the wood on the altar. Then he called to some people close by to take four barrels of water and drench the wood and the sacrifice three times. They did this, and there was so much water that the little trench Elijah had made round his altar was full.

When evening came, Elijah was ready with his sacrifice. The people stood round him. Elijah the prophet raised his voice to God and said,

A LITTLE BIT OF HISTORY

The Kingdom of Israel was divided into two states. In the north it was called Israel, and Jeroboam was the king. In the south it was called Judah, and Rehoboam was the king. This division happened immediately after the death of King Solomon in about the year 930 B.C.

In a short period of time, the economic power of what had been the kingdom of Solomon disappeared, and the two little states became very weak politically.

In the next century King Ahab came to the throne. He had married Jezebel, the daughter of the king of Sidon. She openly worshipped her god, Baal, and she attempted to impose the cult of Baal on the people and do away with the religion of Moses.

King Ahab built an altar and temple to Baal in the northern capital of Samaria. For this homage paid to Baal, the king was condemned by Elijah.

Elijah and later his disciple Elisha were opposed to the pagan and foreign gods whose worship had become widespread in the country.

"Lord God, God of Abraham, Isaac, and Jacob, today I ask You to show that You are God of Israel and that I am Your humble servant and that I have done everything according to Your plan. Answer me now, O Lord, so that these people will know that You alone are God and can change their hearts."

Then fire shot out of the sky onto the sacrifice, and the fire of the Lord was so intense that the wood, the sacrifice, the stones, and the water were all burnt up.

When the people saw this, they fell down on their faces and cried out, "The Lord is God! The Lord is God!"

Elijah said, "Arrest the prophets of Baal. Make sure not one escapes!"

The false prophets of Baal were seized and taken to the dry stream of Kishon, where they were put to death. Then Elijah told King Ahab to eat and drink, for there was rain in the air. And soon a cloud came from off the sea, and rain fell, and the drought was over.

ELIJAH ON MOUNT HOREB

I Kings 19

After this show of God's power, Elijah was forced to escape the violent anger of Queen Jezebel. She wanted revenge for the death of her priests. He hid in a cave in the side of Mount Horeb, intending to spend the night there. But the Lord came to him and said, "Stand on the mountain, and I will be there with you!"

Then the Lord came. A wind sprang up that was so powerful it split the mountain. But the Lord was not in the wind! After the wind blew, the earth shook. But the Lord was not in the trembling of the earth! After the earth shook, there was a great fire. But the Lord was not in the fire!

After the fire, there was a gentle sound like the evening breeze. When Elijah heard this, he covered his face with his coat, because he understood that the Lord was close at hand. He stood up and went to the entrance of the cave. He heard a voice saying, "Elijah, what are you doing here?"

The prophet replied, "The children of Israel have rejected Your covenant. They have destroyed Your altars and killed Your prophets. I alone remain, and they wish to kill me."

The Lord said, "Go into the desert of Damascus. When you meet Hazael, anoint him king of Syria. And when you meet Jehu, anoint him king of Israel. Elisha will be the prophet of Israel after you."

Elijah left that place and found Elisha, who was working with cattle. Then he took off his coat and threw it over Elisha, who knew what this meant. Elisha said, "Let me kiss my mother and father goodbye. After that I will follow you."

Elisha killed two oxen and roasted them and gave the meat to the people. Then he made himself ready, and followed Elijah and became his servant.

Then fire shot out of the sky onto the sacrifice, and the fire of the Lord was so intense that the wood, the sacrifice, the stones, and the water were all burnt up.

When the people saw this, they fell down on their faces and cried out, "The Lord is God! The Lord is God!"

ELIJAH IS TAKEN TO HEAVEN

Elijah and Elisha both went on to Jericho, and when they reached the river Jordan, Elijah took off his coat and struck the water with it. At once the water divided, and the two men crossed the river on dry ground. Elijah said to Elisha, "Soon I will be taken away from you. Tell me now what I can do for you."

Elisha said, "I want a double portion of your spirit to stay within me."

Elijah said, "You have asked for something very difficult. But listen, if you see me when I leave you, your request will be granted. If you do not see me, your request will not be granted."

And as they walked and talked together, a chariot of fire drawn by horses of fire swept to the ground and separated them, and Elijah was carried up to heaven in a whirlwind.

Then Elijah was gone, and Elisha tore his clothes to pieces in anguish and sadness. Elisha picked up Elijah's coat and went back to the river Jordan. He took the coat and did as Elijah had done. The water divided, and Elisha crossed on dry ground.

THE MIRACLES OF ELISHA

One day a woman came running to Elisha in great distress, crying, "My husband is dead! You know he was a good man and feared the Lord. Now people he owed money to are coming to take away my sons and make them slaves!"

The prophet said, "Go to your neighbours and ask them to lend you as many empty containers as possible. Take them back into your house and close the door. Then empty your jug of oil into the containers."

With the help of her sons, the woman did this. First one container was full, then another, then another, until at last the woman cried out to her sons, "Bring more containers, more jugs—cups will do!"

But her sons replied, "Everything we have is full."

Opposite: And as they walked and talked together, a chariot of fire drawn by horses of fire swept to the ground and separated them, and Elijah was carried up to heaven in a whirlwind.

Then Elijah was gone, and Elisha tore his clothes to pieces in anguish and sadness.

The woman left the house and ran to the prophet, and told him what had happened. Elisha replied, "Take the oil and sell it, and pay off your debts. The money that is left over will feed you and your sons."

On another day Elisha met some of his followers on the banks of the river. They were cutting down trees. As one of the men worked, the head of his axe flew off and sank into the water. The man cried out, "Oh no, I borrowed that axe!"

The prophet Elisha said, "Where did it fall?"

The man showed him the spot. Elisha took a little piece of wood and threw it into the river, and the iron head of the axe floated to the surface. The prophet stretched out his hand, took the axe, and gave it to the man.

ELISHA CURES NAAMAN OF LEPROSY

Naaman was a captain in the army for the king of Syria. But he was sick with leprosy.

A LITTLE BIT OF HISTORY
Elisha continued Elijah's fight against the family of Ahab. Ahab was finally overcome by Jehu and army officers faithful to the law of Moses. Jehu became the tenth king of Israel, and reigned from about 842 to 815 B.C.

The new king wiped out the pagan court of Queen Jezebel, devotees of Baal, and killed all the male descendants of Ahab.

There was a little girl from Israel who worked for Naaman's wife. One day, she said to her mistress, "It is a pity your husband is not in Samaria. The prophet Elisha is there, and he could cure him."

When Naaman's wife heard this, she told her husband, and word was sent to Elisha's house. Elisha told the servant, "Tell your master to bathe seven times in the river Jordan. After that, his skin will shine, and he will be well."

Naaman thought about this, and after a while, he went down to the river Jordan. He washed himself seven times. When he came out of the water, his skin was new and shining like that of a child. He was cured!

After this miracle, Naaman went with his men to Elisha. He knocked at the door and was invited to enter. He said to Elisha, "I have learnt that there is no other God except the God of Israel. I beg you now, as a sign of my gratitude, to accept a gift from me."

Elisha replied, "In the name of the Lord, I will accept no gift. Go in peace!"

Naaman left Elisha, and he went back to his country and his duties.

II Kings 8-9

THE DEATH OF JEZEBEL

Following the word of the Lord, Elisha saw that Jehu, the son of Jehoshaphat, was anointed king of Israel.

Jehu had killed both Joram, the son of Ahab, and Ahaziah, the king of Judah. Then he had gone with his army to Jezreel to recover from his battle wounds.

When Queen Jezebel learnt where Jehu was, she put make-up on her face, made her hair beautiful, and went to a window to watch the arrival of Jehu. When he was just through the gates of the city, she called out, "Has everything gone well?"

Jehu looked up to the window and said, "Who is now on my side?"

Two or three servants who were with Jezebel also leant out of the window, and Jehu shouted to them, "Throw that woman out of the window!"

The servants threw her out of the window. Then Jehu entered the house, and ate and drank, and gave instructions that Jezebel, a king's daughter, should be buried.

And all this happened just as Elisha the prophet said it would.

II Kings 13

THE DEATH OF ELISHA

Elisha had been sick for some time before he died and was buried.

In the new year, following the death of Elisha, bands of Moabites crossed the border into Israel to see what they could steal. One of their men had died, and they were looking for a place to bury him, when they saw a group of hostile warriors. Without thinking about it, the Moabites dropped the body into the grave of Elisha and took to their heels.

When the dead Moabite slid down into Elisha's grave, he touched the bones of Elisha. And he came to life and stood up on his feet once more.

When Jehoiada saw
Athaliah in the temple,
he called captains and
officers to his side.
He said to them,
"No blood must be
spilt in the temple,
but as soon as she
leaves and is without
guards, kill her!"

A short time later,
Athaliah was killed
outside in the street.

149

JOASH BECOMES KING OF JUDAH

When Athaliah of Judah learnt that her son Ahaziah was dead, she made up her mind to kill all the other princes, so that she alone could rule the land. The murders began. But Jehosheba, who was the daughter of King Joram and the sister of Ahaziah, stole a boy and hid him in a bedroom, thus saving his life. This boy was named Joash, and he was the son of Ahaziah.

The boy was moved secretly into the house of the Lord and hidden there for six years while Athaliah ruled the country.

In the seventh year of Athaliah's reign, a priest named Jehoiada judged it safe to reveal the hidden boy. He arranged a meeting with rulers and army captains in the house of the Lord. He showed them the late king's son and made them agree to protect the boy. He said, "Make sure there are always armed men surrounding the boy. If any assassin should slip into the circle round the boy, kill him at once. You must not leave his side. You must be with him when he leaves the temple and when he enters it."

The rulers and captains agreed to these suggestions and put them into practice. Jehoiada, the priest, gave out King David's spears and shields to the army captains to defend the boy. These weapons had been in the temple since David's reign.

Guards were placed in the right and left corners of the temple, and there were also guards next to the altar.

When everything was ready, the priest anointed Joash king of Judah. A royal crown was placed on his head and a royal seal in his hands. When the people saw the young king, they clapped their hands and shouted out, "God save the king!"

Athaliah heard the commotion and went to the temple to see what was happening. Then she saw the king! He was standing by a pillar, according to the custom. Round him trumpets of celebration were blown, and the people rejoiced.

Athaliah screamed and tore her clothes, shouting, "Treason! This is treason!"

When Jehoiada saw Athaliah in the temple, he called captains and officers to his side. He said to them, "No blood must be spilt in the temple, but as soon as she leaves and is without guards, kill her!"

A short time later, Athaliah was killed outside in the street.

Then Jehoiada made a covenant between the Lord, the young king, and the people. It stated that the people were to be the people of the Lord God. There were to be no other gods.

People from far and wide entered into the buildings dedicated to Baal. They smashed his altars and broke up his idols. They killed Mattan, a priest of Baal, at his own altar.

The people rejoiced. Joash sat on the throne of kings. He was only seven years old.

A LITTLE BIT OF HISTORY
After he had killed Queen Jezebel, King Jehu killed Ahab and his seventy sons. The cult of Baal was banished from Israel. Jehu also killed Ahaziah, king of Judah and grandson of King Ahab. The kingdom was then governed by Athaliah, the mother of King Ahaziah and the daughter of Ahab and Jezebel. She reigned from about 842 to 837 B.C. and was successful in bringing the cult of Baal into Jerusalem.

THE WARNINGS
OF THE PROPHETS

THE PROPHECY OF AMOS

Woe to those of you
Taking your ease in Zion,
Who only bring the prospect of violence closer.
They lie on their ivory beds
And stretch out on their sofas.
They eat the lambs of the flock
And the calves from the herd.
They sing to the sound of the lute
And make music as though they were David.
They drink large goblets of wine
And rub themselves with precious ointments;
Yet they do not grieve for the fall of Joseph.
The earth will surely tremble because of
These idlers, and they will know sorrow.
There will come a day,
The Lord has said,
When He will put out the sun at noon
And change these false joys to sorrows
And this borrowed music to the sound of grief.
And the Lord has said
That days will follow when
Famine will spread across the earth.
But this famine will not be a hunger for bread
And a thirst for water. It will be a need to hear
The words of the Lord.
And people will wander from sea to sea,
From the north to the east,
Across the face of the earth,
Looking for the word of the Lord.
But they will not find it anywhere.
The Lord said, "I will build the tabernacle of David again.
I will cause the ruins from the past
To become great buildings.
The day will come when the people of Israel
Will build cities and live in them.
They will plant vineyards and drink wine.
They will have gardens and eat fruits from them.
They will live in their own country
And never be forced to leave it.

A LITTLE BIT OF HISTORY
As Elisha had predicted, Israel won three battles against the armies of the king of Syria. But after the successful reign of the son of Joash, Jeroboam the Second (about 783 to 740 B.C.), Israel lost its advantage and fell into a time of political intrigue and assassinations. The beginning of the end of the Kingdom of Israel was vehemently predicted by a prophet of Judah. Amos was the first in a long line of prophets who intervened in the name of the Lord in the history of the two kingdoms. Amos preached in Israel during the end of the reign of Jeroboam toward the middle of the eighth century B.C. He particularly attacked the life of luxury and the injustice to the poor of the politically powerful class of the time. For Amos, these faults were the main reason for the weakness of Israel.

The warnings of Amos were taken up by the prophet Hosea in about 750 B.C. He also preached in the northern part of the Kingdom of Israel, where the Assyrian military power, as it moved its borders ever closer to Israel, was more threatening than the power of Syria.

Although Hosea predicted disaster, he also offered hope for those who repented and found redemption through the grace and love of God.

People of Israel,
Return to your God.
Your sins have taken you away from Him.
Ask Him to forgive you your sins.
Then once again the world
Will be filled with beauty and light.
And those who live under the shadow of God
Will come back to life. They will harvest corn
And cultivate the vine.
He who is wise understands these things;
He who is intelligent knows them.
The ways of the Lord are righteous.
All evildoers will fall by the wayside.

Isaiah 6

THE VISION OF ISAIAH

The prophet Isaiah spoke to the people gathered round him and told them about the vision he had had: "In the year that King Uzziah died, I saw the Lord God seated on a throne high up in the temple, and the folds of his clothes were flowing down. Seraphim attended Him. Each seraph had six wings: two wings covered their faces, two covered their feet, and with two they flew. The seraphim called to each other, crying, 'Holy, holy, holy is the Lord! The earth is full of His glory!'

"The doorposts shuddered at the sound of these voices, and the temple was filled with smoke. I said to myself, 'I am a poor sinner. What chance do I have? I am a man whose mouth has spoken lies. I am a man who lives among liars, even though I have seen the King, the God of the world.'

"Then a seraph took tongs and took a glowing coal from the altar with them, and flew to me with it. The seraph touched my mouth with this coal and told me that I had been made clean and that my sins were forgiven.

"And I heard the voice of the Lord saying, 'Whom shall I send? Who will spread my word?' I answered, 'Here I am. Send me.' Then the voice of the Lord said, 'Go, and tell the people: Keep listening, but do not understand. Keep looking, but do not see. Make the hearts, ears, and eyes of the people heavy, in case they see with their hearts, and turn and be healed of their sins.'

"I spoke to the Lord and asked Him how long it would go on like this. The Lord replied that it would go on like this until the cities were deserted, the houses empty, and the land desolate.

"Until the Lord has sent men far away from where they are in the land and in their spirits. But few—only a few—men will remain. And those that remain will be like the trunk of a giant oak tree that has shed its leaves and only the trunk remains. And from this trunk, a purity and holiness will grow again."

A LITTLE BIT OF HISTORY
Isaiah lived about the time of Hosea. One of the greatest prophets in Israel, he was also an advisor to the state and a councillor to the kings of Judah during years of crisis. Israel was constantly under threat from neighbouring countries. Syria was an enemy, but the worst adversary was Assyria.

Opposite: "And I heard the voice of the Lord saying, 'Whom shall I send? Who will spread my word?' I answered, 'Here I am. Send me.' Then the voice of the Lord said, 'Go, and tell the people: Keep listening, but do not understand. Keep looking, but do not see.'"

WHEN ISAIAH WAS PROPHET

Uzziah, king of Judah, ruled over Jerusalem for fifty-two years, and after his death, his son Jotham ruled. When Jotham died, he was buried in the city of David, and his son Ahaz became king.

While Ahaz was king, both the king of Syria and the king of Israel attacked Jerusalem, but they did not conquer it. Then God spoke to Isaiah, saying, "Go to Ahaz and tell him not to be frightened of this joint force, because they will not be successful."

And God spoke to Ahaz, saying, "You may ask for a sign in the heavens or on earth from the Lord."

But Ahaz replied, "I will not ask for anything. I will not tempt the Lord."

Then Isaiah spoke to Ahaz with these words: "It may be a little thing for you to make men weary, but do you also wish to behave before God in this way? God Himself will now give you a sign. This will be the sign:"

A virgin will conceive,
And give birth to a son,
And his name will be Immanuel.
He will eat butter and honey,
Until he learns to reject evil
And choose what is good.
But before the child learns
To reject evil and choose good,
The country that you fear
Will be abandoned by both kings.
The people who walked in darkness
Have seen a great light.
It shines over the country,
Which lives beneath the shadow of death.
Unto us a child is born; a son is given.
This child takes the weight of the world on his shoulders.
And we will call him
Wonderful, Counsellor, the mighty God,
The everlasting Father,
The Prince of Peace.
And his kingdom of peace
Will be without end,
Now and for ever.
The Lord God does all this.

A LITTLE BIT OF HISTORY
The two kingdoms of Judah and Israel came under the influence of the powerful Assyrian Empire after the second half of the eighth century B.C. The northern state of Israel was in thirty years completely destroyed by Assyrian invasions. The southern state of Judah survived for another 150 years.

Some Assyrian writing discovered by archaeologists bears out what is found in the books of Kings, Hosea, and Isaiah. During the time of Ahaz (eleventh king of Judah, who reigned from about 736 to 716 B.C.), Isaiah spoke of the coming of the Messiah. He said the Messiah would come from the tribe of Judah and be descended from the family of David.

ISAIAH'S SONG FOR IMMANUEL

Isaiah also sang in honour of Immanuel:

A rod will grow from the tree of Jesse;
A branch will grow out of his roots.
The spirit of the Lord will rest upon him,
And the spirit of wisdom and understanding,
And the spirit of advice and power,
And the spirit of knowledge and of the fear of the Lord.
He will not judge by appearance
Or listen to gossip,
But he will judge the poor with justice.
Then the wolf will live with the lamb
And the leopard will lie down with the goat.
The calf and the young lion will walk together,
Led by a little child.
The cow and the bear will feed together,
And their young ones will share the same sleeping places.
The lion and the ox will both eat straw.
Little children will play near nests of snakes;
Older children will stroke lizards.
And no one will come to harm,
Because the country will be covered by the wisdom of the Lord,
As surely as water covers the sea.

A LITTLE BIT OF HISTORY
The Assyrians were not content to capture Damascus and overthrow the king of Syria. Later, in 722 B.C., they captured Samaria, the capital city of Israel, the kingdom in the north. The fall of Samaria in 722 B.C. marks the end of Israel as a nation. The Israelites were sent as prisoners into different regions of the Assyrian Empire. Meanwhile, Jerusalem miraculously survived. The Assyrians attacked Jerusalem in 701 B.C., but their army was struck down by a plague and forced to retire. Isaiah saw this as a sign that the Lord was helping to free his people. To understand the acts of God in history was one of the most important roles of prophets.

AHAZ SEEKS HELP FROM THE KING OF ASSYRIA

Ahaz sent messengers to the king of Assyria, saying, "Come and save me from the king of Syria and the king of Israel, who have joined forces against me!"

And Ahaz took money and gold from the temple and sent it with his messengers as a present for the king of Assyria.

The king of Assyria fought a battle for Ahaz in Damascus and killed the king of Syria.

After this, King Josiah ordered Hilkiah, the priest, to throw out of the temple of God all the idols that had been made for Baal and various other gods. The idols, objects, and pictures were taken to a place outside Jerusalem and burnt.

JOSIAH IS A GOOD KING

Josiah was eight years old when he came to the throne, and he ruled in Jerusalem for thirty-one years. He followed the teachings of the Lord and the example set by his ancestor, King David. He walked a straight path and did not turn to the left or to the right.

In the eighteenth year of his reign, King Josiah sent Shaphan to the temple. He told him to ask the high priest, Hilkiah, to count out the money the people had given to the house of the Lord and then give it to workmen so that repairs to the building could be done.

Shaphan reached the temple and completed his business with Hilkiah, who then handed him a book and said, "I found this book on the law in the house of the Lord."

Then Shaphan went back to Josiah. He reported that repairs to the building were now ready to begin and showed the king the book on the law.

When King Josiah heard what was written in the book, he tore his clothes in anger, because he then understood that his ancestors had not obeyed the laws as set out in the book.

At once he arranged a meeting with the elders of Judah and Jerusalem. He went with them to the temple of the Lord. The men of Judah and Jerusalem—the elders, the priests, the prophets, and the ordinary people—all listened as the book of the law was read aloud. When the reading was finished, King Josiah made a pact before God that in future His commandments, His laws, and His words would be followed by everybody. They were to follow the teachings of the book with their heart and spirit, and to live their lives in this way. And all the people agreed that this should be so.

JOSIAH FORBIDS THE WORSHIP OF IDOLS

After this, King Josiah ordered Hilkiah, the priest, to throw out of the temple of God all the idols that had been made for Baal and various other gods. The idols, objects, and pictures were taken to a place outside Jerusalem and burnt.

Former kings of Judah had appointed priests to burn incense to Baal, the sun, the moon, the planets, and the stars. These priests were banished, as were those who practised magic and pretended to be wizards. Other priests who had set up altars to false gods were put to the sword. Wherever Josiah found places where idols were worshipped, those places were burnt to the ground. Everywhere in Judah and Jerusalem, the word of the Lord was strong again.

There had never before been a king like Josiah. He followed the path of the Lord with all his heart and with all his soul. The law of Moses was his law.

JEREMIAH AND THE FALL OF JERUSALEM

God visited the prophet Jeremiah and said, "Before you were born I knew you and appointed you a prophet."

But Jeremiah replied, "Forgive me, Lord! I cannot speak, I am a child."

God said, "Do not tell me you are too young! Go now, and keep company with those I cause you to meet. Tell them all the things I have told you."

And the Lord God stretched out His hand and touched Jeremiah's mouth so that when Jeremiah spoke, it would be God's word.

God spoke to Jeremiah again with a dreadful warning: "Israel, I will send a distant country to your land to do battle with you. That country will be strong. It will be an ancient nation, whose language you will not understand. They will be ruthless. They will steal your harvest, and the bread meant for your children will go into their mouths. Then they will eat your sheep and cattle. They will strip your vineyards and fig trees. Many will cry out and ask why God is doing this. And you will tell them that it is because they have abandoned Me and worshipped false gods. The children of Israel will become slaves in a country that is no longer theirs. The people of Israel have lost their way. They had eyes, but they did not see. They had ears, but they did not hear."

JUDAH IS CONQUERED

After King Josiah had rid his country of idols and false gods, he went to fight the Pharaoh of Egypt. The battle went against him. He was killed in Megiddo, and his body was brought back to Jerusalem in a chariot. He was buried in his own tomb.

Then his son Jehoahaz was made king. The young man was twenty-three years old when he began his reign, and he ruled for only three months. Pharaoh, king of Egypt, removed him from the throne and made Jehoiakim, another son of Josiah, king in his place.

Then Pharaoh imposed heavy taxes on the country. He demanded silver and gold. Jehoiakim was forced to tax his people to pay Pharaoh.

Jehoiakim was twenty-five years old when he became king, and he reigned in Jerusalem for eleven years. But God was never pleased with this king.

During Jehoiakim's reign, King Nebuchadnezzar of Babylon fought him and made him his servant for three years. Then Jehoiakim rebelled.

When the Lord God saw this rebellion, he sent forces against Jehoiakim. These armies came from bands of Chaldeans, Syrians, Moabites, and Ammonites. They fought the country of Judah and won. And all this was just as God had said when His prophets spoke to the people. Jehoiakim was killed, and his son Jehoiachin became king in his place.

At this time the king of Egypt suffered a loss of power and did not dare go beyond the boundaries of his country. This was because the

A LITTLE BIT OF HISTORY
Another Hebrew prophet appeared during the reign of Josiah. This was Jeremiah, a man inspired by God. He had a mild manner and advised kings, who did not always listen to him. His preaching often provoked a violent reaction and made the heads of state in Judah angry with him. One even sent him to prison.

In the last years of the reign of Josiah, Nineveh, the capital of Assyria, fell into the hands of Babylon. Jeremiah saw the emergence of this new power as a bad sign for Jerusalem and the Kingdom of Judah.

king of Babylon had taken all the land that stretched from the river Nile of Egypt to the river Euphrates.

Jehoiachin was eighteen years old when he began his reign, but he ruled for only three months in Jerusalem. God was no more pleased with his behaviour than with Jehoiakim's.

Nebuchadnezzar, the king of Babylon, brought out his army and camped round Jerusalem. When Jehoiachin saw that his position was hopeless, he went with his family and household, and surrendered to the king of Babylon.

Then Nebuchadnezzar ransacked the temple. He took all the gold and treasures that King Solomon had placed in the house of God. He left nothing. Princes, warriors, craftsmen, smiths, and ten thousand slaves were transported to Babylon. Only the poorest people were left. Even Jehoiachin and his family were taken to Babylon.

Nebuchadnezzar made Mattaniah king in place of Jehoiachin, and he changed Mattaniah's name to Zedekiah.

Zedekiah was twenty-one years old when he began his reign, and he ruled for eleven years in Jerusalem. But he was a bad king, as bad as Jehoiakim, and the Lord God was not pleased with him.

Zedekiah revolted against the king of Babylon. Nebuchadnezzar was furious and led his army to Jerusalem. He surrounded the city and built strong forts all round it.

JEREMIAH TELLS ZEDEKIAH HIS FATE

Jeremiah 37-38

Zedekiah sent two priests to the prophet Jeremiah, asking him whether there was news from the Lord.

At this time Jeremiah was not in prison, although he frequently had been. He was free and among the people.

At the same time, Pharaoh's army left Egypt to do battle with the Chaldeans who were camped round Jerusalem. When they heard that Pharaoh was approaching, the Chaldeans did not attack the city.

Then the word of the Lord reached Jeremiah. He told the two priests, "Listen carefully now, for these are the words of God, and these words you will take to your king. Pharaoh's army, which has come here to help you, will shortly return to their own land, Egypt. Then the Chaldeans will return and make war on the city. They will be victorious and burn it to the ground. Do not deceive yourselves that the Chaldeans will go far away. They will not. Even if you fought them and there were only wounded men left, they would still do battle with you and burn the city."

The two priests took this message to King Zedekiah. He listened to the news, as did the noblemen round him. The noblemen were angry and said to the king, "This man is no good. He should be put to death. All he does is upset people with this kind of talk."

The king replied, "Do what you think is right. I will not stand against what you think is just."

So they took Jeremiah and threw him into a dry well. And there was no water in the dry well, just mud at the bottom. And Jeremiah sank into the mud.

A LITTLE BIT OF HISTORY
Nebuchadnezzar became king of Babylon in 605 B.C. He besieged Jerusalem in 598 B.C., the year in which the Hebrews were first deported into the capital of his kingdom. The revolt of Zedekiah, king of Judah, against the power of Babylon (approximately 587 B.C.) was the origin of later deportations. Historians have estimated that the number of slaves sent abroad was between 15,000 and 20,000. Those deported were especially religious Jews, social leaders, chief priests, wealthy traders, artists, and their families. Archaeologists have discovered information on Hebrew deportations in Babylonian writings of the time.

In the third year of the reign of King Jehoiakim of Judah,
King Nebuchadnezzar of Babylon surrounded the city of Jerusalem
with armed men. A battle took place, and Nebuchadnezzar won.
(See page 170.)

JEREMIAH THE PRISONER

When Ebed-melech, one of the king's slaves, learnt what had happened to Jeremiah, he went to Zedekiah and said, "My lord, these men have done wrong. The prophet should not be in prison. He will die of hunger there."

The king saw the wisdom in Ebed-melech's words. He ordered him to go to the dry well with thirty men. "Get Jeremiah out of that place before he dies," he said, and his servant went at once to rescue the prophet.

The men made ropes from old pieces of cloth and lowered these down to Jeremiah.

Ebed-melech, an Ethiopian, shouted down into the well, "Put this makeshift rope under your arms, and we will pull you up."

Jeremiah did this and was lifted to safety. Afterwards he was allowed to stay in the courtyard of the prison.

Then King Zedekiah sent for Jeremiah, and they met at the third entrance to the temple. The king said, "There is something I wish to know, and I want you to answer me truthfully."

Jeremiah replied, "If I tell you the truth, perhaps you will have me put to death. On the other hand, if you like my advice, you will listen."

When Zedekiah heard this, he swore to the prophet that he would not have him put to death or turn him over to those who wanted to kill him.

Then Jeremiah said, "The God of Israel has spoken to me, and this is what He has said: You must surrender to the king of Babylon. If you do this, you will save your life, and the city will not be burnt down. However, if you do not do this, the city will fall into the hands of the Chaldeans, and they will burn it! And you will be killed!"

Zedekiah thought about this and said, "I am afraid of the Jews who have taken sides with the Chaldeans. If I fall into their hands, they will treat me badly."

Jeremiah's voice rose. "Listen to the voice of the Lord! You will not fall into the hands of these people you fear! Do as I have told you, and you will be saved! I have already told you what will happen if you don't! If you do not give yourself up to the king of Babylon, all the women and children will be handed over to the Chaldeans, you will be a prisoner of the king of Babylon, and Jerusalem will go up in flames."

Zedekiah found it hard to speak. He told Jeremiah, "No one must know this meeting took place. Do not breathe a word, and you will live. If the princes come to you and want to know what you have said to me, you must not tell them. Even if they ask what I said to you and even if they promise to save your life, you must tell them nothing. Pretend you came to see me to beg for mercy."

And so it happened that the princes and noblemen approached Jeremiah with questions. But he told them nothing, and they guessed nothing.

Jeremiah the prophet lived in the courtyard of the prison until the day Jerusalem was captured.

The king saw the wisdom in
Ebed-melech's words. He ordered
him to go to the dry well with thirty
men. "Get Jeremiah out of that
place before he dies," he said, and
his servant went at once to rescue
the prophet.

The men made ropes from old
pieces of cloth and lowered these
down to Jeremiah.

Ebed-melech, an Ethiopian,
shouted down into the well,
"Put this makeshift rope under
your arms, and we will pull
you up."

Jeremiah did this and was
lifted to safety.

JERUSALEM IS DESTROYED

How alone the city feels,
A place once so full of people!
Now the city is like a widow!
She who was formerly great among nations,
Who was thought of far and wide as a princess,
Now is merely a servant.
In the night, she weeps bitterly,
And tears stain her cheeks.
Among all those who loved her,
No one comes to give comfort.
And all have betrayed her
And become her enemies.
Judah is in captivity,
Afflicted with misery and slavery.
She lives with heathens
And finds no rest.
All her persecutors have joined
To torment her.
The streets of Zion are in mourning,
No one attends a solemn feast.
The city gates are dreary places:
The priests sigh, and
Young girls look sad.
Her opponents have become masters,
And her enemies prosper,
For the Lord has made her suffer
Because of her sins.
The enemy has taken her children
Into captivity.
The daughters of Zion have lost their beauty,
And the sons of Zion are like stags
Who cannot find grassland:

They run wearily
Before the huntsmen.
In these days of sorrow and misery,
Jerusalem remembers happier times;
She also remembers times
When her people
Fell into the hands of the enemy
And no one came to help.
Adversaries mocked her and her Sabbaths.
Jerusalem has sinned,
And for this she will be crushed!
All who honoured her
Despise her now,
Because they have seen her for what she is.
She has trailed her skirts in the mud
And thought little of it.
She has fallen dramatically
From a place of grace
To a level where no one may help her.
She cries aloud, "O Lord, see my sorrow!
How mighty the enemy has become!"
The heathens have touched
Everything she held precious.
Her people sigh
And look for bread.
They trade silver and gold
For something to eat.
And she cries aloud, "Was there ever
A sorrow like the one I suffer,
Brought down on me from the Lord
On this day of burning anger?"

A LITTLE BIT OF HISTORY

The Chaldeans (sometimes called the Babylonians in the Bible) laid siege to Jerusalem during the eleventh year of the reign of Zedekiah. On the ninth day of the fourth month of the siege, famine broke out in the town, and there was no bread for the people.

The town fell, and Zedekiah and all his soldiers fled along the path of the king's garden and out of the door between the two walls. They did this under cover of darkness. They fled toward the flat country.

The Chaldean army gave chase and met them on the plain at Jericho. The Chaldeans took the king and dispersed his army (about 586 B.C.). The king was then taken to Nebuchadnezzar in Riblah, where a sentence was passed. Zedekiah's sons were killed in front of their father. The king was put in chains and taken to Babylon after being blinded. The Chaldeans burned the king's house and the houses of the people. They broke down the walls of Jerusalem.

Nebuzaradan, the captain of the guard, deported all the people who had stayed in the town to Babylon. These were the deserters and the rest of the population. But Nebuzaradan left the poor people in Judah and gave them vineyards and fields.

SONGS OF EXILE
IN BABYLON

Psalm 137

THE TEARS OF THE EXILED
WHO THINK OF THEIR HOMELAND

By the rivers of Babylon,
We sat down and wept
When we remembered Zion.
And we hung our harps on the willows there,
And our captors mocked us, saying,
"Give us one of your old songs.
Sing us one of the songs of Zion!"
But how can we sing of the Lord
In a strange land?
O Jerusalem, if ever I forget you,
Let my right hand turn to stone.
If I do not remember you,
Let my tongue stick to the roof of my mouth.
Jerusalem, you will always be my first joy.
Remember, O Lord, the children of Edom,
Who in the days of Jerusalem cried,
"Raze it, raze it to the ground!"
How happy they must be now!

A LITTLE BIT OF HISTORY
This is the psalm of the exiles in
Babylon. It is a hymn to the Lord and
expresses their sadness and deep
longing for their distant country.
The temple and its liturgy disappeared
with the destruction of the city.
The hymn is also a prayer for revenge
on Judah's Babylonian conquerors.

Opposite:
Remember, O Lord, the children of Edom,
Who in the days of Jerusalem cried,
"Raze it, raze it to the ground!"
How happy they must be now!

SONG FOR THE LOST CITY OF JERUSALEM

Remember, O Lord, what has happened to us.
Consider, and look down on our shame.
Our inheritance has passed to strangers,
Foreign people live in our houses.
We are orphans without fathers,
And our mothers are like widows.
We have sold our water,
Our wood no longer belongs to us.
A yoke hangs round our necks,
We work without rest.
Egyptians rule us,
Assyrians take our bread.
Our ancestors have sinned,
And we suffer for that.
Servants rule us,
And we dare not object.
We struggle daily for our bread,
Always beneath the threat of the sword.
The terrible famine was like an oven,
Which burnt our skin to coals.
Our women were raped in Zion,
As were the girls in the cities of Judah.
Princes were hung up by their hands,
The elders became objects of fun.
Young men worked at the grindstone
While children slaved beneath bundles of wood.
The elders have deserted the cosy places,
The young men no longer make music.
There is no laughter in our hearts,
We only dance in mourning.
We no longer wear a crown,
We pay the price for our sin.
Our hearts tremble,
Our eyesight has dimmed.
The mountains of Zion are desolate,
And foxes play there.
O Lord, you remain for ever.
Your throne is secure from one generation to the next.
Why have you forgotten us for so long?

O Lord, return to us!
We will turn to you,
And it will be as it was before.
This is our prayer.
We know we have done wrong,
We know you are bitterly angry with us.

DANIEL IS TAKEN PRISONER

In the third year of the reign of King Jehoiakim of Judah, King Nebuchadnezzar of Babylon surrounded the city of Jerusalem with armed men. A battle took place, and Nebuchadnezzar won.

The king of Babylon stole many of the precious treasures from the temple and took them to the land of Shinar, where he had his own temple for his own god.

Then King Nebuchadnezzar ordered Ashpenaz, the master of his household, to bring certain children of Israel to his court. He wanted children with royal blood who were handsome, skilful, good at science, and eager to learn. These youngsters were to live in the king's palace, where they would learn the wisdom and language of the Chaldeans.

Nebuchadnezzar provided these special children of Israel with a daily portion of his meat and wine. His idea was that after three years, they would be just like his family and live in court with him.

Among these young people were four sons of Judah, whose names were Daniel, Hananiah, Mishael, and Azariah. These boys were given new names.

Daniel became Belteshazzar, Hananiah became Shadrach, Mishael became Meshach, and Azariah became Abednego.

From the start, Daniel decided that he would not eat the king's food or drink his wine. His reason was that doing so would dishonour him, because it was not in keeping with his religion.

He told Ashpenaz about his decision. The head of the household was disturbed by Daniel's words. He had grown fond of Daniel, but the young man had put him in a difficult position. He said, "My king has ordered the food and drink for you. Now if he sees you growing pale and thin, what will he think? Your request puts my life in danger!"

Then Daniel spoke to Mezar, whom the head of the household had appointed to look after the four boys from Judah. He said, "You know what I have asked; let us put it to the test. Give us just pulses to eat and water to drink for ten days. After that time, compare our health and looks with that of the others."

Daniel got his way. When the ten days were up, the health and looks of the four boys were compared with those who had eaten the king's meat and drunk his wine. It was then evident that Daniel and his friends looked stronger and healthier than those who had eaten the king's diet. So Melzar relented. These four children were allowed to eat their own food.

The four boys became strong and wise. God gave them knowledge and skill in learning. Daniel had visions and understood the meaning of dreams.

When the three-year period was up, the head of the king's household brought them before Nebuchadnezzar.

The king questioned all of the children of Israel closely. And he found that no one could compare with the four young men, Daniel,

Hananiah, Mishael, and Azariah. For every question he put to them, they had a wise answer. He realised that they were ten times more intelligent than any of the magicians and astrologers in his kingdom.

KING NEBUCHADNEZZAR'S GOLDEN STATUE

King Nebuchadnezzar had his craftsmen build a massive golden statue. It was sixty cubits tall and six cubits wide. He erected the statue on the Dura plain in the province of Babylon. This done, the king ordered the princes, governors, captains, judges, treasurers, counsellors, and all the rulers from the provinces to attend the ceremony of dedication.

Thus, many royal and official people were standing before the statue when the voice of a herald rang out, saying, "Hear me now, you people of many nations and many languages! When you hear the sound of the flute, the cornet, the harp, and other musical instruments, you are to bow down before the statue of the king. Those who do not worship the statue will be thrown immediately into a fiery furnace."

The herald had no sooner finished speaking than the sounds of many musical instruments blared out. And at once all the people, from every corner of the world, fell to their knees and worshipped the golden statue that King Nebuchadnezzar had erected.

THE CHALDEANS ACCUSE THE HEBREWS

But the Chaldeans were not happy. They made accusations against the Jews, and finally they went to the king. They said, "O King, live for ever! We know you have issued an order that everyone, when he hears the fanfare of music, must fall down and worship your statue. We also know that those who do not worship it will be dropped into the fiery furnace. We are here to tell you that certain Jews who have positions in Babylon have not obeyed your commands. They worship their own god. Their names are Shadrach, Meshach, and Abednego."

Nebuchadnezzar was furious when he heard the Chaldeans' words. His voice roared as he demanded that his servants bring these three to him immediately.

When the three men stood in front of the king, he asked them, "Is it true what I have heard? Is it true that you do not bow down and worship my golden image when you hear the sound of the musical instruments? You know the penalty for this! What god can help you when you are looking into the face of fire?"

The three young men answered as one: "O King, we have no need to discuss this subject! The God we worship will not allow us to burn in the fire. He will save us from you. And even if He did *not* spare us, we would not worship your gods or your golden statue."

THE FIRE DOES NOT HARM THE THREE, *Daniel 3*

When Nebuchadnezzar heard the words of the three young men, his expression changed. His face darkened. His voice rose in fury. He shouted at his servants to stir up the furnace and make it seven times hotter than usual.

While this was being done, the king ordered his strongest and most ruthless warriors to tie up the three men and throw them into the furnace.

A LITTLE BIT OF HISTORY
During the reign of Nebuchadnezzar, the Babylonian Empire took in all of Mesopotamia and stretched from the Arabian Gulf to the Mediterranean. This empire did not last more than a century. It was during this time that Babylon reached the summit of its splendour. The city was surrounded by a double perimeter wall. It was entered by great carved doors. The main door was dedicated to the goddess Astarte and led to the "holy way." The door of Astarte was covered with blue enamel and embossed with pictures of dragons and towers.

The famous hanging gardens of Babylon were also built at this time. They were considered one of the seven wonders of the world. The gardens were made up of terraces enclosed by walls built to a height of 25 metres. The trees and plants were watered by a complex system of fountains.

With their clothes still on, the three young men were pushed towards the furnace, and they stumbled in. And the heat of the fire was so intense that those who pushed the Jews into the fire were themselves overcome by the heat and died on the spot.

And these three men, Shadrach, Meshach, and Abednego, walked in the middle of the flames.

Then King Nebuchadnezzar was astonished. He called his counsellors to him at once. He spoke hurriedly: "We threw three men into the fire. Was it really three men?"

And his men answered, "It was three men, O King!"

The king replied, "There are four men walking in the middle of the fire, and no one is hurt or suffering. The fourth figure is like the Son of God!"

Nebuchadnezzar went as close to the mouth of the furnace as he dared. He called down, "Shadrach, Meshach, Abednego—you three, who serve the highest God—come out of there!"

The three young men walked out of the fire. The king, the princes, and all the officials stood staring. The fire had hurt the men in no way. Their clothes were not burnt nor even their hair. There was not even the smell of burning in the air.

Then Nebuchadnezzar said, "Praise the God of Shadrach, Meshach, and Abednego. For He sent His angel to save them, because they trusted in Him. They did not listen to me! They were prepared only to worship their own God. They have taught me a lesson.

"I now issue a new order: Any man who speaks badly of the God of these three shall be cut into pieces, and his house will be made into a dunghill. There is no God except this one who can save His followers."

And then the king promoted the three young men to higher offices in Babylon.

THE WRITING ON THE WALL

Daniel 5

After the death of Nebuchadnezzar, his son Belshazzar became king. The young king loved to feast and drink. One day, he gave invitations to a thousand lords and ladies, and they all came to celebrate with the new king.

In the middle of the feasting, Belshazzar had an idea. He shouted to his servants to bring the gold and silver drinking cups from his temple. Now these vessels were part of the treasure that the king's father had stolen from the temple in Jerusalem. The cups were brought and they were filled with wine. The king, his princes, his wives, and all his friends drank from the precious vessels. As they drank, they praised the gods of gold, silver, brass, iron, wood, and stone.

In the middle of this toasting and drinking, the fingers of a man's hand were suddenly seen to be writing on the wall of the king's palace.

When the king saw the handwriting, his legs shook and his body trembled. His face fell and dark thoughts raced inside him. He shouted to his servants to bring the astrologers, the Chaldeans, and the fortune-tellers to him at once.

The king addressed his assembly of wise men: "Whoever can read this writing and tell me what it means will in future wear scarlet robes

Opposite: Nebuchadnezzar shouted at his servants to stir up the furnace and make it seven times hotter than usual. While this was being done, the king ordered his strongest and most ruthless warriors to tie up the three men and throw them into the furnace.

and a gold chain. And this will make him the third most powerful ruler in the kingdom!"

One by one, the wise men studied the writing on the wall, but no one could make any sense of it.

Then Belshazzar was deeply disturbed. His face changed as though he were ill. His lords were astonished and anxious. They called for the queen, and when she saw how her husband looked, she said, "O King, live for ever! Put aside your dark thoughts, and let us see a light in your face again! I have news! There is a man in our kingdom who still has the spirit of the old holy gods. In the old days, your father made him chief of all the wise men. He has knowledge and understanding. He knows how to interpret dreams and take all troubles away. This man's name is Daniel. In your father's day, he was known as Belteshazzar."

Daniel was summoned, and he appeared before the king, who said, "Are you the same Daniel my father brought out of Judah?"

Daniel said that he was. The king went on, "I have heard of you. I have heard that the spirit of God lives in your wisdom and understanding. I want you to read this writing on the wall for me. If you can, I will dress you in scarlet and gold, and you will be third highest ruler in the kingdom."

Daniel said, "I do not ask for gifts or favours, but I will read the writing and interpret it for you."

After the death of Nebuchadnezzar, his son Belshazzar became king.
The young king loved to feast and drink. One day, he gave invitations to a
thousand lords and ladies, and they all came to celebrate with the new king.

In the middle of the feasting, Belshazzar had an idea. He shouted to his
servants to bring the gold and silver drinking cups from his temple.
Now these vessels were part of the treasure that the king's father had stolen
from the temple in Jerusalem. The cups were brought and they were filled
with wine. The king, his princes, his wives, and all his friends drank from
the precious vessels. As they drank, they praised the gods of gold, silver, brass,
iron, wood, and stone.

In the middle of this toasting and drinking, the fingers of a man's hand
were suddenly seen to be writing on the wall of the king's palace.

DANIEL INTERPRETS THE WRITING

Daniel said, "God, the Almighty, gave your father, Nebuchadnezzar, a kingdom. And he filled it with glory, honour, and majesty. He was a man feared throughout the world by all people and nations. He held life and death in his hands. But when his heart swelled with too much pride and arrogance, he was removed from his throne and stripped of all his glory. He went through much hardship before he understood that it is the Lord who appoints and governs, not man.

"And you, O Belshazzar, you know all this, but you have not behaved in a humble way. You have insulted the Lord of heaven. You took the holy cups and vessels from your own temple, filled them with wine, and handed them round to your family and friends. You did not stop there! You praised the gods of silver and gold, and of brass, iron, wood, and stone. And yet these things have no life! God alone breathes into the living, but you did not have one word for Him. The Lord saw all this.

"The writing was written by His hand; this is what was written:

"MENE MENE TEKEL UPHARSIN.

"Now I will tell you what this means.

"MENE means God has judged your reign, and it is over.

"TEKEL means you have been weighed in the balance of life and found to be a trivial person.

"UPHARSIN, or PERES, means your kingdom will be divided and given to the Medes and Persians."

When Daniel had finished speaking, Belshazzar told his servants to dress Daniel in scarlet robes and put a gold chain round his neck, for he was now the third highest ruler in the kingdom.

And that same night, Belshazzar, the king of the Chaldeans, was killed.

Darius, a Median, seized the kingdom. He was not a young man. He was probably about sixty-two years old.

DANIEL IN THE LIONS' DEN

Darius decided that a hundred and twenty princes should take care of the affairs of state. Above these hundred and twenty princes, there would be three presidents. The highest of the three was Daniel. Thus, the running of the country was very much in Daniel's hands. Darius was pleased with this man and the spirit he showed. He planned to let Daniel oversee the whole kingdom in the future.

The presidents and princes grew restless and jealous. They wanted to find fault with Daniel, but this proved impossible. Daniel was faithful, showed good character, and did not make foolish mistakes.

Then the men who plotted against Daniel met together and discussed the matter. One said, "It is obvious he is a loyal servant. We cannot fault him there."

Another man said, "That is true. But he is always true to his God, and that is where we can trap him!"

This was considered a good idea. They went to Darius, saying, "O King, live for ever! The princes, the counsellors, and the captains have been discussing things. They wish you to make a law that if any man, within the space of thirty days, offers a prayer to some god or man

Opposite: "Now I will tell you what this means.

"MENE means God has judged your reign, and it is over.

"TEKEL means you have been weighed in the balance of life and found to be a trivial person.

"UPHARSIN, or PERES, means your kingdom will be divided and given to the Medes and Persians."

other than yourself, he should be thrown into a den of lions. We ask that you, our king, sign this petition according to the laws of the Medes and the Persians."

Darius saw no harm in this and signed the petition.

When Daniel heard what had happened and that a petition had been signed, he went to his house. His windows were wide open and looked towards Jerusalem. Daniel fell to his knees as he always did three times a day. He prayed and gave thanks to his God.

Those who plotted against Daniel passed by Daniel's house and saw him at prayer. They were very pleased. They went to Darius and said, "O King, did you not sign a petition saying that every man, within a period of thirty days, must first talk with you rather than with any other god? And that if any man went against this decree, he was to be thrown into a den of lions?"

The king answered at once, "What you say is true. That was my decree, and it is in keeping with the laws of the Medes and the Persians. This cannot be changed."

Then a spokesman for the group said, "Daniel, who was brought in captivity from Judah, is not obeying the decree that you signed. Three times a day we see him praying to his God!"

When the king heard these words, he was greatly troubled. He looked to Daniel to find an answer to the problem. But no word came. All day the king was tortured with the problem. When the sun went

down, the men came to King Darius again. This time they said, "O King, live for ever! We are here only to say that any law made by a king over the Medes and the Persians cannot be changed."

Then Darius ordered Daniel to be brought before him. He told him that he was to be thrown into a den of lions. He said, "I cannot save you, but the God you worship must do that."

Daniel was pushed into the den of snarling beasts. A huge stone was moved on top of the den. Darius himself put a mark on the stone with his own signet ring to show that the law could not be changed.

Then Darius went back to his palace. He could not eat. He could not sleep. No music could calm his troubled soul. Slowly, the night passed.

Darius got up early in the morning, and with a heavy heart he ran to the den of lions. He cried out in a sad and weary voice, "Daniel, Daniel, you servant of the living God, are you alive? Did the God whom you serve save you from the lions?"

The voice of Daniel came out of the pit, "O King, live for ever! God sent His angel, and the mouths of the lions were shut. God found that I had done no wrong to Him or to you."

Darius rejoiced. He ordered Daniel to be pulled out of the den. And when Daniel reached level ground, there was no mark on him from a lion's paw. He was well and safe, because he had kept faith with his God.

Then Darius ordered all the men who had brought accusations against Daniel to appear before him. These same men, and their wives and children, were all thrown into the den of lions and eaten until nothing was left of them.

King Darius wrote to all the nations of the world, wishing them peace. He wrote: "This is my law. Every kingdom must fear the God of Daniel. His God is the living God. If you wish to survive, you must worship this God. He is the God for ever, and He will never be destroyed.

"This God saves and rescues. He performs miracles in heaven and on earth. He saved Daniel from the lions. Praise Him!"

After this, things went well with Daniel. He served Darius and, afterwards, Cyrus the Persian.

Opposite: Then Darius ordered Daniel to be brought before him. He told him that he was to be thrown into a den of lions. He said, "I cannot save you, but the God you worship must do that."

EZEKIEL, THE PROPHET OF EXILE

It was eleven years after the fall of Jerusalem, when the Jews had been in captivity for twenty-five years, that the hand of the Lord touched Ezekiel. And he spoke of his visions:

"In a vision God carried me to the land of Israel and put me down on a very high mountain, which looked south to a city. And God brought me there. And by the gate, I met a man who seemed to be made of brass. In one hand, he held a ruler for measuring, and in the other, a length of twine. He said, 'Son of man, listen to all I tell you as you must tell it afterwards to the people of Israel. That is the reason you have been brought here. Therefore, open your heart, see clearly, and hear everything I say.'

"A divine spirit carried me inside the wonderful temple, where the glory of God filled the whole building. Then the man spoke to me, as though we stood opposite each other. He told me everything there was to know about the temple. He pointed out the place for His throne and even the place where the soles of His feet would rest. He said that he would remain with the children of Israel for ever and that the Hebrews would never again turn away from Him for any reason whatsoever."

And again Ezekiel's voice rose and spoke with the inspiration of God: "If the wicked are truly sorry for their evil ways, if they wish to do what is true and honest, then they will not die but will live. Good actions done now will count for more than evil actions done in the past. A change of heart and proper behaviour will mean that a person will live."

And Ezekiel spoke of another vision: "I felt the hand of the Lord on me, and He carried me to a valley that was full of bones. And there He set me down. I wandered through this valley of bones, and many of them were very dry. Then I heard the voice of the Lord saying, 'Son of man, can these bones come to life?' And I answered that only He, the Lord, knew whether they could or not.

"Then the Lord said, 'Speak to the bones as though in prophecy. Tell these dry bones to hear the word of the Lord. Tell them that through the Lord God, breath may enter them and they may live. Tell them that I will give them sinews and cover them in flesh and skin. And after I have done this, they will know that I am the Lord.' "

Ezekiel went on: "I did as God commanded me to do. And as I spoke, I heard a noise of rattling bones as they joined up together, bone to bone. As I watched, the bones grew flesh and were covered with skin. But there was no breath in these bodies. Then the voice of the Lord came to me again and told me to call up the four winds, so that these bones might live. I made this as a prophecy, and before my eyes, the people stood before me, as dense as an army in number.

"And God spoke to me again, saying, 'Son of Man, these bones were like the children of Israel: dry, without hope, and in many pieces. Tell this army that the Lord will open their graves and bring them living into the land of Israel. And I will wash away their sins and give them a

A LITTLE BIT OF HISTORY
Ezekiel, who came from a family of priests, had been exiled to Babylon in about 597 B.C., the time of the first deportations. After the fall of Jerusalem in 586 B.C., this prophet spoke of the return of the Jews to their country after seventy years of slavery.

In the passage we quote here, the restoration of Israel is compared to the resurrection of the dead. Only God can perform this miracle.

new heart. I will give them a new spirit. I will turn their old hearts of stone to human flesh and blood.

" 'My spirit will live in them, and they will live according to My laws and commandments. They will be My people, and I will be their God.' "

This was Ezekiel's vision of the future of Israel.

THE ROAD TO JERUSALEM

Isaiah 40

Prepare the way for the Lord.
Make a straight road through the desert
For our God to travel on.
Every valley will rise up,
Every mountain and hill will stoop down.
Crooked paths will be made straight
And rough places made smooth.
And the glory of God will be revealed.
All will see it.
And God himself has said these things.
The voice said, "Cry!"
And He said, "What shall I cry?"
Man is like the grass
And his goodness is like the flower in the field.
The grass may wither,
The flower may fade,
But the word of our God
Will remain for ever.
Zion, you bring good tidings!
Jerusalem, you bring good tidings!
Therefore, raise your voice with strength,
Do not be afraid. Tell the cities of Judah
Their God is at hand.
The Lord God will arrive with a strong hand,
His arm will govern, and His work is set out before Him.
He will feed His flock like a shepherd,
He will carry the lambs in His arms
And lead carefully those with young.

THE RETURN
TO JERUSALEM

In the first year of the reign of Cyrus, king of Persia, God made him follow Jeremiah's advice.

Cyrus announced his intentions towards Jerusalem. He said, "The Lord God has given me all the kingdoms of the world, and now He has asked me to build a temple for Him in Jerusalem, which is in Judah. Step forwards now, you people of this faith, for the Lord needs you to build His house! Those who stay behind should help the volunteers with gold, silver, goods, and cattle."

Then the chiefs of Judah and Benjamin, the priests, the Levites, and all those who felt the spirit of the Lord made themselves ready for the journey to Jerusalem to build the house of the Lord.

And the neighbours of the volunteers gave gifts of money and food to help them on their way.

King Cyrus took back all the treasure and holy vessels that King Nebuchadnezzar had looted from Jerusalem. They were put on donkeys and carried from Babylon back to Jerusalem.

THE BUILDING OF THE TEMPLE

In the second year of their arrival in Jerusalem, all those who had left captivity behind them set to work as a mighty team. But the enemies of Judah made life difficult for the builders and officials. Whatever they could do to delay the building of the temple of God, they did. And this state of affairs lasted through the reigns of Kings Cyrus and Artaxerxes.

When Darius became king, he gave orders that no one was to hinder the building of the temple. And the work resumed.

The temple was finished in the sixth year of the reign of King Darius.

BUILDING THE WALLS OF JERUSALEM, *Nehemiah 1-2, 4, 6*

King Artaxerxes had ruled Persia for twenty years. He had a cupbearer who was called Nehemiah. One day in the royal palace at Shushan, Nehemiah noticed the arrival of a number of men from Judah. When the opportunity presented itself, Nehemiah asked them for news of those who were now working in Jerusalem. And they said, "Things are not so good. It is true that the temple is finished, but the walls of the city are still in ruins, and the city gates have been burnt to ashes."

When Nehemiah heard this, he was overcome with grief. He wept and was in a state of deep sorrow for many days. He fasted and prayed to God. He asked the Lord to forgive the people their sins and to go to their aid.

The king had never before seen his cupbearer so sad, and he said to him, "Why do you look so sad? Are you sick? What is troubling you?"

Then Nehemiah was afraid, but he said truthfully, "O King, live for ever! It is impossible for me not to be sad when my city is in ruins and its gates burnt down."

A LITTLE BIT OF HISTORY
There were two other powerful peoples within the Babylonian Empire: the Lydians, who had settled in the northwest, in Asia Minor, and the Medes, originally from Central Asia, who had settled in the northeast with their subjects, the Persians. For about thirty years the Babylonians, the Lydians, and the Medes lived in relative peace. But in 555 B.C., Cyrus the Second became king of the Persians. He did not accept the Medes as masters and rose up against them. He won a victory against their king Astyages (his grandfather) and took territory from the Medes for his kingdom. He also defeated the Lydians (with King Croesus at their head) and surrounded the territories to the east of Babylon. Then he entered Babylon without resistance because the king of Babylon had lost control of his country.

The conquests of Cyrus (reigned 550 to 529 B.C.) were continued by his successor, Darius the First (reigned 522 to 486 B.C.). The Persian Empire

The king thought for a moment; then he said, "What are you really asking me to do?"

Nehemiah, with a quick prayer to God, said, "If the king is pleased with the way I have served him, I will ask a favour. I beg permission to go to Judah so that I can restore my ancestors' city to its former glory."

The king said, "If I give you leave to perform this task, when can I expect you to return?"

Nehemiah gave the king a certain date when he would return, and the king consented to let him go.

After Nehemiah had been in Jerusalem for three days, he inspected the town, going out one night with this purpose in mind. He rode a donkey, and several men accompanied him. But he didn't tell them what he intended to do for the city. He rode round and examined the walls, the gates, the sewage systems, and the fountains.

The next day he went to the priests and governors and said, "You see how the city has fallen, what misery the people live in, how the walls are broken. The time has come to build them up. We should stop being looked down upon."

Nehemiah told them that he had been touched by the hand of God to perform this task. He also described how the king had given him permission to rebuild the city and a date when he had to return. When the priests and governors heard Nehemiah's words, they were thrilled and said, "This is a worthwhile plan! We will rebuild the city!"

Work began at once. Different jobs were assigned to different families.

stretched from the Mediterranean Sea to the Persian Gulf and even as far as the borders of India. The road of the kings, which linked the city of Sardis (in modern Turkey) to Susa (slightly to the north of the Persian Gulf) was about 1,615 miles long. Caravans took ninety days to cross it, but royal messengers made the journey in just nine days. Different nationalities lived in this immense territory, and it was probably due to the way the Persians treated the conquered nations that peace was achieved. They showed mercy and respected the religious customs of the subject peoples.

Judah became part of the great Persian Empire. The Jews were allowed to return to their country in 539 B.C. They began rebuilding the temple and finished it about 515 B.C. However, all the Jews did not return to Jerusalem. Some stayed in Mesopotamia and other countries. This is how the Diaspora started; that is to say, the dispersal of Jews among Gentiles. This dispersal greatly increased after the death (323 B.C.) of Alexander the Great, the founder of the city of Alexandria in Egypt.

Then the chiefs of Judah and Benjamin, the priests, the Levites, and all those who felt the spirit of the Lord made themselves ready for the journey to Jerusalem to build the house of the Lord.

And the neighbours of the volunteers gave gifts of money and food to help them on their way.

King Cyrus took back all the treasure and holy vessels that King Nebuchadnezzar had looted from Jerusalem. They were put on donkeys and carried from Babylon back to Jerusalem.

But when the enemies of Israel learnt that the walls of the city were going up again and that major repairs were successfully under way, they were angry and plotted against Jerusalem.

When Nehemiah heard that enemy forces were gathering, he stationed guards to watch over the building projects. They kept guard day and night. This cut the labour force in two, since while one half worked, the other half kept guard. The guards were in such a state of readiness that they kept their swords unsheathed and held them up in their hands.

A trumpet was placed next to Nehemiah. He explained to the priests, governors, and all the people the purpose of the instrument: "Our task is a huge one. We are separated and working at different points along the wall. When the trumpet is blown, it means that you should all re-group in this position. Have no fear. God is on our side and will fight with us!"

Despite these setbacks, Nehemiah and his people finished building the walls of the city in fifty-two days.

Psalm 23

THE GOOD SHEPHERD
A psalm of David:

> *The Lord is my shepherd,*
> *I will not go hungry.*
> *He makes a place for me to rest in green fields,*
> *He leads me safely to still waters.*
> *He restores my soul,*
> *He shows me the path to walk*
> *To reach Him.*
> *Even when I walk through a valley shadowed by death,*
> *I will not be afraid,*
> *Because I know He walks beside me,*
> *His rod and staff give me comfort.*
> *I sit at a table and dine in front of my enemies,*
> *You anoint my head with oil,*
> *My cup is full and runs over the side.*
> *Then I feel goodness and mercy*
> *Will be with me all my life*
> *And I will live with God in His house for ever.*

Psalm 24

THE KING OF GLORY
A psalm of David:

> *The earth and all that it contains belong to God.*
> *The world and its inhabitants belong to God,*
> *For it was God who made the earth and sea*
> *And caused the floodwaters to subside.*
> *Who will go up the hill to the Lord?*
> *Who will stand with Him in His holy place?*
> *He who has clean hands and a pure heart,*
> *He who has not been vain and deceitful.*
> *This is who will be blessed,*

This is who will receive salvation from the Lord.
Here is a generation who seek you,
Who wish to see your face, O Jacob!
Lift up your head,
Lift up the gates,
Lift up the everlasting doors,
And the king of glory will come in.
Who is this King of glory?
He is the Lord,
And He is strong and powerful in battle.
Lift up your heads,
Lift up the gates,
Lift up the everlasting doors,
And the King of glory will come in.
Who is this King of glory?
He is the Lord of all armies,
He is the King of glory!

A DESIRE TO BE WITH GOD

Psalm 63

A psalm of David, when he was in the wilderness of Judah:

O God, You are my God!
I look for You as early as possible.
My soul is thirsty for You,
My flesh in a dry land longs for you,
Here, where there is no water.
I desire to see Your power and glory
As I have before in Your sanctuary.
Your loving kindness is more than life
And so I utter words of praise.
For as long as I live, I will bless You.
I raise my hands up and speak Your name.
My soul will be satisfied
As though stuffed with food.
My mouth will sing Your praises.
I will think of You when I am in my bed,
I will remember You in the darkness of the night.
Because You have helped me,
I rejoice to live beneath Your wings.
My soul runs after You,
And Your right hand supports me.
Those who seek my soul to destroy it
Will find themselves deep in the earth.
They will find the edge of the sword,
And they will be eaten by foxes.
I rejoice in God!
Those who do will find glory!
But the mouths of those who tell lies
Will be closed for ever.

A LITTLE BIT OF HISTORY
The Book of Psalms is a collection of hymns and prayers composed over a number of centuries. Tradition has it that David wrote most of the Psalms. The Psalms are used in the liturgy of both Judaism and Christianity.

Psalm 100   **A PSALM OF PRAISE**

Let all countries make a joyful sound
For the Lord.
Serve Him with a happy heart
And go to Him singing!
Be sure you know the Lord is God
And He made us; we belong to Him!
We are His people,
Like sheep we feed in His fields.
We enter the gates to His house with thanks,
We enter His courtyard with praise,
We are full of thanks and bless His name.
The Lord is good.
His mercy lasts for ever,
His truth goes from one generation to the next.

Psalm 126   **A SONG FOR FREEDOM**

When the Lord set Zion free,
We were like people in a dream.
Our mouths were full of laughter,
Our tongues sang
And the heathen knew
The Lord had done great things for us.
And we are glad
The Lord has done great things for us.
Make us free again, O Lord,
Like the streams that run south.
Then those who plant tears
Will grow joy.
He who weeps today, but carries precious seeds,
Will return, rejoicing and reaping a great harvest.

THE TALE OF JONAH

God spoke to Jonah, the son of Amittai, saying, "Go to the city of Nineveh, and preach to the people. Tell them how I have observed their wickedness."

But Jonah did not do as God told him. He went to Joppa, and there he found a ship that was setting sail for Tarshish. He paid for his passage and boarded the ship. He was running away from God!

But the Lord caused a huge storm to break. The ship was tossed up and down on the waves, which were as big as mountains. It seemed as though at any moment the ship would be smashed to pieces.

The sailors cried out in fear, each calling to his own god to save him from a watery grave, for the ship was in great danger of sinking. The crew threw overboard anything they could in order to make the ship lighter.

Jonah, however, was fast asleep in the hold of the ship. The captain, finding this mysterious, went to him and said, "How can you sleep now? Wake up! Call to your God and ask Him to save us from this storm!"

Then the sailors started talking fearfully to each other. They agreed to cast lots to find out who had caused the storm. The lot fell on Jonah!

The sailors demanded, "What is your profession? Where are you from? Why is there such a storm? Why is there evil on our ship?"

Jonah replied, "I am Hebrew. I am afraid of my God, who made the sea and the dry land. He told me to go out and preach, but I ran away from Him."

When the men heard this, they were terrified. They cried out, "Why did you do that? Why did you do that? We have to calm the sea or perish! What shall we do with you?"

Then Jonah said, "It is my fault. I have caused this storm. Throw me overboard into the water. This will calm the sea."

At first the men did not want to do this. They brought out oars and tried to row towards shore. But the sea was too strong, and they made no headway. They prayed to God when they saw that the position was hopeless: "We beg You, O Lord, to save us! Must we die for the sins of this one man?"

The storm raged on, and giant waves smashed against the ship. When they could do nothing else, they picked up Jonah and threw him overboard into the raging sea. Afterwards the men were frightened and made sacrifices to the Lord.

But the Lord was prepared for Jonah. He sent a great fish to swallow him. And Jonah stayed in the belly of the fish for three days and three nights.

In the darkness of the fish's belly, Jonah prayed to the Lord. And God heard Jonah's prayer and made the fish spit Jonah out onto dry land.

Then God spoke to Jonah for the second time: "Go to the great city of Nineveh, and preach as I told you to."

This time Jonah obeyed the word of the Lord and went to Nineveh. He walked the length and breadth of the city, calling to the people:

A LITTLE BIT OF HISTORY

The return to law as set out in the Book of Deuteronomy led Ezra and Nehemiah to shun anything that was not Hebrew. Intolerance grew, and the Samaritans were particularly hated for hindering the rebuilding of the temple and for their hostile acts against the city of Jerusalem. It was in this climate of thought that the Book of Jonah was written. It is a book concerned with mercy and divine intervention and has a universal appeal. The book, in fact, reveals the value of repentance. It is a book with a message for both Jews and Gentiles.

Jesus Christ referred to the Book of Jonah twice: once when he spoke of the goodwill of God toward the repentant Ninevites, and once when he compared Jonah's stay in the belly of a great fish to his own burial.

"The Lord will destroy this city in forty days' time!"

The people believed in God, so they began a fast. Men, women, and children dressed humbly in sackcloth. When the king heard what was happening, he left his throne, took off his fine robes, and dressed like an ordinary person. He sat down in a pile of ashes.

A decree was published in the city, which said, "No human being or animal can eat or drink. Every living human and creature must be covered with sackcloth. All must pray to God and turn away from evil and violence. Who knows if God will have mercy and save us? We do not know."

God saw that the people had repented. He saw that they had put an end to their evil ways. Then His anger ceased, and He did not destroy the city.

GOD TEACHES JONAH A LESSON

When God spared Nineveh, Jonah became very angry. He prayed to his Lord: "I knew that You would spare Nineveh. I knew this, and that was why I ran away. You are a merciful God, You are slow to anger, You show great kindness, and You forgive Your people. Therefore, O Lord, I think it is better that you take my life rather than save it."

Then the Lord said, "Do you think you are right to be angry?"

Jonah left the city and sat on a hill on the city's east side. He made a little shelter for himself and hid himself in it. He watched the city to see whether anything would happen to it. And God caused a marrow plant to grow up over Jonah's head so that the rays of the sun would not burn him. Jonah was very pleased to have this plant over his head.

But the next day at dawn, God sent a worm to invade the marrow plant. Then the plant withered and fell down.

As the sun rose, God brought with it a strong easterly wind. The sun beat down on Jonah's head, and the wind cut at him. He fainted. And in his soul, he thought it better to die than to live.

Then God woke Jonah with these words: "Do you think you are right to be angry?"

And he replied, "Yes, I will be angry until the day of my death!"

God said, "You are sorry for the loss of the plant, even though it grew up in a single night and you had no hand in looking after it. Tell me, then, why should I not spare Nineveh? It is a great city. There are more than one hundred and twenty thousand simple souls and great herds of cattle living there. Why should I not spare them?"

Jonah 4

Opposite: They picked up Jonah and threw him overboard into the raging sea. Afterward the men were frightened and made sacrifices to the Lord.

But the Lord was prepared for Jonah. He sent a great fish to swallow him. And Jonah stayed in the belly of the fish for three days and three nights.

The New Testament

The Gospels of
Matthew, Mark,
Luke, and John

The Acts of
the Apostles

The Letters
of Peter

The Book
of Revelation

ZACHARIAS AND ELISABETH

A LITTLE BIT OF HISTORY
After banishment in Babylon the people of Israel were once more back in their own country, and a string of important political events followed. Between the years 334 and 337 B.C., Alexander the Great of Macedonia crushed the Persian Empire, but he did not live to rule it and died at the age of thirty-three. After much fighting these vast lands were divided into three kingdoms. The Promised Land and Egypt belonged to the kingdom of the Ptolemies. Alexandria in Egypt, founded by Alexander the Great, became the centre of Greek culture in the ancient world. Then there were the Seleucids, who ruled the people of Israel during the second century B.C. Rome was the next master, conquering Jerusalem in 64 B.C. However, there was a ruler in Israel who enjoyed a certain amount of freedom within the framework of the Roman Empire. This was Herod, who came to the throne in 37 B.C. In 29 B.C., Augustus became the new emperor of Rome.

This part of the Bible serves as a backdrop to the New Testament.

In the days of Herod, king of Judea, there lived a priest whose name was Zacharias. His wife's name was Elisabeth. Husband and wife were blameless people and followed the law of God. They were elderly and had no children.

One day, Zacharias went into the temple to burn incense, as was his duty. The people were outside praying. As Zacharias was performing his religious duties, an angel of the Lord appeared to him on the right side of the altar. When the priest saw the angel, terror fell upon him. But the angel said to him, "Do not be afraid, Zacharias. Your prayers have been answered: Your wife, Elisabeth, will give birth to a son, and you will name him John. He will bring you and many people great happiness. From the day he is born, he will be filled with the spirit of God. He will bring God to the attention of the people of Israel. He will have power like Elias [Elijah] in the past. He will make the people ready to receive the Lord."

Zacharias was astonished and said, "I do not understand. My wife and I are too old to have a baby."

The angel replied, "I am Gabriel. I come from God with this good news. Because you do not believe me now, you must be silent until these things come to pass."

Meanwhile, the people outside were amazed that Zacharias stayed so long in the temple.

When he eventually came out, he could no longer speak. He made signs to the people, and they understood that he had had a vision in the temple.

When Zacharias had completed his religious duties at the temple, he went home. Sometime later, his wife, Elisabeth, conceived a child. She thought that God had at last noticed her and taken away her feelings of shame at being childless.

As Zacharias was performing his religious duties, an angel of the Lord appeared to him on the right side of the altar. When the priest saw the angel, teror fell upon him. But the angel said to him, "Do not be afraid, Zacharias. Your prayers have been answered: Your wife, Elisabeth, will give birth to a son, and you will name him John."

THE ANNUNCIATION

God sent the angel Gabriel to the city of Nazareth, where a virgin named Mary lived. She was engaged to a man named Joseph, who belonged to the house of David. The angel spoke to her and said, "God is with you. You are blessed among women!"

Mary was troubled by these words and wondered what they could mean. But the angel said, "Do not be afraid, Mary. God is with you. You will conceive a son, and you will name him Jesus. He shall be great, the Son of the Highest. And the Lord God will give him the throne of David, and his kingdom will never end."

Then Mary said, "How can this happen without a man?"

The angel replied, "The Holy Spirit will descend upon you, and the power of the Highest will come upon you. The child conceived will be the Son of God. Your cousin Elisabeth conceived a child, and she was old. With God, everything is possible."

Mary said, "I have heard your words, and I am the servant of the Lord."

The angel left her, and a short time later Mary travelled as quickly as possible through hilly regions to a city named Judah. She went into the home of Elisabeth and Zacharias, and she greeted Elisabeth in such a way that Elisabeth felt her baby move inside her. She said to Mary, "You are blessed among women, and the fruit of your womb is blessed. How is it that you are here with me now?"

Mary said:

My soul praises the Lord,
And my spirit rejoices in God,
My Saviour,
Because He looked with favour
On His humble servant so that
Henceforth generations to come
Will call me blessed.
The Lord has done great things for me,
And His name is holy.
His mercy extends from one generation to the next
For those who love Him.
He has shown strength with His arms;
He has scattered far and wide those
With high and mighty thoughts;
He has removed the powerful from their thrones
And lifted up those in lowly positions;
He gave food to hungry people
And sent the rich away.
He helped His servant Israel,
Remembering His mercy when He spoke
To our fathers, to Abraham, and to all generations.

Opposite: God sent the angel Gabriel to the city of Nazareth, where a virgin named Mary lived. She was engaged to a man named Joseph, who belonged to the house of David. The angel spoke to her and said, "God is with you. You are blessed among women!"

Mary stayed with Elisabeth for three months; then she returned home.

THE BIRTH OF JOHN THE BAPTIST

When the time came, Elisabeth gave birth to a son. Her neighbours and cousins, hearing how the Lord had favoured her and shown great mercy, rejoiced with her.

When the baby was eight days old, circumcision was to take place. It was thought that the child would be named Zacharias, after his father. But his mother shook her head and said that the child would be named John. They all said to her, "But there's no one in your family with that name." They called Zacharias over and asked what he wanted to name the child. Zacharias called for pen and paper, and he wrote down that the boy's name was to be John. And everyone was full of wonder.

Then the silence of the old priest was suddenly broken. His mouth opened, and words of praise for God poured out. Those who saw this happen were afraid, and word of these events spread throughout the hill country of Judea. And when the people heard what had happened, they were full of awe, and they wondered what kind of child had come into the world. They were sure that the hand of God had touched the child.

THE HYMN OF ZACHARIAS

Zacharias, the father of John, was filled with the Holy Spirit and said:

Blessed is the Lord God of Israel,
Who has visited His people and saved them.
He has raised a horn of salvation
In the house of His servant David.
As He said through the mouths of His ancient prophets
Since time began,
We will be saved from our enemies and those who hate us.
He said this to perform the mercy He promised to our fathers
So that we would remember His holy covenant.
He swore an oath to our father, Abraham,
That he would save us from our enemies
So that we might serve Him without fear
In holiness and righteousness
All the days of our lives.
And you, little child, will be the prophet of the Highest,
Because you have come before the Lord to prepare His way
And tell the people about salvation by the pardon of sins.
And this salvation is possible
Through the tender mercy of God,
Who has come down on us like the sun from on high
To light the way of those who live in darkness
And in the shadow of death.
God will lead us in the ways of peace.

The child grew strong in body and spirit, and he stayed in the desert until the day he showed himself to Israel.

Following pages: Filled with joy, the wise men entered the stable. When they saw the child with Mary, his mother, they fell to their knees and worshipped him. They opened their bags and offered him gifts of gold, frankincense, and myrrh.

THE BIRTH OF JESUS

At this time, Caesar Augustus made a law that everyone should be taxed. In fact, this was not a new law. Cyrenius had done the same thing when he was governor of Syria. But now, all the inhabitants of the Roman Empire were forced to return to the cities of their birth to be counted and taxed.

Joseph, for this reason, left Galilee from the city of Nazareth. He entered Judea and reached the city of David, known as Bethlehem, where he had been born. He travelled with his wife, Mary, who was about to give birth.

The city was very crowded, and they found no place to stay except a stable. It was here that Mary gave birth to her firstborn son. She wrapped him tightly in a cloth and laid him in a manger.

In the same part of that country, there were shepherds looking after their flocks of sheep at night. Suddenly the angel of the Lord came into their pasture, and he shone with great glory. The shepherds were startled and afraid.

But the angel spoke softly: "Do not be afraid. I bring good news for you and for all people. Today, in the city of David, a baby is born, and he will be the Saviour. He is Christ the Lord. You will find the baby wrapped tightly in a cloth and lying in a manger."

Then the angel was joined by a throng of heavenly beings, who praised God and said, "Glory to God in heaven. Peace on earth, and goodwill towards men."

The angel and the heavenly beings disappeared. The shepherds said to each other, "We must go to Bethlehem and see what has happened. The Lord has told us."

They went at once. Soon they found Mary and Joseph, and the baby lying in a manger.

The shepherds were filled with wonder at this miracle. And later, when they left, they told everyone they met what had happened and what they had seen. And everyone who heard what the shepherds said was also filled with wonder.

A LITTLE BIT OF HISTORY

The year of the birth of Jesus Christ is considered to be the year zero in the Christian calendar. In reality Jesus was probably born in 7 or 6 B.C. This was the year of the Roman census and of a conjunction between Saturn and Jupiter that may well have formed the star followed by the three wise men on their journey to Jerusalem to worship the Messiah.

JESUS IS TAKEN TO THE TEMPLE OF JERUSALEM

Before he was born, the child was named by an angel of God. His name was JESUS.

When Jesus was eight days old, Mary and Joseph took the child to Jerusalem to show him to the Lord, in keeping with the law of Moses. They also went to offer a sacrifice of a pair of turtledoves, or young pigeons, according to the ancient law.

There was a man named Simeon who lived in Jerusalem. He was a good man, and the spirit of God lived in him. The Holy Spirit had told him that before he died he would see the Christ.

Simeon went to the temple and waited. When Mary and Joseph brought the child into the temple, Simeon took the child in his arms. He praised God and said, "Lord, it is as You said, and now I may die in peace. My eyes have now seen him who will save the world. I have seen

Opposite: So Joseph, Mary, and the child fled by night into Egypt. They stayed there until the death of Herod. Thus, the prophecy of the Lord became true: "I will bring my son out of the land of Egypt."

the child. He is a light to guide the Gentiles, and he will be the glory of Your people Israel."

The parents of the child were astonished when they heard these words. But Simeon blessed them, and he said to Mary, "This child will bring about the fall and the rise of many people in Israel. And you also will be affected. Sorrow, like a sword, will pierce your own soul. The secret thoughts of many hearts will come to light. The truth will be revealed."

THE WISE MEN FROM THE EAST

Matthew 2

Near the time when Jesus was to be born in Bethlehem, wise men were travelling from the East to Jerusalem. They stopped in various places and asked, "Where is the child who is born to be king of the Jews?" Then they added, "We have seen his star in the east, and we wish to worship him."

When news of these wise men and their quest reached King Herod, he immediately felt troubled. He called a meeting of the chief priests and scribes of the people, demanding to know where Christ would be born. The priests answered, "The prophets say he will be born in Bethlehem in Judea. They say he comes from humble origins, but will rise to become governor and will rule the people of Israel."

Herod met the wise men and asked them when the star had appeared. Then he sent them to Bethlehem, saying, "Go, and look carefully for the young child. When you find him, send word to me so that I may also go and worship him."

The wise men left Herod. As they travelled, the star they had seen in the east appeared in the sky before them. They followed it until the star shone down on the stable where the young child was.

Filled with joy, the wise men entered the stable. When they saw the child with Mary, his mother, they fell to their knees and worshipped him. They opened their bags and offered him gifts of gold, frankincense, and myrrh.

That night, God warned the wise men in their dreams not to return to Herod and tell him where the child was. So they went back to their own countries by a different route.

Matthew 2

FLIGHT INTO EGYPT

After the wise men left, the angel of the Lord appeared to Joseph in a dream, saying, "Go quickly now. Take the child and Mary to Egypt. Stay there until I speak to you again. Herod is looking for the child and wants to kill him."

So Joseph, Mary, and the child fled by night into Egypt. They stayed there until the death of Herod. Thus, the prophecy of the Lord became true: "I will bring my son out of the land of Egypt."

When Herod realised that the wise men had fooled him, he became mad with anger. He ordered the deaths of all the children under two years of age who were in Bethlehem and round that city. Thus, he tried to kill the boy who was to become the Saviour of Israel. But the baby Jesus was already safe in Egypt.

The words of the prophet Jeremiah also were true: "In Rama, a voice was heard, and it was filled with sorrow, mourning, and tears. Rachel weeps for her children, but there is no comfort, because her children are no longer with her."

After the death of Herod, the angel of the Lord again appeared to Joseph in a dream, saying, "Those who wished to kill the young child are now dead. It is time for you to return to Israel."

JESUS SPEAKS
TO THE TEACHERS

When Mary and Joseph had done everything God had told them to do, they went back to Galilee and settled in their own city of Nazareth.

Jesus grew in strength of spirit, and he was very wise. And God watched over him and blessed him.

When he was twelve years old, Jesus went with his parents to Jerusalem to celebrate Passover. After the feast was over, Mary and Joseph started back for Nazareth. They were travelling with a company of people, and they thought that Jesus was with them. But after they had been on the road for a whole day, they discovered that he was not there. They immediately turned back and went to look for their child.

In Jerusalem they looked for Jesus for three days. Finally, they entered the temple and saw him. He was sitting in the middle of a group of learned doctors, listening to what the teachers said and asking them questions. The teachers were astonished at what the young man understood and how much he knew.

Mary and Joseph were astonished, too, but they were also worried, as any parents would be. When Jesus had finished speaking to the teachers, Mary cried, "My son, we have been looking everywhere for you! Your father and I have been very worried!"

But Jesus asked, "Why did you look for me? Did you not know that I must do my Father's work?"

Mary and Joseph did not understand what Jesus meant.

Jesus went home with his parents to Nazareth. And his mother, Mary, listened to everything he said, and she stored his words in her heart.

Jesus grew in wisdom and greatness. God looked down on him and blessed him.

JOHN THE BAPTIST PREACHES

In the fifteenth year of the reign of Tiberius Caesar, Pontius Pilate was governor of Judea. Herod was tetrarch of Galilee; his brother, Philip, was tetrarch of Iturea and the region of Trachonitis; and Lysanias was tetrarch of Abilene. Annas and Caiaphas were the high priests at this time.

God spoke to John, the son of Zacharias, when he was in the wilderness. Then John went into the country round Jordan and preached the baptism of repentance for the forgiveness of sins. This was according to the words of the prophet Isaiah, who wrote: "And there was a voice crying in the wilderness, saying, 'Make way for the Lord, and let his paths be straight. Let every valley be filled and every mountain and hill levelled! Let crooked paths be made straight and rough roads made smooth! Then humanity will see the salvation of God.'"

When the people heard these words, they flocked to John to be baptised. But he said to them, "You generation of snakes! Who warned you to run from the anger about to explode? Make yourselves worthy of forgiveness! It does not help that Abraham was your father! God is able to make children for Abraham out of stones! An axe is poised over the root of the tree. Any tree that does not produce good fruit will be chopped down and thrown into the fire."

When the people thought about John's words, many were confused. They asked, "What should we do to be worthy of forgiveness?"

John replied, "If you have two coats, give one to someone who does not have a coat. If you have food, share it with someone who goes hungry."

Tax collectors also went to John to be baptised, and they asked, "What should we do to be worthy of forgiveness?"

And John replied, "Be fair. Do not take more tax from people than is allowed."

Soldiers also asked the same question, and John told them not to be violent, not to lie, and to be content with their pay.

The words and advice of John spread, and people began to wonder if he was the Christ. When John realised what the people were thinking, he said, "I baptise you with water, but someone will come after me who will be far greater than I. And he is so mighty that I am not even good enough to fasten his sandal. I baptise with water, but he will baptise with the Holy Spirit and with fire."

John said these and many other things to the people.

Opposite: In Jerusalem they looked for Jesus for three days. Finally, they entered the temple and saw him. He was sitting in the middle of a group of learned doctors, listening to what the doctors said and asking them questions.

204

JOHN BAPTISES JESUS

Jesus left Galilee and went to the river Jordan to be baptised by John. But John was against this. He said to Jesus, "It is I who must be baptised by you. Why do you come to me?"

And Jesus answered, "Let it be this way for now. We are doing what is right."

So John agreed, and he baptised Jesus. As soon as Jesus left the water, the heavens opened. The spirit of God flew down upon him like a dove. A voice came out of heaven, saying, "This is My beloved Son, in whom I am well pleased."

JESUS IN THE WILDERNESS

The Holy Spirit led Jesus into the wilderness to be tempted by the devil.

Jesus did not eat for forty days and forty nights, and afterwards, he was very weak from hunger. The devil came to him and said, "If you really are the Son of God, turn these stones into bread so you can eat."

But Jesus answered, "Man does not live by bread alone. Man lives through every word that comes from the mouth of God."

Then the devil led him into the holy city and placed him on the highest part of the temple. The devil said, "If you really are the Son of God, jump off this peak. It is written that the angels will look after you. They will catch you if you fall, or even if you just stub your toe on a stone."

Jesus said, "It is also written that you shall not tempt the Lord your God."

But the devil persisted. He led Jesus to the summit of a high mountain and pointed out all the kingdoms of the world and the glory to be found in them. He said, "I will give you all of these kingdoms if you will just bend your knee and worship me."

But Jesus said, "Leave me, Satan! It is written that you should worship the Lord your God, and it is *only* God who is to be served."

So Satan left, and the angels of God came down to serve Jesus.

Jesus left Galilee and went to the river Jordan to be baptised by John. But John was against this. He said to Jesus, "It is I who must be baptised by you. Why do you come to me?"

And Jesus answered, "Let it be this way for now. We are doing what is right."

207

JESUS IN GALILEE

At this time, the tetrarch Herod had thrown John into prison, because John had criticised Herod for marrying the wife of Herod's brother.

When Jesus heard about this, he left Nazareth and went to Galilee. He stayed in Capernaum, which was on the coast near Zabulon and Nephthalim.

He told the people, "Now is the time to repent. The kingdom of heaven is very close."

Jesus was about thirty years old when he began to preach to the people.

One day, Jesus was walking by the sea of Galilee when he saw two men, one named Simon but known as Peter, and his brother Andrew. They were fishermen, and they were throwing their nets into the sea.

Jesus said, "Follow me, and I will make you fishers of men."

When the fishermen heard the words of Jesus, they left their nets and followed him.

Later, Jesus was by the shore, and people crowded round him to hear the word of God. Two ships were on the water, abandoned by fishermen who were washing their nets. Jesus went into Simon's ship and told him to move it a little way from the shore. Then Jesus sat down and preached to the people from the ship.

When Jesus had finished speaking, he said to Simon Peter, "Take the ship out into deep water, and drop your nets."

Simon answered, "Master, I will do what you say, but we have fished all night and caught nothing."

They took the ship out into deep waters and dropped their nets. When they hauled their nets in, there were so many fish that the nets nearly broke. The fishermen called to their partners in other ships to come and help them. And all the ships were so full of fish that they nearly sank!

When Simon Peter saw that the ships were about to sink, he fell on his knees before Jesus and said, "Lord, you should leave me now. I am a sinful man."

All the fishermen were amazed at the great catch. James and John, who were the sons of Zebedee and the partners of Simon Peter, were also astonished and afraid.

But Jesus said, "Do not be afraid. In future you will catch men who will follow the ways of the Lord."

They reached the shore safely. And after removing the fish, the fishermen left their nets and followed Jesus and his teachings. The fishermen became disciples, or followers, of Jesus.

Opposite: Jesus said, "Follow me, and I will make you fishers of men."

When the fishermen heard the words of Jesus, they left their nets and followed him.

THE MARRIAGE IN CANA

There was a wedding in Cana in the land of Galilee. Mary, the mother of Jesus, was present, and Jesus and his disciples were also invited. But there was no wine. When Mary told her son this, Jesus said to his mother, "Why do you tell me that? My time has not come."

When Mary heard these words, she told the servants, "Whatever Jesus asks you to do, do it."

There were six stone waterpots, and each was deep and broad. Jesus said, "Fill the jars with water."

The servants did as they were told. They filled the waterpots up to the brim.

Then Jesus said, "Take the jars to the steward."

The servants did this. The governor tasted it, but it was not water that he was drinking; it was wine! He did not know where it came from, and he said to the bridegroom, "Feasts usually begin with good wine, and then as they continue, the host serves wine that is not so good. But you have kept the best wine for the end. This is wonderful!"

This was the first miracle that Jesus performed in Cana of Galilee. It showed his power and his glory. And the disciples, who were with Jesus, believed in him. They saw that he was the Lord.

There were six stone waterpots, and each was deep and broad. Jesus said, "Fill the jars with water."

JESUS TEACHES IN THE SYNAGOGUE IN CAPERNAUM

After these events, Jesus went to Capernaum with his mother and his disciples. On the Sabbath, he went into the synagogue there and began to teach.

Those who heard Jesus were astonished by his way of teaching. He spoke with authority and did not sound at all like the clerks and interpreters of law.

But there was a man in the synagogue who was possessed by an evil spirit, and he shouted out, "Leave us alone! What do you want from us, Jesus of Nazareth? Have you come here to destroy us? I know who you are. You are the Holy One of God!"

Jesus addressed the evil spirit: "Be at peace with yourself. Come out of him!"

For a moment, the man wrestled with the evil spirit and cried out. Then the evil spirit left him, and he was at peace with himself.

The congregation was amazed, and they asked each other questions such as, "What has Jesus done? Is this a new kind of teaching that enables him to rid a man of the demons inside him?"

And at once, the fame of Jesus spread throughout the land of Galilee.

JESUS CURES SIMON PETER'S MOTHER-IN-LAW

After Jesus left the synagogue, he went to the house of Simon Peter and Andrew. James and John were with him. They told Jesus that Simon Peter's mother-in-law was sick with fever. Jesus went to her and took her by the hand. He helped her to her feet, and immediately the fever was gone. She became a follower of Jesus.

JESUS HEALS THE SICK AND DISTURBED IN CAPERNAUM

At sunset, many people gathered at the door of the house where Jesus was staying. They brought with them their loved ones who were diseased in mind and body. And Jesus went outside and cured many different diseases. And to those who were disturbed in their minds, he brought peace.

JESUS LEAVES CAPERNAUM

Mark 1

The next day, Jesus got up early and went to a quiet place where he could pray. His disciples followed him, and when they found him, Simon Peter said, "Master, everyone is looking for you."

Jesus said, "We will leave Capernaum now and go and preach in the other towns nearby. My purpose is to spread the word of God."

JESUS IN GALILEE

Mark 1
Luke 5

Jesus preached in synagogues throughout Galilee. Whenever a person possessed by an evil spirit came to him, he tore that demon out of him. One day, a man with leprosy approached Jesus and knelt before him, saying, "Lord, I know if you wish to, you can cure me."

Jesus was moved with compassion for this man. He put his hand upon him and said, "I wish it. Be cured."

As soon as Jesus had spoken, the leprosy left the man's body and he was well. Jesus told the man to tell no one what had happened but to go about his business quietly. He told the man to show to the priests that he was well. This was the custom in those days—a custom that went back as far as Moses.

But the man did not do as he was advised. He went everywhere and told everyone the story of how Jesus had cured him. Then the fame of Jesus spread so much that Jesus could no longer walk freely about the city but was forced to live in solitary places. And even here, people came to him from far and wide.

A LITTLE BIT OF HISTORY
It was in Capernaum that Jesus first began to preach in public. His name soon spread throughout the region. After he left Nazareth, Jesus chose Capernaum as the centre of his ministry in Galilee.

THE PHARISEES ASK QUESTIONS

A LITTLE BIT OF HISTORY

The Pharisees were members of a Jewish movement at the time of Christ. They followed Jewish law and ancient traditions very strictly. They were mostly ordinary people with a great deal of influence who in effect were religious leaders. The severe judgment Jesus passed on the Pharisees is well known. He did not condemn their teaching ("do as they tell you") but their pride and behaviour ("do not do as they do"). Christ saw their pride as hypocritical and their obsession with the law as opposed to the growth of a living religion.

Publicans or tax collectors are sometimes mentioned. The Jews did not like them and saw them as traitors because they were paid by the Romans. They were considered sinners. Matthew was a tax collector. Zacchaeus was a tax collector in Jericho. Jesus did not reject them.

One day when Jesus was teaching, there sat before him Pharisees and doctors of the law, who had come from all over Galilee, Judea, and Jerusalem. And the power of God to heal was present in Jesus.

Some men were carrying a paralysed man on a little bed. They wanted to bring this man to Jesus, but there were so many people that it was impossible. So they carried the man up to the top of the house and lowered him down on his bed through an opening in the roof. The bed, with the paralysed man, came to rest just in front of Jesus. When Jesus saw what these men had done, he was moved by their faith. He said to the paralysed man, "Man, your sins are forgiven."

When the Pharisees, clerks, and doctors of law heard Jesus say these words, they thought to themselves, Who is this who blasphemes? Who can forgive sins except God?

Jesus understood what they were thinking, and he said to them, "Why are you thinking like that? Is it easier to say to a paralysed man, 'Your sins are forgiven,' or to say, 'Pick up your bed and walk?' In order to show you that the Son of Man has power on earth to forgive sins, I say now to this man, 'Pick up your bed and go home.'"

And immediately the man got up, picked up his bed, and went home, praising God.

The people round Jesus were amazed, and they praised God and the power He had given to Jesus.

After this, Jesus left the people in that house and met a tax collector named Matthew, who was counting his receipts. Jesus said to him, "Follow me." And at once Matthew left his job and followed Jesus. He took him to his house, and there he made a great feast. Most of the people at the table were either tax collectors or ordinary people.

When the Pharisees heard where Jesus was dining and whom he was dining with, they said, "How can he eat with tax collectors and sinners?"

When these words reached Jesus, he went to the Pharisees and said, "People who are well do not need a doctor. I am not here to preach to people who are good but to remind sinners that they can always repent."

THE SABBATH IS MADE FOR MAN, NOT MAN FOR THE SABBATH

One day, Jesus was crossing a cornfield with his disciples. It was the Sabbath, and as they walked, his disciples picked ears of corn, rubbed it between their fingers to remove the husks, and then ate the grain.

Some Pharisees, noticing this, said, "Why are you breaking the law on the Sabbath?"

Jesus said to them, "Have you not read the story of David and what he did when he and his friends were hungry? He went into the house of God and took the bread that was reserved for priests. He ate it and shared it with his companions."

Then Jesus said, "The Sabbath is made for man, not man for the Sabbath. The Son of Man is also the Lord of the Sabbath."

THE POOL KNOWN AS BETHESDA

John 5

Jesus went to a feast for the Jews in Jerusalem. In that city, next to the sheep market, there was a pool with five porches, which was known in Hebrew as Bethesda.

In these porches, a great number of blind, lame, and paralysed people could always be found waiting, because at certain times an angel visited the pool and stirred up the water. After the angel had done this, whoever entered the pool immediately would be made well, no matter what illness or sickness the person had.

One man had been trying for thirty-eight years to reach the water just after the angel's visit.

Jesus saw this man, and knowing how long he had been waiting, asked, "Do you wish to be cured?"

The man answered, "Sir, I have nobody to help me into the pool when the water is stirred up. Every time I am about to get into the water, someone steps in front of me."

Jesus said to him, "Stand up, pick up your bed, and walk."

Immediately the man was cured. He stood up, picked his bed up, and walked. This miracle was performed on the Sabbath.

The man who was healed did not know who had cured him. Jesus left quickly, because the place was crowded with people.

Later in the temple, Jesus met the man he had cured. He said to him, "Now you are well. Do not sin or else something worse may happen to you."

The man left the temple and told the Jews it was Jesus who had cured him. When the Jews heard this, they persecuted Jesus and wanted to kill him, because he had cured the man on the Sabbath.

But Jesus spoke to them, saying: "My Father has never ceased working, and I am like my Father."

When the Jews heard Jesus say this, they wanted to kill him more than ever. Not only had Jesus ignored the Sabbath, but now he was saying God was his father! He was making himself equal with God!

Jesus spoke to the people, and explained the power of the Father and the proofs about the son of God from the prophets' writings.

JESUS CHOOSES TWELVE APOSTLES

Luke 6
Matthew 10
Mark 3

About this time, Jesus went up a mountain to pray. He spent the whole night in prayer to God. When daylight came, he called his disciples to him and chose twelve. He called these men his apostles. Jesus gave his apostles power to heal and to cast out evil spirits and instructed them to preach.

The names of the twelve apostles were these: Simon, also known as Peter; Andrew, Simon's brother; James and John the sons of Zebedee; Philip; Bartholomew; Thomas; Matthew the tax collector; James the son of Alphaeus; Simon the Canaanite, also known as the Zealot; Judas the brother of James; and Judas Iscariot, who would prove to be a traitor.

Then Jesus went with his apostles, disciples, and a huge crowd of

When Jesus saw what a huge crowd had gathered before him, he went partway up a mountain so he could speak to all the people.

people to a plain. People flocked to him from all over Judea and Jerusalem. They came from as far away as the coasts of Tyre and Sidon. They came to listen to him, and they came to be cured. And those who were tortured by evil spirits *were* cured.

THE SERMON ON THE MOUNT

When Jesus saw what a huge crowd had gathered before him, he went partway up a mountain so he could speak to all the people. His disciples were with him, and he taught the people, saying:

"Blessed are the poor in spirit, for the kingdom of heaven will be theirs.

"Blessed are those who mourn, for they will be comforted.

"Blessed are the meek, for the earth will belong to them.

"Blessed are those who hunger and thirst for righteousness, for they will have food.

"Blessed are the merciful, for they will receive mercy.

"Blessed are the pure in heart, for they will see God.

"Blessed are those who seek peace, for they are the children of God.

"Blessed are those who are persecuted for their righteousness, for the kingdom of heaven will be theirs.

"Blessed are those of you who are cursed and persecuted, and who hear all sorts of false, evil things said against you because you follow me. Rejoice and be glad! Your reward is in heaven. Remember how the prophets of old were persecuted.

"Do not think I have come to destroy the law or the prophets. I am not here to destroy; I am here to see that the law and the words of the prophets are fulfilled. Whoever breaks even the smallest commandment and encourages others to do so will find no place in heaven. But he who follows the commandments and teaches others to do the same will be great in the kingdom of heaven. To enter the kingdom of heaven, you must be more virtuous and good than the officials and Pharisees.

"You have heard it said in the past that you must not kill and that whoever has killed another person will pay the price for it. I say to you now that even if you are angry with your brother without reason, you will be judged for that. He who calls his brother stupid will appear before a tribunal. He who calls his brother a fool will be in danger of hellfire.

"If you bring a gift to the altar and then remember that your brother has something against you, it is better not to leave your gift. First, make friends with your brother, and then bring your gift to the altar. Keep your heart pure in thought and action."

LOVE YOUR ENEMIES

Jesus taught the people further, saying:

"In the past, men have said, 'An eye for an eye and a tooth for a tooth,' and this was the way of justice and revenge. I say to you that there is a different way. If someone hits you on the right cheek, offer him your left cheek as well. If someone takes you to court in order to steal your jacket, give him your coat as well. Whoever forces you to walk a mile with him, walk two. Whoever asks you for something, give it to him. Whoever wishes to borrow something, let him have it.

"In the past, you often heard, 'You must love your neighbour and hate your enemy.' I say to you, 'Love your enemies, bless those who curse you, do good to those who hate you, pray for those who make use of you and persecute you.'

"If you love only those who love you back, what reward do you have? You are no better than a tax collector. Any man can do that, but you should strive to be as perfect as your Father in heaven."

THE LORD'S PRAYER

Matthew 6

"Make sure you do not do good things in order to be admired. There is no reward for this kind of behaviour. If you give money to charity, do not broadcast it like the hypocrites in the synagogues and on the street. If you give to charity quietly, only your Father in heaven will know. That is the proper reward.

"And when you pray to God, do not pray like a hypocrite, publicly in a synagogue or on a street corner. Go to your room and close the door. Then pray to your Father in secret. God will see you praying in secret, and he will reward you in public. That is the way of the Lord.

"And when you pray, remember it is not how many words you say that is important. Words alone are not enough. God knows what you want, even before you ask it.

"Pray to your Father in heaven in this way:

"Our Father, who art in heaven,
Hallowed be Thy name.
Thy kingdom come,
Thy will be done
On earth as it is in heaven.
Give us this day our daily bread,
And forgive us our debts,
As we forgive our debtors.
And lead us not into temptation,
But deliver us from evil:
For Thine is the kingdom, and the
Power, and the glory, for ever.
Amen."

THERE IS NO TREASURE ON EARTH

Matthew 6

"Do not save up treasures for yourself on earth. They will only be eaten by moths or rust, or stolen by thieves.

"Store your treasures in heaven, where there are no moths, rust, or thieves.

"Where your treasure is, that is where your heart is also."

THE LIGHT OF THE BODY

Matthew 6

"The light of the body comes from the eye. If you see well, your body will glow with light. If you see badly, your whole body will stay in darkness. If the light within you is darkness, that must be a very great darkness!"

TWO MASTERS

"No man can serve two masters. If he tries to, he will hate one and love the other. You cannot serve both God and money."

FIRST SEEK THE KINGDOM OF GOD

"I will say this to you: Do not think too much about your life, what you should eat or drink, or what you should wear. Life is more important than food, and the body is more important than clothes.

"Look at the birds in the sky; they do not sow, reap, or store grain in barns. But your heavenly Father looks after them. Are you not better than the birds?

"You cannot make yourself taller by wishing that you were. And why think about clothes? See the lilies in the fields, how they grow without effort. Solomon, in all his glory, was not dressed with such beauty.

"Therefore, if God covers the grass of the fields, which lasts only so long, do you not think he will take care of you, O you of little faith!

"Do not always say things like, 'What shall we eat? What shall we drink? What shall we wear?' That is the way of the Gentiles. But you don't need to say it, because your heavenly Father knows that you need all these things.

"First seek the kingdom of God and His righteousness; then everything that you need will come to you.

"Therefore, do not think about tomorrow, because tomorrow will take care of itself. Each day offers its own difficulties."

JUDGE NOT, FOR YOU MAY BE JUDGED

"Do not judge people, or you will be judged in return. When you judge a person meanly, you will be judged in the same way. And why look at the speck of dust in your brother's eye yet pay no attention to the plank in your own? How can you offer to help your brother when you yourself cannot see clearly? Do not be a hypocrite! First, clear the straw out of your own eye. Only then will you be able to help your brother.

"Do not give to dogs what is holy. Do not throw pearls to pigs. They will only tread them underfoot, then turn on you and try to tear you to pieces."

THE POWER OF PRAYER

"Ask and you will receive; seek and you will find; knock and the door will be opened for you.

"Everyone who asks, receives; he who seeks, finds; for he who knocks, the door is opened.

"Is there anyone so hard-hearted that if his son asked for a piece of bread, he would give him a stone? Or if he asked for a fish, would he give him a snake?

"Even sinners like yourselves know how to give good things to your children. Think how much more God, the heavenly Father, can give to those who ask.

"Therefore, treat others as you would like them to treat you. This is the law and the prophets."

"Enter by the narrow gate! The gate to ruin is big and wide, and it is all too easy for thousands to enter the wide gate. But because the gate that leads to life is narrow, and the path to the gate is likewise narrow, few will find their way to it.

"Beware of false prophets, who approach you in sheep's clothing while underneath they are as savage as wolves. You will recognise them by the fruits of their work. Do men gather grapes of thorns, or figs of thistles?

"A good tree produces good fruit, but a corrupt tree produces rotten fruit. A good tree cannot produce rotten fruit, and a corrupt tree cannnot produce good fruit. Every tree that does not bear good fruit is cut down and thrown into the fire. You will know a tree by the kind of fruit it bears.

"Not everyone who cries, 'Lord, Lord!' will enter the kingdom of heaven. But people who do as I ask will enter the kingdom of heaven.

"There will come a day when some will say to me, 'Lord, Lord, did we not make predictions in your name? And did we not cure people of their demons in your name? And did we not perform many good deeds in your name?' And I will tell them that I have never known them and that they should leave me alone. These are wicked people.

"But whoever hears my teachings and follows them is like a man who builds his house upon a foundation of rock. The rain falls, the

When the Lord saw her, he was moved with compassion and said to her, "Do not weep." Then he went to the stretcher on which the dead man lay, and he touched it. The men who carried the stretcher stopped and stood still. Jesus said, "Young man, I say to you, arise."

Instantly the young man sat up and began to talk, and he was reunited with his mother.

A LITTLE BIT OF HISTORY
In Ezra's time, scribes or writers were those who knew the law and could explain it. Their honorary title was "rabbi," which survives today and means "master." The rabbis came from all classes of people and lived by their writing skills. These educated men became a class close to that of the priests and were highly respected.

Luke 7

floodwaters rise, the wind blows and beats at the house, but the house does not fall, because it is built on a firm foundation.

"But whoever hears my words and does not act upon them is like a foolish man who builds his house on the sand. The rain falls, the floodwaters rise, the wind blows and beats at the house—and the house falls! It sinks to nothing."

When Jesus had finished speaking, the people were astonished. They were astonished because Jesus taught with authority and was not like a scribe or an official.

THE HEALING OF THE SERVANT

After teaching the people, Jesus went to Capernaum. In that place, there lived a centurion whose much-loved servant was sick and on the point of death. When the centurion heard that Jesus was close by, he sent elders of the Jews to plead with Jesus for the life of his servant.

The elders found Jesus and said, "This is a good man. He deserves help. He loves our nation, and he has even built a synagogue for us."

When Jesus heard them speak so favourably about the Roman centurion, he went with them.

When the group had nearly reached the house, friends came running out to meet Jesus. They told him that the centurion had said, "Lord, I am not worthy enough for you to enter my house. I am not worthy enough to come out to meet you. But if you will, just say the word, and I know that my servant will be healed. For like you, I am a man who has authority. I have soldiers who come and go as I command."

When Jesus heard these words, he turned to his followers and said, "This is a good man! I have not found such great faith, not even in Israel."

Then the friends of the centurion went back to the house and found that the servant who had been sick was now well.

Luke 7

THE WIDOW'S SON

The next day Jesus went to a city called Nain. His disciples were with him, and many people followed them. As Jesus approached the gates of the city, a dead man was carried out. He was the only son of his mother, and she was a widow. She was accompanied by a great crowd of people from Nain.

When the Lord saw her, he was moved with compassion and said to her, "Do not weep." Then he went to the stretcher on which the dead man lay, and he touched it. The men who carried the stretcher stopped and stood still. Jesus said, "Young man, I say to you, arise."

Instantly the young man sat up and began to talk, and he was reunited with his mother.

All the people were filled with fear, and they praised God, saying, "Here is a great prophet who has brought God to us."

And stories of Jesus spread through Judea and all the neighbouring areas.

JOHN THE BAPTIST ASKS A QUESTION

The followers of John the Baptist told him what miracles Jesus had done. John listened, and then he sent two of his disciples to Jesus with the question, "Are you the one we are waiting for, or should we look for somebody else?"

As John's disciples asked this question, Jesus cured people of disease, blindness, and evil spirits.

Jesus answered, "Return to John, and tell him what you have seen and heard. Tell him that the blind see, the crippled walk, the lepers are cured, the deaf hear, and the dead come back to life. And tell him that the poor hear the gospel, and that those who find no fault in what I do are blessed."

John's messengers left, and Jesus spoke to the people about John: "Why did you bother to go out into the desert? Was it just to see a reed shaken by the wind? Why did you really go there? Did you wish to see a man in beautiful clothes? If it was for that reason, you should have gone to a king's court! Ask yourselves why you really went there. Was it to see a prophet? I say it was, and that you have seen more than a prophet. For John is the messenger sent by God. He prepares the path before me. There is no greater prophet than John the Baptist; yet he who is least in the kingdom of God is greater than he."

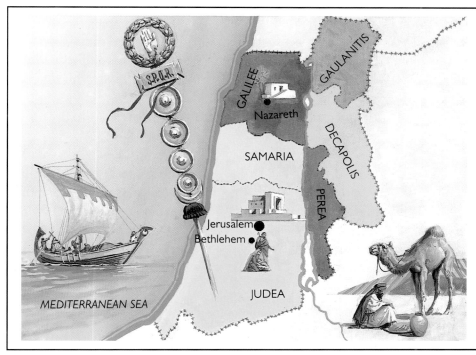

The map shows the main areas and the most important centres in Israel. In the time of Jesus, the country was known as Palestine.

The three regions that made up the country this side of the river Jordan were, from north to south, Galilee, Samaria, and Judea. It was in these regions that Jesus spent most of his life. He rarely travelled beyond the Jordan.

The river Jordan divided the Holy Land into two parts, which were known as Jordan and Transjordan.

JESUS PREACHES THE GOSPEL OF FORGIVENESS

One day, some Pharisees and officials known as scribes led to Jesus a woman who was accused of adultery. They said to Jesus, "Master, this woman is sinful. According to the law of Moses, she should be stoned to death. What is your opinion on this?"

The scribes and Pharisees had hoped that by asking this question they would trap Jesus and reveal how he would break an ancient law. Jesus answered, "Let the person who has never sinned be the first to throw a stone at this woman."

Then each man looked at himself and thought back on his own life. And there was not a man present who could say that he had never sinned. They left one by one, until only Jesus and the woman remained. Jesus said to her, "Woman, where are the men who accused you? Is there no one here to condemn you?"

She replied, "There is no one, Lord."

Jesus said, "I do not condemn you either. Go on your way, and do not sin any more."

At another time, a Pharisee named Simon begged Jesus to come and eat with him. Jesus went to this man's house and sat down at his table. Now, there was also in this town a woman who was well-known as a sinner. When she heard that Jesus was at Simon's house, she hurried there, taking with her an alabaster box of ointment.

This woman stood behind Jesus and wept. She washed his feet with her tears, and then she dried them with her hair. She kissed his feet and rubbed ointment into them.

When Simon saw this, he thought to himself, Surely, if this man is a prophet, he knows what kind of a woman this is!

Then Jesus said, "Simon, I have something to say to you."

Simon said, "I am listening, Master."

Jesus said, "There was a certain man who was owed money by two other men. One owed him five hundred pence; the other, fifty. When neither could pay, he let them both off. So explain to me, who do you think was most grateful?"

Simon said, "I suppose it must be the man who owed him the most money."

And Jesus replied, "You are right, Simon."

Then he turned to the woman and said to Simon, "Look at this woman. I came into your house, but you gave me no water to wash my feet. This woman washed my feet with her tears and dried them with her hair. You gave me no kiss or hug when I entered your house, but this woman has kissed my feet endlessly. You did not anoint my head with oil, but this woman has rubbed my feet with ointment.

"I have to tell you that although her sins are many, she is forgiven. She is forgiven because her heart is full of love. He who forgives little, loves little."

Then Jesus said to the woman, "Your sins are forgiven."

And those who sat at Simon's table wondered who this person was

Opposite: A Pharisee named Simon begged Jesus to come and eat with him. Jesus went to this man's house and sat down at his table. Now, there was also in this town a woman who was well-known as a sinner. When she heard that Jesus was at Simon's house, she hurried there, taking with her an alabaster box of ointment.

This woman stood behind Jesus and wept. She washed his feet with her tears, and then she dried them with her hair. She kissed his feet and rubbed ointment into them.

that he could forgive sins. But Jesus said to the woman, "Your faith has saved you. Go in peace."

Mark 3
Luke 6

THE MAN WITH THE PARALYSED HAND

One day, Jesus went into the synagogue on the Sabbath, and there was a man there with a paralysed hand. As usual, the scribes and Pharisees tried to trick Jesus. They said to the Lord, "Is it permitted to heal on the Sabbath?"

But Jesus knew what they were thinking and that they were trying to trick him. He said, "Is it lawful to do good or evil on the Sabbath? If you had a sheep and it fell in a ditch on the Sabbath, would you leave it there or pull it out? You would pull it out, of course! Surely this man I have healed is worth more than a sheep? Is it not permitted, then, to do good on the Sabbath?"

He called the man with the paralysed hand to his side and told him, "Stretch out your hand!"

The man stretched out his hand, and Jesus made the hand well.

And this made the Pharisees mad with anger. Once again they had failed to trick Jesus! They looked for another way to bring about his downfall.

Matthew 12
Mark 3

JESUS CURES A VERY SICK MAN

On another day, the people brought to Jesus a man who was blind and dumb, and who seemed to have a devil living inside him. Jesus healed him so that he saw and spoke properly. The people who saw this were amazed and said, "Surely Jesus must be the son of David!"

But the Pharisees said, "This man is only able to bring devils out of a body with the help of Beelzebub, and this man himself is the prince of demons!"

Jesus knew what they were thinking, and he told them, "Every kingdom that is divided ends in ruin. Every city or family that is divided will not last long. Even if Satan casts out himself, he is divided and therefore ruined. His own kingdom will perish. If I am Beelzebub and I am destroyed, then who will cast out devils for your children? Think about this. If I cast out devils from a body in the name of the Lord, the spirit of God comes to you.

"How can a thief enter the house of a strong man and steal his possessions? First he must tie up the strong man in order to steal his things.

"He who is not with me is against me. He who does not understand what I say wanders in his thoughts.

"So I say this to you: All sins and blasphemy may be forgiven. But when you sin and blaspheme about the Holy Spirit, you will not be forgiven.

"You may speak badly about the Son of man and be forgiven. But if you speak badly against the Holy Spirit, you will not be forgiven, either in this world or in the next."

THE PARABLES OF JESUS

Jesus went from town to town and from village to village. Everywhere he went, he preached and told the people the good news about the kingdom of heaven. The twelve apostles travelled with him, as did a number of women who had been cured of sickness and evil spirits.

A great crowd of people gathered round Jesus while he was on the seashore. So he got into a boat and spoke to the people from there, while they remained on the beach. Then Jesus preached many things. The things he said were parables, which are stories that make people think.

THE SOWER

"There was once a sower who went out one day to sow seeds. He threw his seeds into the earth. But some seeds fell to one side, and the birds came down and ate them up. Other seeds fell on stony ground, where there was little earth. These seeds sprang up quickly, because they were in shallow ground. But as soon as the sun rose, they were scorched and withered away, because they had no roots.

"Other seeds fell among thorns. And as soon as they sprang up, they were choked by the thorns.

"Other seeds dropped into good ground, and these grew and produced fruit."

Then Jesus raised his voice and said, "He who has ears to hear, open them and listen."

When the disciples heard the Lord speaking to the people in this way, they went to him and said, "Master, why are you speaking to the people in parables?"

Jesus answered, "You know the mysteries of the kingdom of heaven, but there are people here who do not. The person who has everything gains even more, but the person who has nothing will be robbed and have less than nothing. That is why I speak in parables. There are those who see without seeing and hear without hearing. They understand nothing.

"Now listen, and I will tell you what the parables mean. When a person hears words about the kingdom of heaven and understands nothing, the Evil One comes and steals what was sown in the heart. This person's seeds fall to one side.

"Then there is the person who hears, but his seeds fall in stony places. At first he is full of joy. But this joy is short-lived, because he has no roots. It is not long before the smallest thing makes him give up.

"Think next about the person who hears in the middle of thorns. He receives the word of God, and then worldly troubles, lies, and riches choke him. He cannot go on.

"But the person whose seeds fall into good earth is he who hears and understands, and he produces a mighty crop."

"There was once a sower who went out one day to sow seeds. He threw his seeds into the earth. But some seeds fell to one side, and the birds came down and ate them up. Other seeds fell on stony ground, where there was little earth. These seeds sprang up quickly, because they were in shallow ground. But as soon as the sun rose, they were scorched and withered away, because they had no roots.

"Other seeds fell among thorns. And as soon as they sprang up, they were choked by the thorns.

"Other seeds dropped into good ground, and these grew and produced fruit."

228

THE KINGDOM OF HEAVEN

Then Jesus told another parable:

"The kingdom of heaven is like a man who sows good seeds in his land. Then the sower goes to bed, and while he sleeps, an enemy comes and plants weeds among his wheat. The crop grows, and when it is ripe, the weeds and wheat are mixed together. When the servants of the household see this, they run to their landlord and say, 'Sir, you sowed good seeds on your land. We cannot understand why the fields are so full of weeds.'

"The landlord says, 'This is the work of an enemy!'

"Then the servants say, 'Shall we go and tear out the weeds?'

"The landlord replies, 'No. When you pull up the weeds, you may damage the wheat. Let both grow together until harvest time. Then gather everything in and separate the weeds from the wheat. Then burn the weeds and put the wheat into our barns.' "

Jesus taught everything to the crowds in parables. When he had finished preaching, he went back to his house.

It was there that his disciples approached him and said, "Master, please explain to us what the parable about the weeds and the wheat means."

Jesus replied, "The one who sows good seed is the Son of man; the field stands for the world; the good seeds are those who follow the path to the kingdom of heaven; the weeds are the followers of evil; the enemy who sowed the weeds among the wheat is the devil; the harvest is the end of the world; and the harvesters are the angels of God. As one cuts and burns weeds, so it will be for sinners at the end of the world. The Son of man will send his angels to tear out all sin and evil from his kingdom and throw it into a fiery furnace. On that day, many tears will be shed.

"But the good people will shine like the sun in the kingdom of their Father."

ANOTHER PARABLE ON THE KINGDOM OF HEAVEN

And Jesus continued to speak in parables. He said, "The kingdom of heaven is like a treasure hidden in a field. When a man finds it, he is filled with a great, secret joy. He sells everything he has in order to buy the field and keep his treasure.

"And the kingdom of heaven is like a merchant who wants to buy fine pearls. When he finds a pearl of great value, he sells all his lesser pearls in order to keep it.

"The kingdom of heaven is like a net that is thrown into the sea. The net catches every variety of living thing from the water, and when the net is full, it is hauled to shore and emptied. The good is kept, but the bad is thrown away. This is the way it will be when the world comes to an end. The angels will separate the good from the bad. And the bad will be thrown into an intense fire."

Then Jesus asked if they had understood the parable, and they said that they had.

JESUS IN NAZARETH

After he had told these parables, Jesus went to Nazareth, where he had been brought up. As was his custom, he went into the synagogue on the Sabbath and stood up to read.

He was given the book of the prophet Isaiah to read from. He opened the book and read: "The Spirit of the Lord is with me because He has anointed me to teach the gospel to the poor. He sent me to heal the brokenhearted. He sent me to preach freedom for prisoners, the recovery of sight for the blind, and liberty for the oppressed. He sent me to announce a year of favour from the Lord."

Jesus closed the book, returned it to the minister, and sat down. All eyes in the synagogue were on him, and Jesus said, "Today, the words of this Scripture have come to pass."

Then the congregation were amazed by the gracious things he said. And they said to one another, "Is this really the son of Joseph? Is this the carpenter, the son of Mary?" And they began to doubt themselves.

But Jesus said, "A prophet is honoured, but in his own country, among his relatives, and in his own house, he is scorned."

And Jesus, shocked by their lack of faith, performed no great miracle there unless it was the healing of sick people. Some people who helped in the synagogue were angry with him. They tried to lead him to the top of the mountain on which their town was built so that they could push him off. But Jesus disappeared into the middle of the crowd and went on his way.

JESUS CALMS THE STORM

One day, Jesus was in a boat with his disciples. He had just finished preaching to a huge crowd on the seashore. He said to his disciples, "Let us now cross over to the other shore."

They pushed off, and while the disciples navigated the boat, Jesus slept.

Suddenly a huge storm blew up. The waves rose, and the boat filled up with water.

Jesus was in the stern of the boat, lying fast asleep on a pillow. The disciples woke him up and cried out, "Master, don't you care that we are about to drown?"

Then Jesus stood up. He commanded the wind to fall, and he said to the sea, "Peace! Be still!" And the wind fell, and there was a great calm at sea.

Jesus said to his disciples, "Why are you so afraid? Have you lost your faith?"

And then the disciples were extremely afraid. They asked one another, "What kind of man is this? Even the wind and the sea obey him!"

MIRACLES OF HEALING AND RESURRECTION

Jesus and his disciples reached the other shore, where a great crowd had gathered. Jairus, one of the ministers of the local synagogue, came to Jesus and threw himself at his feet. He prayed to the Lord, saying, "My little daughter is about to die. I beg you to lay your hands on her and save her life."

Jesus went with him, and a great crowd followed him, so that he was pressed on all sides.

And there was also a woman there who had suffered losses of blood for twelve years. She had been examined and treated by many doctors and spent her savings seeking a cure. But she had had no success and was always close to the point of death.

This woman had heard of Jesus, and she now threaded her way through the crowd and touched the hem of his cloak. For she thought, If I can just touch his clothes, I will be healed.

And in the same moment that she touched Jesus' cloak, she was healed. She stopped losing blood, and she felt well.

Jesus also felt something, and he turned to the crowd and said, "Who touched my clothes?"

The disciples said, "Master, you see the great crowd pressing in on you, and you wonder who has touched your clothes?"

But Jesus stood and looked round him to see the person.

Then the woman, trembling with fear, threw herself at the feet of Jesus and told him the truth.

Jesus said, "Daughter, your faith has saved you. Go in peace, and be well from now on."

While Jesus was speaking to the woman, men came running from the house of Jairus to inform him that his daughter was dead. They said, "There is no point in the Lord's going on any farther to the house."

When Jesus heard these words, he said to Jairus, "Do not be afraid; only have faith."

Jesus entered the house with the mother and father of the girl, and with Peter, James, and John. Inside the house and outside there was crying and sorrowing. Then Jesus said, "Do not weep. She is not dead; she is only asleep."

When they heard Jesus say this, many made fun of him. They had seen death before, and the girl was clearly dead. Jesus asked these doubters to leave the house. Then he went to the girl. Taking her by the hand, he said, "Young girl, I say to you, rise up!"

At once, the girl got up and began to walk round.

All those present were stunned into silence, and Jesus told them not to speak of what had happened. He told them to bring food and drink for the girl.

THE MARTYR, JOHN THE BAPTIST

King Herod heard everything that was being said about Jesus, and he wasn't sure what to think. Some said that Jesus was John the Baptist, back from the dead, and that this was what gave him the power to work miracles. Others said that he was Elias or one of the prophets of old.

King Herod thought, I beheaded John. He must have come back from the grave!

Earlier, Herod had imprisoned John because the prophet did not approve of the king's marriage. The king had married Herodias, his brother Philip's wife. John had told the king, "It is not lawful for you to marry your brother's wife." At that time, Herodias had a quarrel with John and wanted him killed, but she dared not order his murder.

Herod himself was afraid of John. He knew the prophet was a good and just man. He knew he could not always understand the prophet, but he always listened to him.

On his birthday, Herod gave a feast for his landlords, chiefs, captains, and all the high-ranking officials of Galilee. At this feast, the daughter of Herodias danced and charmed the king so much that he said to her, "You may ask what you wish from me, and I will give it to you. You may even ask for half the kingdom."

Then the girl went to her mother and said, "What do you think I should ask from the king?"

And Herodias replied, "The head of John the Baptist."

Then the girl, Salome, went back to the king and said, "I want you to give me the head of John the Baptist at once, and I want it served on a platter!"

King Herod was filled with sorrow. But he had given his word to Salome, and he could not go back on that.

He sent an executioner to John's prison, and there John was beheaded. The head of the prophet was put on a platter and brought to the young woman, who took it to her mother.

When the disciples of John heard what had happened, they went to the prison. They took the body of John and placed it in a tomb.

Then the apostles gathered round Jesus and told him what had happened.

Jesus said, "We will go now into an isolated place and rest there. So much has happened that you have scarcely had time to eat."

And Jesus prepared to leave with his apostles.

Opposite: He sent an executioner to John's prison, and there John was beheaded. The head of the prophet was put on a platter and brought to the young woman, who took it to her mother.

THE PROMISE
OF THE EUCHARIST

Mark 6
John 6
Matthew 14

FIVE LOAVES AND TWO FISH

But when the people saw the apostles make ready to leave, they recognised Jesus and ran down the shore to him. When Jesus saw this, he was filled with compasssion for the people. They seemed to him like sheep without a shepherd. Then he began to teach them many things.

When it was late, the disciples went to Jesus and said, "This is a deserted place. The people have nothing to eat. Should we send them away now so that they can go to the nearby villages and buy bread?"

Jesus answered, "Give them what you have to eat."

The disciples said, "Shall we go and buy two hundred pennies' worth of bread and feed them with that?"

Jesus said, "How many loaves do you have?"

They went to look, came back, and told him, "We have five loaves and two fish."

Then Jesus told the people to sit down on the grass. And the people sat down in groups of hundreds and fifties.

Jesus took the loaves and the fish and looked up to heaven. He blessed the food and broke the bread. Then his disciples gave out the food, and everyone had enough to eat.

After the meal, when the remainder of the bread and fish was collected, it filled twelve baskets. About five thousand people had eaten that day.

Mark 6
John 6
Matthew 14

JESUS WALKS ON WATER

Then Jesus sent the crowd away and told his disciples to get in the boat and set out for the other side, towards Bethsaida.

Jesus went up a mountain to pray. When evening fell, he was still there and quite alone. He went down the mountain and stood on the seashore. Out at sea, he spotted the little vessel tossed here and there by a wind that was against them.

Towards the fourth watch of the night, Jesus saw that his disciples had trouble in rowing the boat. He then walked to them across the surface of the water. When the disciples saw him walking on the water, they were filled with terror. Thinking he was a ghost, they shouted out in alarm. But Jesus heard them at once and said, "Calm yourselves. It is I. Do not be afraid!"

Peter said, "Is that really you, Lord? If it is, order me to cross the water to you!"

And Jesus said, "Come!"

Then Peter got out of the boat and began to walk across the water to Jesus. But realizing how strong the wind was, he grew afraid and cried out, "Master, save me!"

Jesus stretched out his hand, and taking Peter's hand, he said, "Man of little faith, why did you doubt me?"

When they got into the boat, the wind dropped at once. Those on board threw themselves at Jesus' feet and said, "You are truly the Son of God!"

Then they crossed the water and reached the land of Gennesaret. The people in that area, knowing the work of Jesus and his disciples, brought Jesus their sick and diseased. They begged him to let them touch the hem of his cloak so that they might be cured. And everyone who touched his clothes was cured.

Then the scribes and Pharisees from Jerusalem went to Jesus and said, "Why do your disciples disobey the ancient laws? They do not wash their hands before they eat bread."

Jesus replied, "Why do you break God's commandments with your tradition? God said, 'Honour your father and mother.' If you curse your father and mother, you deserve to die. In your tradition, you have gone against God's commandments. You are hypocrites! The prophet Isaiah knew you well when he said, 'These people say nice things and honour me with their lips, but their heart is far removed from me. They worship me in vain.'"

Then Jesus called the crowd to him and told them, "It is not what goes into a man's mouth that defiles him; it is what comes out of his mouth."

Jesus went into a house that was far away from the crowd. His disciples went to him and said, "Master, do you know that the Pharisees have been shocked by your words?"

And Jesus told them, "Every plant that has not been planted by my Father in heaven will be uprooted. Leave these men alone. They are the blind who lead the blind, and when a blind man leads another, they both fall into the ditch."

When Peter heard this, he asked Jesus to explain the parable. And Jesus said, "Do you still not understand what I am trying to tell you? Do you not understand that whatever goes into your mouth goes into your stomach and is then rejected? But the things that come out of your mouth stem from your heart. And out of the heart come evil thoughts, murders, adulteries, thefts, falsehoods, and blasphemies."

Jesus took the loaves and the fish and looked up to heaven. He blessed the food and broke the bread. Then his disciples gave out the food, and everyone had enough to eat.

JESUS AND PETER

Jesus travelled with his disciples to the coast of Caesarea Philippi. It was here that he put a question to them: "I am the Son of man, but who do the people think I am?"

The disciples replied, "Some think you are John the Baptist, some think Elias, others think Jeremias [Jeremiah] or one of the prophets."

Then Jesus said, "But who do *you* think I am?"

And Simon Peter answered, "You are the Christ, the Son of the living God."

Jesus said, "Simon, you are blessed, because nobody told you this except my Father, who is in heaven. I say to you, Peter, you are like a rock, and it is a rock on which I will build my church. I will give you the keys to the kingdom of heaven."

Then he told his disciples that they should tell no one that he was Jesus the Christ.

JESUS WARNS HIS DISCIPLES

From that day on, Jesus spoke openly with his disciples. He told them how he must go to Jerusalem, where he would suffer at the hands of the elders, the chief priests, and the scribes. He told them that he would be killed, but he would come back to life after three days.

When Peter heard this, he began to scold him, saying, "Do not say this, Lord. This cannot happen to you!"

Jesus replied, "Get behind me, Satan! You are an offence to me. You do not think of the things that come from God but only of those things that come from man."

Jesus turned to his disciples and said, "If there is any man who wishes to follow me, he will have to forget about himself and carry his own cross. Whoever saves his life on earth may lose it in heaven. Whoever loses his life for my sake will find it again. What good is there in gaining the world but losing your soul? You cannot put a price on the soul of a human being.

"The Son of man will come in the glory of his Father and his angels. Then every person will be rewarded according to what he has done.

"Some of you standing before me now will live to see the Son of man entering the kingdom of heaven."

Opposite: Peter said, "Is that really you, Lord? If it is, order me to cross the water to you!"

And Jesus said, "Come!"

Then Peter got out of the boat and began to walk across the water to Jesus. But realizing how strong the wind was, he grew afraid and cried out, "Master, save me!"

Jesus stretched out his hand, and taking Peter's hand, he said, "Man of little faith, why did you doubt me?"

THE TRANSFIGURATION

Six days later, Jesus took Peter, James, and his brother John up a high mountain, where there were no other people round. On the mountain, Jesus was transfigured before their eyes. His face shone like the sun, and his clothes were as white as light. Moses and Elias appeared and spoke to the Lord.

Then Peter said, "Lord, we should make three tabernacles: one for you, one for Moses, and one for Elias."

As Peter spoke, a bright cloud overshadowed them. A voice came out of the cloud and said, "This is My beloved Son, in whom I am very pleased. Listen when he speaks."

When the disciples heard this voice, they were terrified. They fell to the ground and hid their faces.

Then Jesus went to them and touched them. "Do not be afraid," he said. "Get up now."

Then the disciples got up and looked around, but they saw no one except Jesus himself.

On their way down the mountain, Jesus said, "Do not tell anyone about what you have seen until the Son of man has risen from the dead."

The disciples asked, "Why is it that the scribes say Elias must come first?"

Jesus replied, "Elias will indeed come first and make things ready. But Elias has already been here, and he was not well treated. People did whatever they liked with him. The Son of man will suffer in a similar way."

Then the disciples realised that Jesus was speaking about John the Baptist.

Opposite: Six days later, Jesus took Peter, James, and his brother John up a high mountain, where there were no other people around. On the mountain, Jesus was transfigured before their eyes. His face shone like the sun, and his clothes were as white as light. Moses and Elias appeared and spoke to the Lord.

JESUS TEACHES HIS DISCIPLES

The following day, a great crowd of people came to Jesus. Out of this group stepped a man who knelt before the Lord and said, "Lord, have mercy on my son. He is deaf and dumb and mad and troubled inside. He is so out of control that he often throws himself into the fire or into the water. Your disciples have seen him, but they were able to do nothing."

Then Jesus said, "O faithless and wicked people, how long must I stay with you? How long must I suffer? Bring the boy to me."

The young man who was sick in his mind was led to Jesus, and as he approached the Lord, his face contorted and he fell to the ground, foaming at the mouth.

Jesus asked the boy's father, "How long has he been like this?"

And the man replied, "Since he was small. Often the evil spirit makes him jump into fire or water as though to destroy him. Lord, if you can, have pity on him and help us."

Then Jesus said, "If you can believe, all things are possible."

At once the father of the child, with tears in his eyes, cried out, "Lord, I believe, but help my miserable lack of faith!"

The people round Jesus shifted uneasily. He turned to the child and said, "Deaf and dumb spirit, come out of this body and never enter it again!"

Then the body of the boy was racked by tortured cries until at last he fell down as though dead. In fact, many thought he was dead. But Jesus took the boy by the hand and lifted him up. And the boy was well.

Later when Jesus was with his disciples in a house, they asked him why they were unable to cure the boy.

Jesus said, "Because you lack faith! If you have as much faith as a grain of mustard seed, you can move a mountain from one place to another. Nothing is impossible. But the sort of demon that was in the boy only leaves after much prayer and fasting."

Then they left that area and went to Galilee. Jesus did not want anyone to know of his presence there. He said, "The Son of man will be betrayed and taken by men. They will put him to death, but on the third day he will rise again."

The disciples did not understand the meaning of these words, and they were afraid to ask for further explanation.

FURTHER TEACHINGS OF JESUS

They reached Capernaum, and when they were safely housed, Jesus asked his disciples, "What were you talking about on the way here?"

The disciples said nothing, because on the way they had discussed who would be the most important of the apostles.

Jesus sat down and called the twelve apostles to sit with him. He told them, "If any man here wishes to be the first, he shall be the last. In fact, he will be the servant of the others."

He called to a child, and the child came to him. Taking the child in his arms and seating him on his knee, Jesus said, "Whoever is kind to a child is kind to me. He who receives me does not receive me without God."

Then John said, "Master, we saw a man, who was not one of us, healing people in your name. When we heard this, we told him to stop, because he does not follow us."

Jesus said, "Do not forbid him, for no man can do a miracle in my name and then speak badly of me. He who is not against us is for us. Whenever a person gives you a cup of water to drink because you belong to Christ, I say, take the cup and drink. You will both be the better for it.

"And as for a person who hurts a child who believes in me, he would be better off if a boulder were hung round his neck and he was thrown into the sea.

"If your brother has hurt your feelings, make it up with him. If he listens, you have saved your brother; if he does not listen, bring in a few people to see both sides of the dispute. If he refuses to see these others, speak to the community about him. And if he refuses to listen to the community, then treat him as you would a pagan and a collector of taxes.

"Also, I tell you, when two people gather together in my name and ask for something, their prayer will be answered by my Father in heaven. Wherever two or three people meet together in my name, I am with them. Their prayers will be answered."

Then Peter went up to Jesus and said, "Lord, how many times should I forgive my brother if he sins against me? As many as seven times?"

And Jesus said, "I did not say seven times; it is more like seventy times seven."

THE PARABLE OF THE CRUEL SERVANT

Matthew 18-19
Luke 9

Jesus told this parable:

"The kingdom of heaven is like a certain king who wished to find out how much money his servants owed him. He did his accounts and requested that a particular servant be brought to him. This servant owed him ten thousand talents.

"The servant could not pay his debt, so the king said that he would have to sell everything he had and become a slave. When the servant heard this, he fell down on his knees and pleaded with the king. 'Master,' he said, 'be patient with me, and I will pay you everything as soon as I can.'

"The king was moved with pity, and he forgave the man his debt.

"Shortly afterwards, this same servant happened to meet a fellow servant who owed him a hundred pence. The servant grabbed the other servant by the throat and shouted into his face, 'Pay me what you owe me!'

"His fellow servant fell down at his feet and pleaded, 'Have patience with me, and I will pay you everything as soon as I can!'

"But his words fell on deaf ears. And the servant who owed a hundred pence was thrown in prison and told that he would stay there until the money was repaid.

"When the other servants of the household heard about this, they were very sad. They went to the king and told him about the poor servant in prison.

"Then the king was full of rage. He summoned the servant whose debt he had forgiven. He said, 'You are a wicked and cruel servant! I forgave you for the money you owed me because you pleaded with me. Why did you not have pity on your fellow servant as I had pity on you?'

"The king was so angry that he handed the servant over to heartless men, who tortured him for the debt he owed.

He called to a child, and the child came to him. Taking the child in his arms and seating him on his knee, Jesus said, "Whoever is kind to a child is kind to me. He who receives me does not receive me without God."

"My heavenly Father will behave as that king did, if you do not forgive those who trespass against you."

After Jesus had told this parable, he left Galilee and went to the shores of Judea, beyond the river Jordan. A huge crowd followed him, and on the way he cured many who were sick.

While they were still travelling, a certain man approached Jesus and said, "Lord, I will follow you wherever you go."

But Jesus replied, "Foxes have holes, and birds have nests, but the Son of man does not know where he will sleep at night."

To another man, Jesus said, "Follow me!" And the man said that he would, but first he had to bury his father.

Jesus told him, "Let the dead bury their dead. Go anyway, and preach the word of the kingdom of God."

Another man said to Jesus, "Lord, I will follow you, but first I must say goodbye to those at home."

And Jesus answered this man, "No man who has put his hand to the plough and then looks back is fit for the kingdom of God."

JESUS APPOINTS SEVENTY DISCIPLES

The Lord appointed seventy disciples to go ahead of him. He sent them in twos to go to those places where he himself would eventually arrive. He told them:

"The harvest will be great, but there will be few workers to help you. You must therefore pray to the Lord of the harvest to send you workers. Be on your way. I am sending you out like lambs to a place where wolves live. Do not carry money or papers; do not wear shoes or greet anyone on your journey. If you enter a house, the first thing you must do is bless the house. If your blessing is received, you may rest; if not, you must go on. But if you find a house that offers food and hospitality, stay there. The worker is worth his pay. You will not need then to go from house to house.

"In whatever city you find yourselves, if you are offered food, accept it. Wherever you go, heal the sick, and tell the people that the kingdom of God is close at hand.

"If you go into a city and the people do not want you there, go out into their streets. Shake the dust of their city from your clothes, and say that the kingdom of God is close at hand.

"This I tell you: The city that rejects you will be worse off than Sodom was in ancient times. Woe to Chorazin! Woe to Bethsaida! If the miracles that were performed before you had been done in Tyre and Sidon, they would have asked for mercy long ago. On the day of judgement, those places will be better off than those towns that reject you now.

"And Capernaum, a place that is so pleased with itself, will drop like a stone into hell.

"Those who listen to you hear the Son of man. Those who despise you hate both the Son of man and my Father who has sent me here."

OTHER PARABLES JESUS TOLD

THE YOUNG RICH MAN
Matthew 19
Mark 10
Luke 18

A man went to Jesus asking, "Master, what must I do to live for ever?"

Jesus replied, "If you wish to live for ever, keep the Lord's commandments."

The man asked, "Which commandments, Master?"

Jesus said, "Do not kill. Do not commit adultery. Do not steal. Do not tell lies about other people. Respect your father and mother. Love your neighbour as you love yourself."

The young man replied, "I have kept those commandments since I was a boy. What must I do next?"

Jesus looked at the young man and said, "If you wish to be perfect, sell everything you own, and give the money to the poor. Your treasure will be in heaven. When you have done that, leave it all behind and follow me."

When the young man heard this, he became sad. He was very rich, and it would hurt him to give everything away.

Jesus turned to his disciples and said, "It is easier for a camel to go through the eye of a needle than for a rich man to enter the kingdom of God."

When the disciples heard this, they were shocked. They said, "Then who can be saved?"

Jesus looked at them and said, "To men, things appear impossible, but with God, everything is possible."

THE GRAPE GROWERS
Matthew 20

"The kingdom of heaven is like a man who owns a vineyard. This man got up early one morning and went off to find some men to gather his grapes. The man found a number of workers, and they agreed that their wage would be a penny a day.

"Three hours later, the owner of the vineyard was in the market, where he saw other men who were not doing anything. He said to them, 'Go and work in my vineyard, and I will pay you a wage.' The men agreed and went off to work in his vineyard.

"Later the owner went out again and hired more workers. Then he went once more and hired even more workers for his vineyard.

"When evening came, the owner called his chief servant and said, 'Bring all the workers here and pay them their wages. Start with those who arrived last of all.'

"The chief servant did as he was told, and he paid those who had started late in the day a penny. Every worker received a penny, even those who had worked the whole day long.

"Those who had worked the whole day long were not happy. They did not think it was fair that they had worked for the entire day for a penny while those who had worked for just one hour had also received a penny. They said, 'We worked all day in the heat of the sun. There are men here who worked for just one hour, and yet they received the same wage as us!'

"The owner of the vineyard said, 'Take your penny and go on your way. I pay the last in the vineyard the same as the first. I may do what I like with what is mine. You agreed to work for a penny a day, and now you are complaining!'

"It may happen that those who will arrive last are equal to those who arrived first. Many are called, but few are chosen."

THE LOST SHEEP

Tax collectors and all kinds of sinners pressed round Jesus to hear his words. The scribes and Pharisees were disgusted to see this, and they said, "This man keeps company with sinners. He even eats with them! What sort of a person is he?"

When Jesus heard what was being said of him, he told this parable:

"If a man owns a hundred sheep and loses one, what does he do? He leaves his ninety-nine sheep to look after themselves in the desert. He looks for his lost sheep until he has found it. When he has found it, he picks it up, puts it on his shoulders, and joyfully carrries it home. He calls out to his friends and neighbours, 'Rejoice with me! I have found the sheep that was lost.'

"And so I tell you this: There is more joy in heaven when a single sinner repents than when there are ninety-nine who do not need to repent."

THE PRODIGAL SON, Luke 15

Then Jesus continued with his parables, and he told this story:

"There was once a man who had two sons. The younger of the sons said to his father, 'Father, I would like to have my portion of your wealth now.' The father agreed and divided up his wealth. A few days later, the younger son left with his inheritance and set off for a distant land. There this son spent all his money enjoying himself. But there came a day when he had nothing left. And at just the same time, his country was stricken by famine.

"So the younger son was forced to work for a man who sent him into the fields to feed his pigs. The young man was so hungry that he often wished he could eat what he fed the pigs, because no one gave him anything to eat.

"After some time, the young man thought to himself, At home even my father's servants have enough to eat, but here I am starving to death. I must go home and tell my father that I have sinned and am not worthy to be called his son. I will ask him to hire me as one of his servants.

"Then the young man travelled back to his father's country. He had no sooner entered that country than his father saw him in the distance. Feeling sorry for his son, he ran to him, took him in his arms, and kissed and hugged him.

"The son said, 'I have sinned against heaven, and I have sinned against you. I know I am not worthy to be called your son.'

"But the young man's father called his servants to him and said, 'Put on my son the best clothes you can find. Put shoes on his feet and a ring on his finger. Prepare a feast so that we may eat and be merry! This is my son, who I thought was dead! But now he is here and alive!'

"There was great happiness in that household. There was music

Luke 15
Matthew 18

Opposite:
The Good Samaritan *(Luke 10)*
"A man who was travelling from Jerusalem to Jericho was attacked by a group of thieves. They beat him, robbed him, and ran away, leaving him half-dead on the road.

"By chance, a priest came down the same road and when he saw the injured man, he crossed to the other side and kept going. Then a preacher came along and when he saw the man, he, too, crossed to the other side of the road.

"But a Samaritan, who was travelling by, saw the man and took pity on him. He went to him and bandaged his wounds, pouring oil and wine on them. Then he set the man on his horse and led him to an inn where he took care of him.

"The next morning he paid the innkeeper and said: 'Please take good care of this man. When I return, I will pay you back whatever money you spend on him.'

"Which of these three do you think was the most neighbourly to the man who was beaten by the thieves?"

"It was the man who took pity on him," responded the lawyer.

And Jesus said to him, " Go out and do the same."

and dancing.

"The elder son was at this time working in the fields. At the end of the day, he went back to the house and heard all the merriment. He asked a servant what all this celebration meant. The servant said, 'Your brother has returned. Your father is full of joy. He has made a feast because he is so happy to see his son safe and sound.'

"This made the elder son angry. He was so angry that he would not go inside the house. When the father heard this, he went out to his son and begged him to come indoors.

"The elder son said, 'I have worked for you all these years, but you have never made a feast for me! I never had a party like this for my friends. He went away and spent all his money on just enjoying himself. Then the minute he comes back, you bring out the best meat and drink!'

"The father looked at his elder son and said, 'My son, you are always with me, and everything I own belongs to you. We should make merry now. Your brother has returned! Your brother was dead to us, and now he is alive! He was lost, and now he is found!' "

THE RICH MAN AND THE BEGGAR

Jesus told another parable to his disciples:

Luke 16

"There was once a rich man who wore the finest purple clothes made of the best linen. Every day, this man ate the best food there was to be had.

"One day, a wretched beggar named Lazarus, who was covered in sores and scabs, lay down at the rich man's door. The beggar was there because he needed food, even if it were only leftovers from the rich man's table. While Lazarus waited at the door, dogs came and licked his sores and scabs.

"After some time, the beggar died, and he was carried by angels into the arms of Abraham. The rich man also died and was buried.

"And the rich man found himself in the torture chamber of hell. But when he looked up, he saw the beggar Lazarus cradled in the arms of Abraham. Then he cried out in his pain, 'Father Abraham, have mercy on me! If you would, just have Lazarus dip the tip of his finger in water and bring it to me, so that for a moment I might be relieved of this flaming torture!'

"Abraham answered, 'Son, remember that in your lifetime, you received everything that was good. Lazarus had a wretched life. Now he is comforted, and you are tormented. You are in hell, and you cannot ever enter the gates of heaven.'

"Then the man who had been rich on earth said, 'Father, could you not send Lazarus to my house? I have five brothers, and he could tell them about the pains of hell.'

"Abraham said, 'They do not need Lazarus. They have the warnings from the prophets and from Moses.'

"The man said, 'But, Father Abraham, if one who was dead warned my brothers of the pains of hell, they would ask for forgiveness!'

"But Abraham replied, 'If they do not listen to Moses and the prophets, they will not listen to one who has risen from the grave.' "

JOURNEY TO JERUSALEM

THE TEN LEPERS

Luke 17

Jesus set out for Jerusalem and travelled through the heart of Samaria and Galilee. On the way, he went into a village, and there he saw ten men who were lepers. They stood at a good distance from the Lord, as lepers carried a fatal disease. So they called out to Jesus, "Jesus, Master, have mercy on us."

Then Jesus said, "Go, and show yourselves to the priest. He will find that you have been cured."

The ten set off to show themselves to the priest, and on the way, they were healed and became healthy. When one of these lepers saw what had happened, he turned back. He glorified God and returned to Jesus. He fell at Jesus' feet and thanked him from the bottom of his heart. This man was a Samaritan.

Jesus said to him, "But there were ten of you! Where are the other nine? Is it only you, a Samaritan, who has returned to give glory to God?" Then Jesus said, "Stand up, and go on your way. Your faith has made you a healthy man."

THE PHARISEE AND THE TAX COLLECTOR

Luke 18

Jesus told this parable to certain men who thought they were holy and who looked down on others:

"Two men went to the temple to pray. One was a Pharisee; the other, a tax collector.

"The Pharisee prayed with his head held high: 'Lord, I thank you that I am not like other men, who are unjust and sinners, just like that tax collector praying over there. Twice a week I fast, and I always give a portion of my money to the poor.'

"The tax collector, some distance away from the Pharisee, did not dare to lift even his eyes to heaven. He beat his fists against his chest and cried out, 'Lord, I know I am a sinner. Have mercy on me!'

"I can tell you this: The tax collector went home and knew that he had prayed. But the Pharisee did not know anything.

"He who assumes he is high and mighty will fall. He who makes himself humble will rise to the heights of heaven."

JESUS CONVERTS ZACCHAEUS THE TAX COLLECTOR

Luke 19

Jesus entered Jericho, where there was a man whose name was Zacchaeus. He was the chief tax collector, and he was very rich.

When this man learnt the path that Jesus was taking, he climbed into a sycamore tree so that he would be able to see Jesus over the crowd.

When Jesus passed by the sycamore tree, he looked up and said, "Hurry down from that tree, Zacchaeus, for today I must stay in your house."

The tax collector quickly climbed down the tree and went home to welcome Jesus. This did not please the people. They thought Jesus was eating with a sinner.

In his house, Zacchaeus explained himself to Jesus. He said, "Half of my money I give to the poor. If I ever feel that I have done someone a wrong turn, I make sure they get back four times what they deserve."

Then Jesus said, "Today you and your household have been saved. You are truly a son of Abraham. The Son of man is here to save those who might otherwise have been lost."

Luke 10

JESUS IN THE HOUSE OF MARTHA AND MARY

On his way to Jerusalem, Jesus stopped in a village where he was welcomed into the house of a woman called Martha. Martha had a sister whose name was Mary. Jesus spoke, and both sisters sat at his feet. But then Martha started to prepare food, and she said to Jesus, "Lord, does it not bother you that I am preparing food while my sister sits with you? Tell her to come and help me."

But Jesus replied, "Martha, you take care of the food. Your sister, Mary, has chosen what is most important. You cannot take that away from her. She must be the way she is."

John 11

THE RESURRECTION OF LAZARUS

Lazarus, the brother of Mary and Martha, became sick. The sisters sent word to Jesus: "Lord, your friend Lazarus is sick."

By the time Jesus returned to Judea, he learnt that his friend had been in his grave for four days. As soon as Martha heard that Jesus was coming, she ran to meet him, while Mary stayed in the house. And Martha said to Jesus, "Lord, I know that if you had been here, my brother would not have died. Even now I know that whatever you ask of God, it will be given."

Jesus said, "Your brother will live again."

Martha said, "I know he will live again in the resurrection on the last day."

Then Jesus said to her, "I am the resurrection, and I am life. He who believes in me, even in death, will live. And whoever believes in me will never die. Do you believe this?"

She said, "Yes, Lord, I believe you are the Christ, the Son of God, who has come into the world."

Then she went into the house and called her sister, Mary, and said, "The Master has come and is calling for you."

As soon as she heard these words, Mary hurried to Jesus. And the Jews who had come to the house to comfort Mary thought she was rushing off to weep at her brother's grave. They followed her.

Jesus was a short distance out of town, and it was here that Mary met him. She fell down at his feet, crying, "Lord, if you had been here, my brother would not have died!"

When Jesus saw her weeping, and saw the tears and sorrow of the Jews with her, he was troubled. He said, "Where have you put him?"

And they said, "Come and see."

Jesus reached the grave of his friend, and his heart was heavy. Lazarus was buried in a cave, and a stone blocked the entrance.

Jesus wept.

When the Jews saw this, they remarked how much Jesus must have loved Lazarus. Some of them even said, "Surely, this man who can make the blind see, could have kept him from dying?"

Jesus said, "Roll away the stone."

The stone was then rolled away from the entrance to the cave where Lazarus was laid. And Jesus lifted his eyes to heaven and said, "Father, I thank You for answering my prayer. I know You always listen to me. I say it because there are so many people here, and they will know that it is You who has sent me."

After Jesus had spoken in this way, he cried out in a loud voice, "Lazarus, come out!"

Then the man who had been dead emerged from the cave. And he was still wearing grave clothes and had a cloth over his face. Jesus said, "Take those things off him and let him go."

Many of the Jews, seeing what Jesus had done, believed in him at once. Others ran to tell the Pharisees what had happened.

THE ENEMIES OF JESUS PLOT HIS DEATH

John 11

The chief priests and Pharisees called a meeting to discuss Jesus. They said, "What shall we do? This man is performing miracles. If we leave him alone, the people will believe in him. And when this happens, the Romans will come, and we will lose our nation."

Caiaphas, who was high priest that year, said, "You do not understand anything. Have you not considered that it may be better that Jesus should die, so that a nation can survive? And I am not speaking only of our nation; his death will unite all the children of God who are scattered throughout the world."

From that day on, the council plotted to kill Jesus.

THE SUPPER AT BETHANY

John 12

Six days before Passover, Jesus went to Bethany. He stayed at the house of Martha and Mary, and Lazarus dined with them.

Then Mary took a pound of precious ointment, and she anointed the feet of Jesus and wiped them with her hair.

Then one of the disciples spoke. It was Judas Iscariot, Simon's son, who would later betray Jesus. He said, "This is a very expensive ointment. Why was it not sold for three hundred pence and the money given to the poor?"

Judas said this not because he cared for the poor, but because he was a thief. He carried the sack in which offerings for the poor were kept, and he often stole from it.

Jesus replied, "Leave her alone. She has saved this ointment so long for me now. There will always be poor people, but I will not always be with you."

ENTRY INTO JERUSALEM

Luke 19
Matthew 21
Mark 11

Jesus continued his journey. When he was approaching Bethphage, not far from Bethany and near the Mount of Olives, he sent two disciples on ahead of him. He told them, "Go into the village opposite. As you enter, you will see a donkey that has never been ridden before. Untie it and bring it back here."

So the two disciples left and found the donkey, just as Jesus said they would. They untied the animal, and the owner said, "Why are you taking my donkey?"

The disciples replied, "The Lord needs it." Then all was well. They

brought the donkey back to Jesus, and Jesus rode the animal. Wherever he went, the people threw their clothes before him; others cut down branches off the trees and spread them in his path to show their respect.

As Jesus descended from the Mount of Olives, all his followers raised their voices and praised God.

But some of the Pharisees in the crowd said to Jesus, "Master, tell your disciples to quieten down."

Jesus replied, "I tell you, if they were to be silent, the stones themselves would cry out!"

As he approached the city, he wept over it, saying, "If you knew those things which regard your peace! But all those things are now hidden. Days will come when you will be surrounded by your enemies. And after that, the city will fall and be as flat as the ground. And your children will perish with you, because you did not recognise the day of visitation."

They brought the donkey back to Jesus, and Jesus rode the animal. Wherever he went, the people threw their clothes before him; others cut down branches off the trees and spread them in his path to show their respect.

JESUS RIDS THE TEMPLE OF TRADERS

Luke 19
Matthew 21
Mark 11

Then Jesus went into the temple. And when he saw men buying and selling there, he ordered them out. He threw over their tables and chairs, crying out, "It is written, 'My house is a house of prayer,' but you have made it a den of thieves!"

THE WITHERED FIG TREE

One morning as Jesus went into the city, he became hungry. When he saw a fig tree on the way, he stopped by it. But the tree had no fruit, only leaves. Then Jesus said, "Let no fruit grow on you for ever." And at once the tree withered away.

When the disciples saw this, they were astonished and said, "The tree just withered away!"

Jesus said, "I say this to you: If you have faith and put aside your doubts, you can do even more than this. With faith, you may move mountains and throw them into the sea. If you believe, whatever you ask for in prayer will be answered."

THE GREEDY GRAPE GROWERS

One day while Jesus was teaching in the temple and preaching the gospels, the chief priests, the scribes, and the elders approached him. "Tell us," they said, "by what authority do you do the things you do? And who gave you this authority?"

He replied, "I will ask you one thing and get an answer. Did John baptise by God or by man?"

They were forced to consider this question carefully. They knew that if they said that John baptised by God, then Jesus would ask them why they had not believed in him. On the other hand, if they said that John baptised by man, the people would stone them to death, because the people considered John to be a prophet.

Finally, they answered Jesus that they did not know.

Then Jesus said, "And I cannot answer your question either."

Jesus went on to tell this parable:

"A man planted a vineyard. He rented the vineyard to some grape growers and travelled to a distant country.

"When the time for the harvest of the grapes drew near, he sent his servants to the vineyard so that they might receive their portion of the harvest. But the grape growers captured his servants. They beat one, killed another, and stoned a third.

"The owner of the property sent more servants, but they were treated in a similarly violent way. Finally, the owner sent his son to his property. He thought they would at least show respect for his son.

"But when the grape growers saw the owner's son, they thought, 'Here is the heir to the property! Let us kill him, and the vineyard will be ours!'

"And then they seized the young man, killed him, and dragged his body off the property."

Then Jesus asked his listeners what the owner of the vineyard would do to the grape growers when he arrived. Those who heard Jesus said, "The owner will kill those wicked men, and he will rent out his vineyard to different grape growers who will behave fairly."

Then Jesus said, "The kingdom of heaven will be taken from you and given to the nation that will produce fruit."

When the chief priests and Pharisees heard these words, they knew that Jesus was speaking about them. So they tried to capture Jesus, but the crowd round him was too thick.

GOD AND CAESAR

Matthew 22
Mark 12

The Pharisees still tried to trap Jesus by making him stumble in his words. They said to the Lord, "Master, we know you are truthful and preach the ways of God, but we have a question: Do you think it is lawful that we should pay tax to the Roman Caesar or not?"

Jesus knew that they were trying to trick him, so he said, "Why are you trying to trap me? Show me the money that you pay your taxes with."

Then the Pharisees brought Jesus a penny, and he held it up and asked, "Whose picture and handwriting are on it?"

At once they replied, "Caesar's."

Then Jesus said, "You must give to Caesar the things that belong to him, and you must give to God the things that belong to God."

THE WIDOW'S DONATION

Luke 21
Mark 12

Another time, Jesus saw rich men throwing money into the treasury that was for the general good of the nation.

He also saw a poor widow throw in two mites, or two small coins. Then he was moved to say, "This poor widow has given more than all the others put together. The others could easily afford what they gave, but this woman has given her last penny."

THE PARABLE OF THE UNWORTHY GUEST

Matthew 22

Jesus told another parable:

"The kingdom of heaven is like a king who prepared a wedding feast for his son. He instructed his servants to call those who were invited to the wedding. But they did not want to come.

"Then the king sent other servants. He said, 'Tell them that everything is ready for the feast. I have killed a whole ox and other animals. Tell them to come to the wedding.'

"But the guests were not interested in the invitation, and they went about their own lives—some to their farms, some to business. Others were ruthless and seized the king's servants and killed them.

"When the king learnt what had happened, he became very angry. He sent out his army, and they killed the murderers and burnt down their city.

"Afterwards, he said to his servants, 'The wedding is ready, but those who were invited were not worthy guests. Go then along the highways and invite the people you find there.'

"The servants went out and returned with enough people to provide the wedding with guests. And some of those invited were good people, and some bad.

"Then the king went to inspect his guests, and he found among them a man who was not wearing a wedding suit. The king said, 'My friend, how is it that you are not wearing a wedding suit?' The man did not answer.

"Then the king said to his servants, 'Bind him hand and foot, and throw him out into the darkness where there is much pain and torture.'

"For many are called, but few are chosen."

SIGNS OF CHRIST'S COMING

As Jesus left the temple, his disciples came to him and pointed out the construction of the building. But he said to them, "Do you see all that? I say this to you in truth: Not one stone of the building will be left. All of it will be pulled down."

Then he went up the Mount of Olives and sat down there. The disciples came to him in private and asked, "When will these things happen? What will be the sign of your coming and the end of the world?"

And Jesus said, "Be careful that you are not tricked. Many will come, using my name, and they will deceive masses of people. You will hear of wars, and there will be rumors of wars. Do not be disturbed by this. Wars will happen, but it will not mean the end of the world. One country will fight another country, and there will be famines, plagues, and earthquakes in different places. These are just the beginnings of many sorrows.

"You will be captured, tortured, and killed. Many who speak my name will be hated by whole nations. There will be times of hatred and betrayal. False prophets will deceive many. But those who remain true up to the end will be saved. Then the gospel of the kingdom of heaven will be preached throughout the world, and the end will come."

THE COMING OF THE SON OF MAN

"Then you will see the Son of man on a cloud, and he will come in power and great glory. And he will send his angels to call in his Chosen People from places throughout the world. Take care, since you do not know which day the Lord will come! Think of this: If the owner of a house knew at what time thieves were going to rob his house, he would certainly not leave his house empty. And you too must always be ready, for the Son of man will come when he is least expected."

THE PARABLE OF THE WISE AND FOOLISH VIRGINS

"The kingdom of heaven is like ten virgins who took their lamps and went out to meet a bridegroom. Five were wise, and five were foolish.

"Those who were foolish took their lamps, but they took no oil to fill them with.

"But those who were wise took jars of oil to refill their lamps.

"The bridegroom was late, and all the virgins fell asleep. Then at midnight, the virgins awoke with a start, for the bridegroom was on his way, and they needed to hurry to meet him. They made their lamps ready, but the foolish virgins realised that they had no more oil to light their lamps. They asked the wise virgins for oil, but they were refused. The wise virgins said, 'We cannot give you oil. If we do, we will have none left to light our way to the bridegroom. You must go and buy oil from those who sell it.'

"While the foolish virgins went to buy oil, the wise virgins met the bridegroom and were escorted to his house, and the door was shut.

Opposite: When they were eating, Jesus took the bread. Then having blessed it, he broke it and handed it to his disciples, saying, "Take this and eat it. This is my body."

"Later, after they had bought oil, the foolish virgins arrived at the door of the house and called out to be let in. But the householder replied that he did not know who they were.

"So, be advised! You do not know the day or the hour when the Son of man will come. You must always be prepared."

THE PARABLE OF THE WORTHLESS SERVANT

"The kingdom of heaven is also like a man who was about to depart for a distant country. Before he left, he called a meeting of all his servants. Then he divided his talents, or goods, among them. To one, he gave five talents; to another, two; to another, one. Each received something depending on his skill. After he had done this, the man went abroad.

"The servant who had received five talents went and traded with them, and made five more talents. And the one who had received two talents also managed to double his money. But he who had received only one talent buried the money in the earth.

"After some time, the lord of the household returned and called his servants to him. He wanted to know what they had done with the money they had received. The one who had received five talents told his lord, 'You gave me five talents, and I have made another five talents out of it.'

"Then the lord replied, 'Well done! You are a good and faithful servant. You have been faithful over this little amount, and I will now make you ruler of a lot more. You have brought me much joy.'

"The servant who had received two talents appeared before his lord and explained how he had turned the two into four. And once again, the lord was pleased and gave this servant more power in his household.

"Then he who had received one talent came before his lord and said, 'Master, I know you are a hard man who finds money where there is none. For this reason I was afraid. I hid my talent in the earth, and there it remains for you to this day.'

"The lord answered, 'You are a wicked and lazy servant! You knew I find money where there is none. Therefore, you ought to have invested your talent, for this would have pleased me. Take that talent, and give it to the servant who now has ten.

" 'And remember this: Everyone who has something will receive more. He who has nothing will receive less than nothing.' "

THE DAY OF JUDGEMENT

"When the Son of man comes in all his glory with his angels, he will sit on his throne of glory. And all the countries of the world will gather before him, and he will separate them, one from the other, as a shepherd separates his sheep from his goats. He will put the sheep on his right and the goats on his left.

"Then the king will say to those on his right, 'Step forwards, you whom my Father has blessed. The kingdom belongs to you. When I was hungry, you gave me something to eat. When I was thirsty, you gave me water. I was a stranger, and you welcomed me into your house. I had no clothes, and you found me some. I was sick, and you visited me. I was thrown into prison, and you found me there.'

"Then the righteous were confused. They did not think that they had seen the Lord, fed and clothed him, and given him something to drink. They did not think that they had seen him as a stranger, taken him in, and visited him when he was sick or in prison.

"But the king answered them, 'Whenever you have behaved to the most unimportant of my people in these kind ways, it was as though you were looking after me personally.'

"Then he spoke sharply to those on his left, saying, 'Leave my sight! You are cursed. The everlasting fire and the devil and his angels await you.

" 'When I was hungry, you gave me no food. When I was thirsty, you gave me no drink. When I had nowhere to stay, you offered me no shelter. When I had no clothes, you found nothing for me. When I was sick or in prison, you did not visit me.'

"And the people on the left of the king were troubled and told the king that they had never seen him in the states of hardship that he had mentioned.

"He answered them, 'You showed no mercy or compassion for the ordinary people, and that was the same as turning your back on me. For this, you will be punished for ever, but the righteous will live for ever in peace.' "

JUDAS ISCARIOT
Matthew 26

Then the chief priests and the elders of the people met in the palace of Caiaphas, the high priest. They discussed ways of secretly trapping Jesus and killing him.

One of the twelve apostles, Judas Iscariot, went to this meeting. He asked the high priest, "What will you give me if I trap Jesus for you?"

He was promised thirty pieces of silver, and from then on Judas looked for a chance to betray Jesus.

THE LAST SUPPER
John 13

Before the celebration of Passover, Jesus knew that he would soon die. He knew he would leave this world for his Father's kingdom.

When the feast was over, the devil entered the heart of Judas Iscariot, the son of Simon. He would betray Jesus as soon as he could.

Jesus left the supper table and put a towel round himself. Then he poured water into a basin, washed his disciples' feet, and dried them with the towel.

When he came to Simon Peter, Peter asked, "Lord, is it right that you are washing my feet?"

Jesus answered him, "You do not understand what I am doing now. But you will understand later."

Peter said, "You should never wash my feet."

But Jesus replied, "If I do not wash your feet, you have nothing to do with me."

Then Peter said, "If that is so, then my hands and head as well as my feet should be washed."

Jesus said, "That is not necessary. You are clean. But not everyone is clean."

And Jesus was referring to the one who would betray him.

After he had washed the feet of the disciples, he sat down again.

He said, "Do you know what I have done? You call me Lord and Master, and you are right to do so, because that is who I am. If your Lord and Master can wash your feet, then surely you ought to be able to do this for each other. I have done this as an example of how you should behave towards one another.

"Let me say this to you: A servant is not greater than his master. I am not greater than my Father who sent me.

"If you know these things and put them into practice, you will be happy."

Matthew 26
Mark 14
John 13

THE TRAITOR IS UNMASKED

When Jesus had finished speaking, he became troubled in spirit and said to his disciples, "I must tell you the truth: One of you will betray me."

Then they looked at one another and wondered which of them was the traitor. "Is it me, Lord?" they asked.

Then Jesus said, "It is he to whom I shall give a piece of moistened bread."

Having said this, Jesus took a piece of bread, dipped it in wine, and gave it to Judas Iscariot. And at that very moment, Satan entered into the heart of this disciple.

Jesus said to him, "What you do, do quickly!"

But none of those at the table understood what Jesus meant with these words. But Judas understood. He took the piece of bread and left immediately. He went out into the darkness of the night.

Matthew 26
Mark 14

THE LORD'S SUPPER

When they were eating, Jesus took the bread. Then having blessed it, he broke it and handed it to his disciples, saying, "Take this and eat it. This is my body."

After they had eaten, Jesus took a cup of wine. He gave thanks and blessed it with these words: "Drink this. This is my blood of the new testament, which is shed to forgive sins."

John 13

JESUS SAYS FAREWELL TO HIS DISCIPLES

After Judas had left, Jesus said, "My children, I am with you for a short time. You will look for me, but as I told the Jews, where I am going, you cannot follow me.

"I have a new commandment for you, and it is this: Love one another as I have loved you. If you love one another, people will know that you are my disciples.

"There is no greater gesture of love than giving up your own life for a friend. If you do as I ask, you are my friends."

Then Peter asked, "Master, where are you going?"

And Jesus replied, "You cannot follow me where I am going now, but you will follow me later."

But Peter continued, "Why can't I follow you now, Master? I will give my life for you."

Jesus said, "You say you will give your life for me, but listen to me now! Tonight, even before the cock crows, you will deny that you know me three times."

THE GARDEN OF GETHSEMANE

Matthew 26
Luke 22

Then Jesus went with his apostles to the Mount of Olives, and here he told them, "Tonight, because of me, you will all be disgraced."

But Peter said, "Even if all men are disgraced because of you, I will not be one of them!"

Jesus said, "This very night before the cock crows, you will deny me three times."

Peter replied, "Even if I have to die with you, I will not deny you."

And all the disciples said the same thing.

Then Jesus went with them to a place known as the Garden of Gethsemane. Here he told his disciples, "Sit here. I am going on a little farther to pray."

Jesus went with Peter and the two sons of Zebedee. And Jesus felt full of sadness, and his heart was heavy. He said to the three apostles, "My soul is dying of sadness. Stay here and watch with me."

JESUS PRAYS

Matthew 26
Luke 22
Mark 14

Then Jesus went on a few steps and lay face down on the earth. He prayed, saying, "Father, if it is possible, let this cup pass me by. However, it must not be as I wish but as You desire."

He went back to his disciples. Finding them asleep, he woke Peter and said, "Could you not stay awake for one hour with me? Keep watch, and pray that you do not enter into temptation. The spirit may be willing, but the flesh is weak."

And he went away a second time and prayed, saying, "Father, if I must drink from this cup, I will. Let Your will be done."

Then Jesus went back to his disciples and found them fast asleep.

He left them for the third time and prayed, using the same words. Then he went back to his disciples and said, "Sleep on now; take your rest. The hour is at hand when the Son of man is betrayed and delivered into the hands of the sinners."

Then he said, "Get up now. It is time. He who will betray me is coming."

JUDAS BETRAYS JESUS

Matthew 26
Luke 22
Mark 14

Even as Jesus spoke, Judas Iscariot, one of the twelve apostles, appeared. He was not alone but was surrounded by men with swords and clubs. This force of men had been sent by the chief priests and elders of the people.

Judas, who was to betray Jesus, had told these men that the man he kissed would be the man they must capture.

Then Judas went up to Jesus and kissed him on the cheek, saying, "Greetings, Master."

And Jesus said to him, "Judas, do you betray the Son of man with a kiss?"

Then the armed men seized Jesus. Peter drew a sword and cut off the ear of one of the high priest's servants. But Jesus said, "Put away your sword. Those who live by using a sword will in the end die by using it. Do you not know that even now I can pray to my Father, and He can send forth twelve legions of angels? But if I do this, how would the Scriptures be fulfilled as they must be?"

Then all the disciples abandoned Jesus and ran away.

John 18
Luke 22
Mark 14

PETER DENIES JESUS

Then those who had seized Jesus took him to the high priest, Caiaphas. Scribes and elders of the people were also present.

Peter had followed Jesus at a distance. He went into the courtyard of the high priest and sat down with the servants.

The chief priests and those gathered there were looking for ways in which they might bring charges against Jesus. If they could do this, then they could condemn him to death. But they could find no way of trapping Jesus with lies, although many tried. At last two men came forwards and said, "Yes, that is the one! He said he could destroy the Temple of God and build it up again in three days."

The high priest rose to his feet and said to Jesus, "Have you nothing to say against these serious charges?"

But Jesus kept silent.

Then Caiaphas, the high priest, said, "I command you in the name of the living God to tell us if you are the Christ, the Son of God."

Jesus said, "It is as you have said. I do not need to speak more about it. Soon you will see the Son of man seated on the right of the Almighty, and he will be riding on the clouds in the sky."

At these words, the high priest ripped his own clothes in a fit of annoyance. He cried, "He has spoken blasphemy! Why should we investigate him any further? You have heard his blasphemy with your own ears! What do you think?"

And they replied, "He deserves to die!"

Then they spat in his face, and kicked and punched him. They yelled things like, "Prophesy to us now, Christ! Who is hitting you now?"

While this was happening, Peter was seated just outside by the door with the servants. One of the maids, seeing Peter, said to him, "Aren't you one of the disciples of this man?"

Peter replied, "No, I have nothing to do with him."

It grew cold. The servants and guards lit a fire and stood round it, warming themselves. Peter warmed himself by the fire, too. Then other men asked him, "Surely you are one of those followers of Jesus?"

Peter denied it. But one of the servants of the high priest was the father of the man whose ear had been cut off in the Garden of Gethsemane. And it had been Peter who had done this. Now this servant said, "Didn't I see you in the Garden of Gethsemane?"

Once again Peter denied this. And at that moment the crow of the cock was heard. Then the Lord turned and looked at Peter, and Peter remembered the words of Jesus:

"Before the cock crows, you will deny that you know me three times."

Then Peter left that place and wept bitterly.

Opposite: Then Pilate saw he was getting nowhere. The crowd was becoming noisier and more restless. He asked for a bowl of water to be brought to him. Then he washed his hands in front of the crowd and said, "I am innocent of the shedding of this innocent man's blood. His death is your doing."

JUDAS KILLS HIMSELF

Meanwhile, Judas Iscariot, seeing that Jesus had been condemned, repented. He went back to the chief priest and elders with the thirty pieces of silver that he had received from them when he betrayed Jesus. He said, "I have sinned! I have betrayed an innocent man! I have blood on my hands!"

But they replied, "That is not our concern."

Then Judas left them. He took the money with him and threw it into the temple. He went off to a lonely spot and hanged himself.

The chief priests picked up the money and said, "We cannot put this money into the treasury, because it is blood money."

They discussed the matter and came up with the idea that they would buy a field from a potter and use this field to bury foreigners.

This field became known as the Field of Blood.

JESUS IS PUT ON TRIAL

In the morning the chief priests and the elders of the people decided to condemn Jesus to death. They tied him up and led him to Pontius Pilate, who was the Roman governor in that district.

Pilate looked at them and asked, "What are you charging this man with?"

And they replied, "If he weren't a criminal, we wouldn't have brought him to you."

To this, Pilate replied, "Take him away and judge him for yourselves."

The Jews said, "We do not have the power to put a man to death."

Pilate went back into his courtroom and ordered Jesus to be brought in for questioning.

Pilate asked him first of all, "Are you the King of the Jews?"

And Jesus said, "My kingdom is not in this world. If it were, my guards would have fought for me long before I was handed over to the Jews. My kingdom is not here."

"But you are a king, then?" asked Pilate.

Jesus said, "It is as you say: I am a king. I was born and came into this world to show people the truth. Whoever is on the side of truth hears my voice."

"What is truth?" asked Pilate.

And after he had asked this question, Pilate went outside to where the Jews were waiting. He said, "I can find nothing wrong with this man. I know it is a custom to release a condemned man at Passover. Do you want me to release Jesus?"

When the chief priests and elders heard Pilate speak in this way, they made signs to the people. They told them to ask for the release of Barabbas, who was a robber and murderer. They said Jesus should be put to death. The voices of the people rose: "Don't release Jesus! Give us Barabbas!"

Pilate was still uncertain, and he asked the people grouped there, "Whom do you want me to set free? Barabbas or Jesus, who calls himself the Christ?"

He knew they had brought Jesus to him merely out of envy and spite. Not only this, but when he was sitting at the tribunal, he received a message from his wife. This message read: "I had a dream about him which has greatly upset me. Jesus is innocent. Do him no harm."

Still the people cried, "Crucify him!"

Pilate asked, "But what wrong has he done?"

But the people shouted even louder, "Crucify him!"

Then Pilate saw he was getting nowhere. The crowd was becoming noisier and more restless. He asked for a bowl of water to be brought to him. Then he washed his hands in front of the crowd and said, "I am innocent of the shedding of this innocent man's blood. His death is your doing."

And once again the voices of the people rose as one: "His blood is on us and our children!"

Then Pilate released Barabbas. Jesus was beaten and whipped, and given to the soldiers to be crucified.

Pilate's soldiers led Jesus into the courtyard. There, they stripped him of his clothes and wrapped a scarlet cloak around him. They put a crown of thorns on his head and a reed in his right hand. They started making fun of Jesus, calling out things like, "Greetings, King of the Jews!" They spat at him. They mocked Jesus by bowing down before him and pretending to worship him.

When they grew bored with making fun of him, they took away the scarlet cloak and gave him back his clothes. Then they led him outside to be crucified.

DEATH AND RESURRECTION

Luke 23
Mark 15
Matthew 27

JESUS IS CRUCIFIED

There was a man from the country outside the courtyard. His name was Simon, and he was a Cyrenian. The Roman soldiers made him carry the cross of Jesus.

A huge crowd followed Jesus. Women lamented and wailed for him. There were two other men, who were criminals, also being taken to be crucified at the same time as Jesus.

When they reached a place called Golgotha, which means "place of a skull," they gave Jesus a drink of vinegar mixed with gall. He tasted it but would not drink it.

Then they crucified him and the other two men—one on his right and one on his left.

Jesus said, "Father, forgive them, for they know not what they do."

John 19
Luke 23
Mark 15
Matthew 27

THE SOLDIERS SHARE THE CLOTHES OF JESUS

After they had crucified Jesus, the soldiers took his clothes and divided them into four piles. Each soldier received a pile.

His cloak could not be shared without tearing it to pieces, so they drew lots to decide who should have it.

Thus, the words of the holy Scriptures came true: "They have shared out my clothes and have drawn lots for my cloak."

Gathered round the cross of Jesus were his mother; his mother's sister; Mary, wife of Cleophas; and Mary Magdalene.

When Jesus saw his mother and a disciple he loved, he said, "Woman, now you see your son!" To the disciple he said, "This is your mother!" And after that the disciple took Mary to stay in his house.

Luke 23
Mark 15
Matthew 27
John 19

THE CROWD MOCKS JESUS

The people gathered at the foot of the cross and looked up at him. But there were those who mocked him and shook their heads, saying, "Hey, you who can destroy the temple and rebuild it again in three days! Save yourself now! Come down from that cross!"

The chief priests and scribes also made fun of Jesus. They called out, "He saved others, but he could not save himself! If you are the Christ, the king of Israel, come down from the cross. Then we will see and believe! He trusted in God; let us see God save him now. God will do that much if He loves Jesus! He said himself, 'I am the Son of God.'"

Then, from the sixth hour to the ninth, darkness filled the earth. And towards the ninth hour, Jesus cried, "My God, my God, why have You forsaken me?"

After that, Jesus knew that everything was as it should be. What was written in the Scriptures had come to pass. He said, "I thirst."

There was a jug of vinegar at the foot of the cross. Someone standing nearby dipped a sponge in the vinegar and put it on the end of a long stick. He pushed the wet sponge up to Jesus' mouth and said, "Let us see if his God will come take him down."

Above the head of Jesus there was a notice written in Latin, Greek, and Hebrew, which read: THIS IS JESUS THE KING OF THE JEWS.

One of the criminals who was also being crucified spoke roughly to Jesus, saying, "If you are Christ, save yourself and us!"

But the other criminal said, "Do you not fear God? We deserve to be crucified for what we have done, but he is innocent." Then he said, "Jesus, remember me when you reign as King!"

And Jesus gave him this answer: "I will remember you. You will join me in paradise today."

THE DEATH OF JESUS

Luke 23
Mark 15
Matthew 27

Towards midday a darkness fell over the world. This lasted until three o'clock in the afternoon. Then Jesus cried out with a loud voice, "Father, I put my spirit into Your hands!"

After that, he said, "Everything has been done."

And after saying this, he lowered his head and died.

The curtain before the holiest place in the temple was torn in two. The earth trembled. Rocks sprang out of the earth. Graves opened, and holy bodies that were buried came to life.

When the Roman centurion who was present saw the trembling of the earth, he praised God and said, "This man really was the Son of God."

The others who were present at the crucifixion went home. And their hearts were heavy with great sorrow.

THE BURIAL

John 19
Mark 15
Luke 23
Mattthew 27

The Jews did not want the bodies to stay on the crosses during the Sabbath, since this was a holy day. So they asked Pilate to break the legs of those crucified, as was customary, and take the bodies down. The soldiers arrived and broke the legs of the two criminals who had been crucified with Jesus.

But they saw that Jesus was dead already, so they did not break his legs. One of the soldiers pierced Jesus with a spear, and blood and water came out of his side.

And all this happened as it had been written in the Scriptures: "A bone of his body shall not be broken. They will look on the man whom they have pierced."

When evening came, a good and honest man named Joseph arrived. He was also a disciple of Jesus, and from a Jewish town called Arimathea.

Joseph begged Pilate to let him have the body of Jesus, and Pilate gave him permission to take it away. Another good man, Nicodemus, helped Joseph. He brought a mixture of aloes and myrrh, weighing about a hundred pounds. This was for Jesus' body.

Together these men wrapped the body in linen clothes and used the spices to keep everything fresh. This was the usual way the Jews buried their dead.

There was a garden not far from where Jesus had been crucified. The garden was new and had not yet been used as a burial ground. It was here that Joseph and Nicodemus took the body of Jesus. The grave itself was made out of a rock. Jesus was laid inside, and a rock was used to seal the tomb.

The women who had come with Jesus from Galilee followed

There was a garden not far from where Jesus had been crucified. The garden was new and had not yet been used as a burial ground. It was here that Joseph and Nicodemus took the body of Jesus. The grave itself was made out of a rock. Jesus was laid inside, and a rock was used to seal the tomb.

Joseph and Nicodemus, and they saw the care taken with the body and noted the tomb where Jesus was laid.

Meanwhile, the chief priests and Pharisees went to see Pilate and said to him, "We have remembered what this imposter Jesus used to say when he was alive. He used to say that he would come back to life after three days. We ask you therefore to place a guard round the tomb. We do not want his disciples to go in the night and take away his body and then start saying things like, 'He has risen again!' "

Pilate did not want to be a part of any of this. He said, "If you want, you may station your own guard and keep watch over the tomb."

So the chief priests and Pharisees went to the tomb and sealed the stone that served as a door. They kept watch day and night. The guards never took their eyes off the place where Jesus was buried.

JESUS RISES FROM THE DEAD

Matthew 28
Luke 24
Mark 16
John 20

After the Sabbath, as dawn was breaking on the first day of the week, Mary Magdalene and the other Mary went to the tomb. As they approached the spot, the earth shook, and an angel of the Lord came down from heaven. The angel rolled back the stone and sat down upon it. His face was like lightning, and his clothes were white as snow.

When the guards saw the angel, they trembled with fear and ran away.

But the angel spoke softly to the women, saying, "Do not be afraid. I know you are looking for Jesus who was crucified. He is not here. He has risen, as he said he would. You may see the place where he lay. But go quickly, and tell his disciples that he has risen from the dead. Tell them the Lord has gone on ahead of them into Galilee, and it is there that they will see him."

Then the two women quickly left the tomb and ran to tell the disciples the news. And in their hearts they felt a mixture of fear and joy.

But as they ran to tell the news, Jesus met them and greeted them. At once they fell at his feet and worshipped him. Then Jesus said again, "Do not be afraid. Go and tell my disciples that I will see them in Galilee."

Opposite: Jesus met them and greeted them. At once they fell at his feet and worshipped him. Then Jesus said again, "Do not be afraid. Go and tell my disciples that I will see them in Galilee."

THE APPEARANCES
OF JESUS

Luke 24

THE APPEARANCE AT EMMAUS

On that same day, two disciples were travelling to a village called Emmaus. The village was about sixty furlongs from Jerusalem. As the two walked, they discussed the many things that had happened over the last few days. While they were talking, they were joined by a third person. It was Jesus himself, but they did not recognise him. He said to the disciples, "What are these things that you are discussing as you walk, and why are you so sad?"

One of them, whose name was Cleopas, answered, "You must be the only stranger in Jerusalem who does not know what has been happening for the last few days."

And Jesus said, "What things are you talking about?"

They replied, "We are talking about Jesus of Nazareth. He was a powerful prophet, both in what he did and in what he said. He spoke for God and for the people. But the chief priests and our rulers condemned him to death, and he was crucified. We thought he would free Israel, but it is now the third day since he left us.

Then Jesus went to Thomas and said, "Look at my hands and put your fingers in my wounds. Touch my side and feel the wound. Now, you may believe."

"Not only that, but certain women whom we know have astonished us. They were at his tomb early this morning, but they didn't find his body. They came from that place, saying that an angel had told them that Jesus had risen from the dead. Then some of us went to the grave, and everything was just as the women had said: The body was not there!"

Then Jesus said, "Oh, you are a pair of fools! And your hearts are slow to believe everything the prophets have predicted! Are you saying Christ should not have gone through these things? Are you saying he should not reign in glory now?"

Then Jesus preached to the two disciples. Beginning with Moses, he mentioned all the prophets and how they related to the life of Christ.

By now they were near the village, and it seemed as though Jesus were travelling farther. They said, "It is evening; the day is gone. Stay with us." And Jesus stayed in their house.

They sat down to eat at their table. Jesus took the bread, blessed it, broke it, and gave it to them.

Suddenly their eyes opened as though they had been sealed. They recognised Jesus, and a moment later, he disappeared from their sight.

Then they said to each other, "When he was speaking to us on the road, I felt as though my heart were on fire! He made the Scriptures come alive!"

They went back immediately to Jerusalem and found the eleven apostles and their friends there. They told them what had happened.

"The Lord has risen! He appeared to Simon!"

They told the story of their journey on the road and the stranger who had joined them. They said that it was only when he broke bread that they recognised him.

Luke 24
John 20

JESUS APPEARS TO THE APOSTLES

While the two disciples were telling their story, Jesus himself appeared in the middle of the group, and said, "Peace be with you!"

The apostles were terrified. They thought they had seen a ghost. But Jesus said, "Why are you so disturbed? Why are there doubts in your hearts? Look at my hands and feet! You can see it is I. Touch me. A ghost has no flesh and bones as I have."

And Jesus showed them his hands and feet, and they were overcome with joy. They could hardly believe their eyes! Then Jesus asked them, "Do you have food here?" And they gave him a piece of broiled fish and a honeycomb. And Jesus sat with them and ate.

Then Jesus said to them, "The holy Scriptures say that Christ would suffer death and that on the third day he would rise again. The Scriptures also say that the gospel of the forgiveness of sins would be preached throughout the world, beginning in Jerusalem. You are here to witness this. And I will send you everything my Father has promised. You will stay in the city until you receive the power from heaven."

Thomas was not present when Jesus appeared. When he joined them, the apostles told him what had happened. They cried, "We have seen the Lord!"

But Thomas replied, "Unless I can see the mark of the nails in his hands and see his side where the sword pierced him, I will not believe it!"

It was eight days later that Thomas found himself with the other apostles in the same house. The doors of the house were all locked, but Jesus entered and said to them, "Peace be with you!"

Then Jesus went to Thomas and said, "Look at my hands and put your fingers in my wounds. Touch my side and feel the wound. Now, you may believe."

Thomas exclaimed, "O my Lord and my God!"

Then Jesus said to him, "Thomas, because you have seen, you believe. Happy are those who have not seen but still believe."

JESUS APPEARS BY THE SEA OF TIBERIAS

After this, Jesus appeared again by the sea of Tiberias. Peter had told the other disciples that he was going fishing, and the others had said they would come with him.

They pushed off in a boat and fished all night, but they caught nothing. In the morning, Jesus stood on the shore, but the disciples did not recognise him. He called out to them, "My children, do you have anything to eat?" And they told him they had nothing.

Then Jesus said, "If you throw your nets over the right-hand side of the boat, you will find fish."

The disciples followed this advice, and when they began to pull in the nets, it was impossible because the nets were so full.

John, the disciple whom Jesus loved, said, "That is the Lord!"

When Peter heard this, he threw off his clothes and jumped into the water, since he was so anxious to get back to shore. The others stayed on board, dragging the nets behind the boat.

When they reached dry land, they saw a fire. Fish were being cooked, and bread was set out.

Jesus said, "Bring some of the fish you have caught."

Peter pulled in the net, which was bulging with fish. But even though there were a hundred and fifty-three fish in the net, it did not break. Then Jesus said, "Come, let us eat!"

The disciples knew it was the Lord, and not one of them dared to ask him who he was.

Jesus took the bread and the fish, and he gave it to them.

THE ASCENSION

Jesus appeared to his disciples over a period of forty days. He spoke to them of things that had to do with the kingdom of God.

He told them not to leave Jerusalem, but to wait until everything his Father promised came true. He said, "John baptised you with water, but soon you will be baptised with the Holy Spirit. With this power, you will spread my word in Jerusalem, in Judea, and to the ends of the earth."

After Jesus had said this, he rose up into the sky. As they watched, a cloud received him and he was lost from sight.

While they were still staring into the sky, two men who were dressed all in white came to them and said, "Men of Galilee, why do you keep staring into the sky? This Jesus who has risen into heaven will come back to you one day from heaven."

Then the disciples worshipped the Lord and went back to Jerusalem, full of joy.

THE COMING OF
THE HOLY SPIRIT

Acts 2

PENTECOST

When the day of Pentecost arrived, the apostles were together in the same place. Suddenly a sound like a great wind came out of heaven and filled the house in which they were sitting.

Then twisting tongues, which looked as though they were made of fire, fell upon the apostles. The Holy Spirit entered them, and they began to speak in many languages.

At this time, there were devout Jews staying in Jerusalem who had come from all over the world. When these men met those who had received the gift of the Holy Spirit, they were amazed. The apostles spoke to them in their own languages!

Then Peter said to them in a strong voice, "Men of Israel, listen to me now! Jesus of Nazareth was sent to you by God. He was known for his miracles and wonderful actions. But what did you do? You took him and nailed him to a cross! But God has caused His Son to rise from the dead, and we are here to witness that truth. We have received the Holy Spirit that God promised us. He has given it to us, as you may now see and hear. From now on, let all of Israel know that God is the Lord, and Jesus is the Christ whom you crucified!"

When the people present heard these words, their hearts were moved. They said to Peter and the other apostles, "Brothers, what must we do?"

And Peter told them, "Repent, and each one of you will be baptised in the name of Jesus Christ. Ask for your sins to be forgiven, and you will receive the gift of the Holy Spirit."

That day, three thousand people were baptised in the name of Jesus Christ.

These people followed the teachings of the apostles. They loved one another, they shared their bread together, and they said the prayers.

They praised God and lived peacefully with their neighbours. And the power of the church grew daily, and those who were saved found mercy.

Acts 3

THE HEALING OF A LAME MAN

One day, Peter and John went to the temple to pray, because it was the ninth hour. At one of the gates of the temple known as Beautiful, there lay a man who was placed there daily. He had been crippled since birth and was forced to beg. When he saw Peter and John, he asked them for a few coins.

Peter and John stared at the man, and Peter said, "Look at us!"

The man looked, expecting to receive some money. Then Peter told him, "I have no gold or silver, but what I have I will give to you. In the name of Jesus Christ of Nazareth, stand up and walk!"

Peter extended his right hand to the crippled man and lifted him to his feet. At once, strength poured into the man's feet and ankles, and

Opposite: Then twisting tongues, which looked as though they were made of fire, fell upon the apostles. The Holy Spirit entered them, and they began to speak in many languages.

the man jumped for joy. He leapt in the air, he walked, he praised God, and then he went into the temple with the apostles.

And the people who saw him walking praised God. They recognised the man who had always sat begging at the gate of the temple known as Beautiful. He had been lame, but now he could walk. Such was the power of the Holy Spirit!

Acts 4-5

THE APOSTLES ARE ARRESTED

The apostles spoke to the people, but the priests, the captains of the temple, and the Sadducees watched and disapproved. These groups did not like that the apostles were preaching that Christ had risen from the dead. They arrested them and put them in prison for the night.

However, many who had heard the words of the apostles believed them. That day, about five thousand people were converted to the ways of Christ.

The next day, the rulers, the elders, the scribes, the high priest Annas, Caiaphas, John, Alexander, and many more who wanted to stop the apostles met in a public place in Jerusalem to discuss the matter. They asked each other, "What are we going to do with these men? A miracle has taken place in this city, and we cannot deny it! Word of it, however, must not spread! We will order them to speak no more about Jesus Christ."

They called the apostles to them and ordered them to stop preaching the word of Jesus.

But Peter and John replied, "Should we listen to you or to God? We are speaking about the things we have seen and heard."

The apostles were again threatened, but they were released. Those who wanted to stop the apostles could find no real reason to punish them. Besides, they feared the feelings of the crowd, which praised God for His glorious deeds.

The apostles went on to perform many miracles, and more and more people converted to the ways of Christ.

The sick were carried outside and into the streets on beds and stretchers. People thought Peter was so holy that if only his shadow fell over them, they would be cured!

The sick and those who were disturbed in their minds gathered in towns and villages close to Jerusalem, and the apostles cured them.

For this reason, the high priests and others, such as the Sadducees, threw them in prison once more.

Acts 5

THE APOSTLES ARE SET FREE

But an angel of the Lord opened the doors of the prison during the night and set the apostles free. And he told them, "Go into the temple and preach to the people; tell them the truth about life."

When the apostles heard these words, they went to the temple and taught.

Meanwhile, the high priest, the council, and the senate of the children of Israel met. They sent officers to the prison to get the prisoners. But they did not find the apostles, and they hurried back to make their report, saying, "The prison looked normal. All doors were locked, and

Opposite: Then Peter told him, "I have no gold or silver, but what I have I will give to you. In the name of Jesus Christ of Nazareth, stand up and walk!"

the guards were stationed outside. But when we actually went into the prison cell, there was no one there!"

The high priest, the captain of the temple, and the chief priests did not know what to think. Then an officer came running in with news: "The men you put in prison are preaching in the temple, come and see!"

The captain went with a number of his men and brought the apostles back to the council. They were careful not to hurt the apostles, because they feared that the people might stone them if they did.

The high priest lost no time in telling them what was on his mind. He said, "Did I not tell you that you are not allowed to teach in the name of Jesus Christ? Now look what you have done! You have filled Jerusalem with his teachings! Are you trying to bring this man's blood upon us?"

Then Peter answered, "We must obey God rather than men. The God of our fathers has brought Jesus back to life. The same man you nailed to a cross, God has raised from the dead to be a prince and the Saviour. Through him, Israel may ask for mercy, and her sins will be forgiven. We are here to witness these things, and so is the Holy Spirit, which God has given to those who obey Him."

This was not what the high priest and his company wanted to hear. Anger blazed in their hearts, and they at once discussed how they could murder the apostles.

Then a Pharisee named Gamaliel, who was a member of the council and a doctor of law, rose to his feet. This man was respected by the people, and the assembly listened closely to what he had to say. Gamaliel said, "We should not be concerned with these men. We should let them go. If their teachings and actions come from themselves, they will not last long. But if their teachings and actions come from God, they will last for ever, and you will not be able to destroy them. Do not run the risk of fighting against God!"

The assembly saw the wisdom in Gamaliel's words, and they agreed to let the apostles go. Then the apostles were brought out and beaten, and they were told not to preach the word of Jesus Christ any more. Then they were set free.

The apostles were full of joy that they had suffered in the name of Christ. Every day they preached in the temple and taught in the houses of the people. They did not stop preaching in the name of Jesus Christ.

Acts 6-7

STEPHEN, THE FIRST MARTYR

To help them with their everyday affairs, the apostles chose seven men. Among these was a man named Stephen. He was full of faith, and the Holy Spirit shone in him.

Stephen performed great wonders and miracles for the people. When words of his deeds came to the attention of certain members of the synagogue, they were jealous of him and tried to find fault in what he did and said. But Stephen behaved and spoke to them with such wisdom and spirit that they could find no fault in him. So they made a plan.

They paid some men to lie and say that Stephen had said bad things about Moses and God. They stirred up the people against Stephen. Then the elders ordered Stephen to be brought before the council. False witnesses were produced, and these bribed men said, "This man is always blaspheming and saying things against the law. Once we heard him say that Jesus of Nazareth will destroy this place and change the way of life that we inherited from Moses!"

And those who sat in the council looked at Stephen while these things were said. And the face of Stephen shone like an angel.

Being filled with the Holy Spirit, he looked up into heaven and saw Jesus standing on the right side of God. Stephen said, "I see the heavens open and the Son of man standing on the right side of God."

When the council and the elders heard Stephen speak like this, they put their hands to their ears so that they would not have to hear his words. Others took hold of him and dragged him out of the town and stoned him to death. Some men threw his clothes to a young man named Saul.

While Stephen was being stoned, he prayed aloud, "Lord Jesus, receive my spirit!"

Then he fell to his knees and cried out in a firm voice, "Lord, forgive them this sin!"

These were the last words of Stephen before he died.

PETER AND PAUL

Saul had been active in bringing about the death of Stephen. He also persecuted those who belonged to the church in Jerusalem. He threatened to kill those who followed the teachings of Christ.

One day, Saul went to the high priest and asked him for his approval to investigate the synagogues of Damascus. He told the priest that if he found any men or women speaking of Christ there, he would arrest them and send them in chains back to Jerusalem.

Saul was given his letters of authority, and he set off on the road to Damascus. When he was not far from this city, a light suddenly came from the sky and wrapped him in its brilliance.

Saul fell to the ground, and he heard a voice saying, "Saul, Saul, why are you persecuting me?"

And he asked, "Who are you, Lord?"

The Lord said, "I am Jesus, the one you are persecuting."

Then Saul trembled, but he found words to ask, "Lord, what must I do?"

And the Lord replied, "Stand up and go into the city, and there you will find out."

The men who were travelling with Saul were speechless because they had heard a voice but had seen no man.

Saul got up, but when he opened his eyes, he could see nothing. He was blind and had to be led by the hand into Damascus. He stayed in the city for three days. During this time he neither saw anything nor ate or drank anything.

In Damascus there was a disciple whose name was Ananias. The Lord appeared to him in a dream and said, "Ananias!"

And the disciple answered, "I am here, Lord."

Then the Lord said, "Go into the town and find a street known as Straight. There you will find the house of Judas. Ask for a man named Saul of Tarsus. He is there, and he is praying. He has seen a man named Ananias in a vision, and you are this man who will restore his sight."

Ananias said to the Lord, "Master, I have heard of this man and how he has persecuted the faithful people in Jerusalem. Now he has the approval of the high priest to persecute anyone in Damascus who speaks your name!"

But the Lord replied, "Go at once. I have chosen this man to bring my name before the nations of the world, before their kings, and before the children of Israel. And I will show him everything he must suffer in my name."

Ananias followed the Lord's instructions and found Saul in a house in the street called Straight. He put his hands on Saul and said, "Saul, my brother, the Lord Jesus has sent me to restore your sight and to see that you are filled with the Holy Spirit."

Then it was as if scales fell from Saul's eyes, for he could suddenly see again. He got up from his bed and was baptised.

He stayed with the disciples in Damascus. But he was now a changed man. He went daily to preach in the synagogues, and he told the people that Jesus was the Son of God.

One day, Saul went to the high priest and asked him for his approval to investigate the synagogues of Damascus. He told the priest that if he found any men or women speaking of Christ there, he would arrest them and send them in chains back to Jerusalem.

Saul was given his letters of authority, and he set off on the road to Damascus. When he was not far from this city, a light suddenly came from the sky and wrapped him in its brilliance.

After Saul's baptism, certain Jews decided to kill him. But their plan reached the ears of Saul and the disciples. As the city was well guarded, they made their escape by night. Saul himself was lowered down the city wall in a basket.

He made his way back to Jerusalem, where he tried to join the disciples. But Saul was still feared. They did not believe he was a true disciple.

Seeing the way things were, Barnabas took Saul to the apostles and told them how Saul had been walking on the road to Damascus when the voice of the Lord spoke to him and the light blinded him. Barnabas pointed out that Saul had preached boldly in the synagogues of Damascus and that he had preached in the name of Jesus Christ.

So Saul became one of the disciples in Jerusalem and was called Paul. Wherever he went, he spoke publicly in the name of Jesus. He spoke frankly with the Jews who were Grecians. But they did not like what Saul said and looked for ways to murder him. When the disciples learnt that Saul was in danger, they sent him to Caesarea and then on to Tarsus. Then the churches entered a time of peace that spread into Judea, Galilee, and Samaria. The people respected the Lord and found comfort in the Holy Spirit.

THE TEACHINGS OF PETER

Acts 9-10

There was a man in Caesarea named Cornelius who was a Roman centurion and a religious man, as was all his household. He gave alms to the poor and always prayed to God.

One day, at about the ninth hour, Cornelius had a vision in which he saw an angel of the Lord coming towards him and heard it calling his name. Cornelius was afraid, but he answered, "What do you want from me, Lord?"

The angel said, "God has heard your prayers and has seen how you give alms to the poor. Now the Lord wants you to send men to Joppa. There they will find a man named Simon, whose name is also Peter. He is staying in a house by the sea with Simon, a tanner of leather."

As soon as the angel disappeared, Cornelius summoned two of his servants and a devout and faithful soldier. He told them everything, and they set out for Joppa.

Finally, this group of three reached the house of Simon, and Peter came out to meet them. He said, "I am the man you are looking for. Why have you come here?"

They replied, "The centurion Cornelius is a just and God-fearing man. It was he who sent us. He was advised by an angel in a dream to send for you. He wishes that you visit his house, so that he can hear your words."

The following day, Peter went with the three men and some other Christians to Joppa.

PETER AND THE CENTURION

Acts 10

When they reached Caesarea the next day, they found Cornelius waiting for them. As soon as Cornelius saw Peter, he knelt down and worshipped him. But Peter gently pulled him to his feet, saying, "Stand up. I am only a man, the same as you."

They went into the house, where many guests were at the table. Then Peter said, "You know it is unlawful for a Jew to keep company with foreigners or to go into their houses. But I am here. God has shown me that I should not call any man foreign or unclean. That is the reason I came here as soon as you sent for me. Now I am here, and we are all of us in the sight of God. I am ready to listen to what the Lord has commanded you to tell me."

Then Cornelius replied, "Four days ago, when I was fasting and praying in my house, a man appeared. He was dressed in very bright clothing. He told me that God had heard my prayers and that God was pleased that I gave alms to the poor. He told me where you were living in Joppa and that I should send for you. He said you would speak to me. I did everything I was told, and you came immediately. Now we must hear from you what God wishes."

Then Peter said, "I see now that God does not just favour one people. I see that whoever respects God and lives an honest life will please Him. It does not matter what country he comes from."

Acts 12

PETER IS ARRESTED

It was about this time that King Herod was persecuting certain disciples of Jesus. James, the brother of John, was killed by a sword.

Herod saw that his violent behaviour and attitude to the church pleased some of the people. So he had Peter arrested and thrown into prison. But on the night he was taken, many prayed for Peter in the churches.

Herod was to judge Peter the next day. Outside the prison, guards were on duty.

Suddenly the angel of the Lord appeared. He woke Peter up and said, "Be quick! Get up!" The chains fell away from Peter's hands. He dressed himself and followed the angel, not knowing whether he was still asleep or awake. He left the soldiers and passed the guards at the door. When he came to the iron gate that led into the city, it opened as if by magic. Peter went out into the streets, and the angel left him.

Then Peter came to his senses. He knew that the Lord had sent an angel to free him from Herod. He was thinking about this when he came to the house of Mary, the mother of John, whose last name was Mark. Inside the house, many people were praying.

Peter knocked at the door, and a young woman named Rhoda went to answer it. She heard Peter's voice and recognised it, but she was so overcome with joy that she ran back into the house. She told everyone that Peter was waiting outside, but they did not believe her and called her mad.

Peter continued to knock on the door, and when at last a number of them went to open it, they saw Peter and were astonished. But Peter waved his hand and told them to remain silent. He explained to them that the Lord had freed him from prison.

At dawn, when the soldiers woke up, they were shocked that Peter was missing. They did not know how he could have escaped.

Herod was in a rage. He searched everywhere for Peter, but he could find no trace of him.

Meanwhile, Peter left Judea and went to Caesarea.

THE TRAVELS OF PAUL

BARNABAS AND PAUL

Acts 13

There was a church at Antioch where certain doctors and prophets were meeting. Among those present were Barnabas, Simeon (also called Niger), Lucius of Cyrene, Manaen (who had been brought up with Herod, the tetrarch), and Saul (who was also called Paul).

While they were fasting and praying, the Holy Spirit spoke to them, saying, "I have work for Barnabas and Paul."

After they had finished praying and fasting, Barnabas and Paul blessed the others and then left. Then Barnabas and Paul, who had been called by the Holy Spirit, went to Seleucia, and from there they took a ship to Cyprus.

THE FIRST JOURNEY OF PAUL

Acts 13-14

When they reached Cyprus, Paul and Barnabas spoke about God to the people. Then they travelled to Perga, which is in Pamphylia. From there they went to Antioch, in Pisidia. Arriving on the Sabbath, they went into the synagogue and sat down. The laws and the sayings of the prophets were read. Afterwards, Paul spoke to the people about Jesus, and about how he died and then rose again from the dead.

On the next Sabbath, almost the entire town came to hear Paul and Barnabas. The two men preached in the synagogues and in the streets. They spoke of Jesus to Jews and Gentiles, for as they said, "The Lord has told us that we must carry His message to all the nations of the world."

When Paul and Barnabas reached a place called Iconium, they went to the synagogue and found a huge crowd of Jews and Gentiles. But some of the Jews did not believe what they heard, and they stirred up the Gentiles against the apostles. The population of the town became divided. Some supported the Jews, others supported the apostles.

It soon became clear that the apostles were to be stoned to death. The two apostles fled to Lystra and Derbe, cities in Lycaonia, where they continued to preach the gospel.

After they had preached in these places and made a number of disciples, they went back to Lystra, then to Iconium, and finally to Antioch.

They crossed Pisidia and reached Pamphylia. And everywhere they went, they spoke of Jesus Christ. They went to Attalia and from there to Antioch. And here they stayed for some time with followers of Jesus Christ.

A LITTLE BIT OF HISTORY
Paul and Barnabas returned from Antioch and stayed in Jerusalem for some time. A meeting with the apostles and certain elders of the Church was arranged. They needed to solve the problem that was bothering the churches of Galatia: Did pagans have to become Jews before they became Christians?

Paul and some others persuaded the heads of the church of Jerusalem that pagans could become Christians straightaway as long as they observed certain rules of behaviour and ritual.

Afterwards, Paul and Barnabas returned to Antioch and continued to preach the word of the Lord.

THE SECOND JOURNEY OF PAUL

Acts 15-17

Paul said to Barnabas, "Let us go back and visit the towns where we made converts of those to whom we preached the word of the Lord. Let us see how things are with them."

They could not agree on the best way to make this journey, so they separated. Barnabas set sail for Cyprus, while Paul went through Syria, Cilicia, and part of Galatia, and wherever he went, he strengthened the

THE LETTERS OF PAUL
TO THE GALATIANS

Some time after he left the Roman province of Galatia, Paul wrote a letter to the Christian church that he had helped to found there. It is one of many letters that he sent to various communities. Together they make up a little more than a quarter of the New Testament. The Letters (or Epistles) give warnings and offer encouragement to those concerned with the Christian way of life. Paul wrote this letter to the Galatians with great passion because he had just learnt that their church was at the point of abandoning the purity of the Christian doctrine. The text that follows is drawn from several parts of the Letter.

GALATIANS 3

" O foolish Galatians, come to your senses! Who has put a spell on you? Can you not see that Jesus Christ was crucified? I would like to know one thing, did you receive the Holy Spirit from the law or from hearing of the faith? Are you really so foolish? You began with the Spirit; will you now end with the flesh? Have you suffered so much in vain? He who grants you the Spirit and performs miracles for you, does he do this through the works of the law or by hearing the faith? You must know that the children of Abraham were born out of faith. You are all children of God by your faith in Jesus Christ. There is no longer Jew or Greek, slave or free man because you are all one in Jesus Christ. And if you belong to Christ, then you are the descendants of Abraham and his heirs according to the promise."

THE LETTERS TO
THE THESSALONIANS

Paul fled alone to Athens. He was increasingly occupied with threats to his ministry in the north of Greece, as we see from a passage from one of the two letters to the Thessalonians. He had written to one of his closest friends to give him encouragement. The fact that the news he received from Thessalonica sometime later was good is borne out by the two letters. Here are some extracts from the first one.

church. He crossed Mysia and reached Troas. And here Paul had a vision during the night, in which a Macedonian came to him and prayed to him, saying, "Come to Macedonia. We need your help!"

After this vision, Paul set out for Macedonia.

He left Troas and reached Samothracia. The next day, he was in Neapolis. From there he went on to Philippi, the chief city of Macedonia and a Roman colony.

Silas, who had become a disciple of Paul in Jerusalem, was with Paul on this journey. On the Sabbath day, they sat down to pray at a favourite spot beside a river. It was here that they met a woman who was a fortune-teller. She made a lot of money for her masters in this way. But after Paul and Silas showed the woman the ways of Jesus Christ, she stopped telling fortunes. This angered her masters, because they could no longer use the woman to make money.

They were so angry that they seized Paul and Silas and dragged them into the public square, where they appeared before the leaders of the town.

They accused Paul and Silas, saying, "These men are making trouble in our town. They are Jews, and they are preaching things we Romans cannot accept."

Then the crowd became angry and excited. The magistrates ordered that the two men be stripped of their clothes and whipped. Paul and Silas were beaten until they were black and blue. Then they were thrown into prison, and the jailer was told to keep a close eye on them. He locked them up in the deepest prison cell, putting their feet in stocks.

At midnight, Paul and Silas prayed and sang praises to God. And their voices rose so that the other prisoners heard them.

Suddenly there was a great earthquake. The foundations of the prison building shook. Locked doors sprang open, and stocks loosened and fell away.

The keeper of the prison woke with a start. Seeing that the doors of his prison were open, and knowing that he was responsible for the prisoners, he guessed that they had all escaped. He decided to kill himself and drew his sword. But just as he was about to take his own life, the voice of Paul rang out: "Do not harm yourself! We are all still here!"

Then the keeper of the prison took a light and found Paul and Silas in their dungeon. He led them out and fell at their feet. He asked, "Sirs, what must I do to be saved?"

And they answered, "Believe in the Lord Jesus Christ, and you and your family will be saved."

That night, the keeper bathed the wounds of his prisoners, and afterwards, they took him and his family to be baptised.

Then they went back to his house, and he served them food. He rejoiced with his family, because he now believed in God.

When day broke, the magistrates sent word to the keeper to let the men go.

Paul and Silas left the keeper and his family, and they travelled on through Amphipolis and Apollonia.

PAUL AND SILAS IN THESSALONICA

They reached Thessalonica, where the Jews had a synagogue. There Paul, in his usual way, spent three Sabbaths reasoning with the people and discussing holy texts. He openly stated that Christ had suffered death on the cross but had risen again from the dead. He said that Jesus was the Christ.

Some believed the words of Paul and were converted. But others, who did not believe, were full of jealousy. They got together with a number of rough men and stirred up trouble in the city. They shouted, "These men are making trouble in our town! They go against Roman law! They say there is another King, and they call him Jesus!"

There was such an uproar that the people stormed the house of Jason, where they believed the two men were staying. But they did not find them, and later Jason and his brothers were able to get word to Paul and Silas and help them escape by night to a place called Berea.

When they reached Berea, they went into the Jewish synagogue there. They found the Jews to be more noble and open to the holy Scriptures than were those in Thessalonica. There were daily discussions and careful readings of texts. But it was not long before the Jews in Thessalonica learnt where Paul and Silas were. They sent men to Berea to stir up the people once again against these two men.

The followers of Paul saw that it was wise to send him on to Athens. Once there, Paul was to tell Silas and another disciple, Timotheus, to join him.

PAUL PREACHES TO THE ATHENIANS, Acts 17

Paul waited in Athens for Silas and Timotheus. He was angry to see that the city was so full of idols. However, he continued to speak and argue with the Jews in the synagogues. He also spoke to devout people in public places, such as the market square.

Paul said: "Men and women of Athens, I find you to be a religious people! In walking about the city, I have even found an altar with an inscription that reads, TO THE UNKNOWN GOD. I will tell you who this God is that you do not know. God, who made the world and everything in it, does not live in temples constructed by human hands. Nor does He receive service by man's hands as something He needs. After all, it is God who breathes life into the world and makes things live! He has made all men and women of flesh and blood. He has put us on earth. God has said that we must repent of our sins and that there will come a day of judgement. He sent His Son into the world to assure us of this. Then He raised His Son from the dead."

When the people heard Paul speak of resurrection from the dead, some people mocked him. Others said, "We would be interested to hear more on this subject."

Paul left them, but some people believed and followed him.

PAUL CONTINUES HIS TRAVELS AND REACHES CORINTH

Paul left Athens and went to Corinth, where he spoke in the synagogue on every Sabbath and tried to convert Jews and Greeks.

When Silas and Timotheus reached him from Macedonia, Paul's

I THESSALONIANS 2-4
"To the Church of the Thessalonians: may grace and peace be with you!

"We forever thank God for you all. We think of you in our prayers. We call to mind the works of your faith, the sacrifices you have made, and your steadfast belief in our Lord, Jesus Christ. O beloved brothers in God, you have set an example for all the believers in Macedonia and Achaia. You know that the growth has brought forth fruit. After suffering much hardship in Philippi, as you know, we put our faith in our God and preached the gospels despite opposition. We give thanks to God for entrusting us with the word of the gospel. You have heard it, and it is not like the words of men because it is the truth as God has spoken it, and this is what stirs the hearts of the believers. As for us, O brothers, after having been separated from you in body but not in heart, we long to see you again. We decided at several meetings that at least I, Paul, should go to see you; but Satan has got in our way. We have sent Timotheus, our brother, minister of God and fellow labourer in the gospel of Christ, to give you comfort concerning the faith. We do not wish you to remain in ignorance, my brothers, of those who have died. We must believe that God, in the name of Jesus Christ, will bring back to us all those who have died in his name. Thus, we will remain for ever with the Lord.

"Take comfort from these words. May the grace of our Lord Jesus Christ be with you. Amen."

When Paul left Corinth, he left behind
a strong and healthy group of disciples.
However, no sooner was Paul gone
than serious conflicts broke out. This
accounts for the severe tone of voice
in the Letters to the Corinthians. The
following text is taken from parts of
those letters.

I CORINTHIANS 1, 12-13
*"My brothers, I call upon you in the name
of Jesus Christ to hold fast to our common
beliefs and to end the divisions among you.
I say this because I have heard that there
are disputes among you. I wish you to
speak in this way: 'I am for Paul! I am for
Apollos! I am for Cephas! I am for Christ!'*

*"Would Christ be divided? Has Paul
been crucified for you, or is it in the name
of Paul that you have been baptised?*

*"Christ is one body. He has one body
with many limbs, but all these limbs only
make one body. Jew or Gentile, free man
or slave, we have all been baptised with
one spirit to form a single body, and we are
all fed by the same Holy Spirit. Our bodies
are made up of different parts, but they
still make one body. God has given our
body different parts, but each part must
look after the other. If one limb is in pain
then the others suffer with it; if one limb
grows strong, then the others rejoice in that
strength. You are the body of Christ,
and you are like limbs of the same body.
Each part is important...*

*"When I speak the language of men
and angels, if I do not have the mercy of
charity, I am only the sounds of worthless
music.*

*"And if I have the gift of prophesy and
all the knowledge of the faith so that I can
move mountains, if I do not have compassion and charity, I am nothing.*

*"And when I give away all my
material things and finally give up my
body to be burnt, if I do not have charity,
everything was in vain. Charity is patient
and full of goodness. Charity is not
jealous. It does not flaunt itself. It is
respectful. It is not looking for its own
ends. It does not grow angry. It does not
listen to evil. It does not rejoice in
injustice. But charity rejoices in the truth.
It forgives all, it believes all, it lives in
hope and bears troubles. Charity will live
for ever. So three things remain: faith,
hope, and charity. But the greatest of these
is charity."*

spirits rose, and he preached powerfully to the Jews that Jesus was the Christ.

But the Jews were against him. Then Paul stayed in the house of a man called Justus. This was a man who honoured God and whose house was next to the synagogue. Crispus, the chief ruler of the synagogue, also believed in the Lord, as did many Corinthians who had heard Paul speak. And many were baptised.

Paul stayed quite a long time in Corinth. Then he set sail for Syria. He reached Ephesus, where he left his companions and went on to Caesarea. From there, he went to Jerusalem, then to Antioch, and then back to Ephesus.

THE THIRD JOURNEY OF PAUL, Acts 19
In Ephesus, God gave Paul the power to work miracles. He took hand-kerchiefs and touched the sick with them, and the sick were cured. Some who practised magic gave it up and became followers of Jesus Christ. They burnt their books in public, and there were so many books that they were valued at fifty thousand silver pieces.

The word of the Lord grew and spread from one place to another.

THE ANGER OF THE SILVERSMITHS, Acts 19-20
About this time, the words that Paul preached caused great trouble. A man named Demetrius, a silversmith, made little models of the temple of Diana. These silver models provided work and a good living for a number of men.

Demetrius called a meeting of all the workers in this profession. He said to them, "Fellow workers, you know our livelihood depends on making models of Diana's temple. As you have seen and heard, this fellow Paul is persuading people, not only in Ephesus but throughout Asia, that sculptures of gods made by the hand of man are not really gods! This is bad for our business!"

These words filled the workers with anger, and they shouted, "Long live Diana of the Ephesians!"

Then the whole city was in an uproar. The workers marched to the open theatre to protest. Paul understood what was happening, and he wanted to go there and meet them. But the disciples stopped him, and some leaders of that region, who were friends of Paul, also begged him not to go.

In the theatre there was confusion. Some shouted one thing, others something else. Most of the people no longer even remembered why they had come to the theatre in the first place.

Then a man named Alexander was pushed to the front of the meet-ing by some Jews. Alexander signalled to the people that he wished to speak to them. But the people saw that he was a Jew, and they shouted, "Long live Diana of the Ephesians!"

Then the town clerk was called to calm the people down. When he had done this, he said, "People of Ephesus, we all know that we wor-ship Diana and that her shrine is in this city. We know that the image of Diana fell from the sky, and that this is a fact. You know this, so there is no need to shout or act rashly. These men who have come here do not rob churches, nor do they blaspheme. If Demetrius or any of his fellow workers have anything against these men, they may bring charges in the proper way through the courts. If there is anything else that you wish to debate, it should be done in a proper and legal way. We are behaving badly today. There is no reason for this meeting."

With these words, the town clerk dismissed the crowd.

After the uproar had died down, Paul called a meeting of his disciples. He embraced them and set out for Macedonia.

When he had preached in that area, he went back to Greece and stayed there for about three months. He was about to leave for Syria when news reached him that the Jews were waiting to trap him. He therefore travelled through Macedonia instead.

Later, Paul and his friends started out from Philippi. In five days, they reached Troas, where they stayed for seven days.

EUTYCHUS FALLS FROM THE WINDOW

Acts 20

On the first day of the week, the disciples met to break bread together. Paul spoke at length with them, because he was going to leave Troas the next day. He talked until midnight.

In the lofty room where the disciples were meeting, there were many lamps. A young man named Eutychus was seated high up on a window ledge, listening to Paul talk. The apostle spoke for so long that Eutychus fell fast asleep and fell out of the window from three floors up, down onto the ground. At first he was thought to be dead. But Paul went to him and took him in his arms. He said, "Do not be alarmed; he's still alive."

Paul waited in Athens for Silas and Timotheus. He was angry to see that the city was so full of idols. However, he continued to speak and argue with the Jews in the synagogues. He also spoke to devout people in public places, such as the market square.

Then everyone went back indoors, and Paul broke bread and they ate. Paul spoke until dawn before leaving.

Acts 20-21

PAUL HURRIES TO REACH JERUSALEM

Paul had decided to be in Jerusalem if possible for Pentecost. So they left Troas, set sail for Syria, and landed in Tyre. Then they went on to Caesarea. They had been there for a few days when a prophet named Agabus arrived from Judea. He visited the disciples, and then he did a strange thing. He took Paul's belt and tied the apostle's hands and feet with it, saying, "The Holy Spirit has said that the owner of this belt will be tied up by the Jews in Jerusalem. He will then be handed over to the Gentiles."

When they heard these words, all present begged Paul not to go to Jerusalem. But Paul replied, "Why are you crying? Do you wish to break my heart? I am ready not just to be tied up in Jerusalem; I am ready to die in the name of Jesus Christ."

When the disciples saw that Paul could not be persuaded to stay, they said only, "Let the Lord's will be done!"

A few days later, they were on the road for Jerusalem.

Acts 21

PAUL IS ARRESTED

When the Jews from the provinces of Asia saw Paul in the temple of Jerusalem, they stirred up the people against him. They took hold of him and shouted, "Men of Israel, this is the man who preaches against the people, against the law, and against this place!"

Then the temple was filled with confusion, and people ran everywhere. Paul was dragged out of the temple, and its doors were shut.

They were about to kill the apostle when word reached the Roman captain of that area that Jerusalem was in an uproar. The captain went with his centurions and soldiers to see what was happening. When they saw the soldiers, the people stopped beating Paul. The captain tied Paul up with two chains and demanded to know who he was and what he had done.

Voices came out of the crowd, some saying one thing, and others something quite different. The noise was too great for the captain to understand exactly what was said. He therefore ordered Paul to be taken into the castle. Because of the violence of the crowd, Paul was protected by the Roman soldiers on the steps to the castle. The people pressed in on all sides, shouting, "Kill him!"

II CORINTHIANS 3
"You are our letter, and you are written in our hearts. You are known and read by all men. You are like a letter written by Christ for our ministry. You are not written with ink but with the spirit of the living God. You are not written on pieces of stone, but you are written on the flesh of our hearts."

Acts 21-22

PAUL DEFENDS HIS ACTIONS

As soon as Paul was within the castle walls, he was taken to the chief captain. Paul asked at once, "May I speak to you?" He was given permission. Then Paul said: "I am a Jew from Tarsus, one of the main cities in Cilicia. I ask you to let me speak to the people."

The chief captain gave him permission to do so. Paul went to the castle steps and beckoned the people to him. A great silence fell, and Paul addressed the crowd in Hebrew:

"Men, brothers and fathers, please listen to what I have to say in my defence." When the people heard the apostle speaking in Hebrew, they kept silent. Paul continued: "I am a Jew from the city of Tarsus, but I was brought up in this city and went to the school of Gamaliel. I was taught according to our ancient laws and worshipped God as you do to this day. I was a fierce man. I condemned people to death and had men and women thrown in prison. And why? Because they were following the same doctrine I preach today! The high priest and the elders may be my witnesses. I received letters of approval from them. With these letters, I went to Damascus to bring back followers of Christ to Jerusalem, where they would be punished.

"When I was once again back in Jerusalem, I prayed in the temple and went into a trance. I saw the Lord, and he told me to leave Jerusalem at once, for the people would not believe my words about the Lord."

The crowd had listened quietly up to this point, but now they began to shout, "Wipe him off the earth! He does not deserve to live!"

The shouts of the crowd grew stronger, and the chief captain ordered Paul back within the castle. Then he ordered Paul to be whipped until he explained why the people hated him so much.

PAUL APPEARS BEFORE THE COUNCIL, Acts 22-23

While the soldiers were getting the instuments of torture ready, Paul said to a centurion, "Are you allowed to whip a Roman citizen before he has been judged?"

Then the centurion went to the chief captain and said, "We must be careful. This man is a Roman."

The chief captain became alarmed when he heard that Paul was a Roman. He was also afraid, because he had tied Paul up. So punishment was delayed, and Paul was kept in the castle.

During the night, the Lord came to Paul and said, "Have courage. You have spoken about me in Jerusalem; now you must speak about me in Rome."

PAUL'S ENEMIES PLOT AGAINST HIM, Acts 23

When day came, the Jews made a plot against Paul. They vowed to eat and drink nothing until he was put to death. There were more than forty men involved in this plot.

But Paul's nephew learnt about their plans and hurried to the castle to inform Paul. Then Paul called a centurion and said to him, "Take this young man to the chief captain. He has something to tell him."

The chief captain listened to the young man in private. Then he said, "Do not breathe a word of what you have said to anyone else."

The young man left, and the chief captain called for two centurions. He gave them instructions: "I want two hundred soldiers ready to go to Caesarea, as well as seventy horsemen and two hundred spearmen. They are to leave at the third hour of the night. Put Paul on a horse, and see that he reaches Felix the governor safe and sound."

The soldiers obeyed their orders. They brought Paul safely to Antipatris, a province of Caesarea.

PAUL APPEARS BEFORE FELIX THE GOVERNOR
Acts 24

Five days later, the high priest Ananias, some elders, and a lawyer named Tertullus brought charges against Paul. Felix the governor listened to what they had to say. He knew how the charges had come about and

LETTERS TO THE ROMANS
Paul wished to visit Rome, the capital of the huge empire in which he had been preaching. With this in mind, he wrote to the Christian community that lived and worked there.

After he had written this letter from Corinth, persecution befell him, and he arrived in Rome in chains. Here are some extracts from his letters to the Romans.

I ROMANS 8, 15
"To all those in Rome who are loved by God and called to be his saints. I always remember you in my prayers, and I ask God in his goodness to send me to you when the time is ripe. I wish to see you so that I may give you some spiritual gift. Brothers, you should know that I have often planned to visit you but have always been prevented. It would be good to have fruit with you.

"If God is for us, who will be against us? Who will separate us from the love of Christ? Will it be tribulation, distress, persecution, famine, nakedness, peril, or the sword?

"But we are more than a match for these things, and we are made victorious by he who loves us.

"I am convinced that neither death nor life, neither the present nor the future, neither the heights nor the depths, nothing at all, has the power to separate us from the love of God, which is in Jesus Christ, our Lord.

"I yearn to see you. I have so often been prevented from going. But now there is nothing to hold me back, and as I have been burning to see you for several years, I will make the journey when I return from Spain.

"I know that I will visit you with the full blessing of Christ.

"I ask you, my brothers, in the name of our Lord Jesus Christ and in his generosity of spirit, to help me in this fight. Pray to God for me so that I may happily reach you if it be the will of God. I wish to be with you in joy and comfort. May the peace of God be with you! Amen!"

EPHESIANS 6
*"Make yourself strong in the Lord, and
draw on his almighty strength. Put on the
armour of God so that you can resist the
tricks of the devil.*

*"Stand firm and wear a belt of truth,
make justice your breastplate, put shoes on
your feet with the preparation of the gospel
of peace.*

*"Always carry in your hands the shield
of the faith. With this you will be able to
put out the flaming arrows of the wicked.
Take with you the helmet of salvation and
the sword of the spirit, which is the word
of God."*

Acts 27

why Paul had been brought to him. He told Ananias and his supporters, "I will look into these accusations when the chief captain, Lysias, is present."

Then he gave orders to a centurion to look after Paul and to allow him some freedom. After that, Felix spoke a great deal to Paul about his faith in Christ.

Two years went by. Paul remained a prisoner. Then Porcius Festus became governor after Felix.

PAUL MUST APPEAR BEFORE CAESAR, Acts 25
Three days after Festus reached Antipatris, he left for Jerusalem. Back in Caesarea, he ordered a meeting and stated that Paul should be present.

When some Jews from Jerusalem saw Paul, they surrounded him and shouted things against him. But they were unable to prove anything.

Festus did not want trouble with the Jews. He was the governor and wanted to keep things calm. Hoping to please the Jews, he asked Paul, "Do you want to go to Jerusalem and be judged there?"

Paul answered, "I stand before you, and you represent Caesar. It is he who must judge me. You know I have done the Jews no harm. If I have committed a crime worthy of death, I do not refuse to die. But if there is no truth in these charges brought against me, no one has the right to condemn me and hand me over to the people. I should appear before Caesar."

Then Festus thought long and hard about Paul's words. Finally, he said to Paul, "That is the way it will be. It is to Caesar you will go."

PAUL IS TAKEN TO ROME
Julius, a centurion who belonged to the band of Caesar Augustus, took charge of Paul and some other prisoners. Julius had to take these men to Italy.

They all boarded a ship, but the sailing was slow, and there were many problems at sea. When they reached Sidon, Julius allowed Paul to see his friends there.

But the time for safe sailing was past. Winter was fast approaching, and the seas were rough. Paul said, "I do not think we can sail without many dangers. We, the cargo, the ship, and the men will be in peril."

But the centurion put his trust in the captain and the owner of the ship, and he did not follow Paul's advice. It was not safe to spend the winter in the port where they were, because it offered little shelter. So they set sail for Phenice, which is a port in Crete.

A gentle wind rose as they set sail, and soon they were close to the coast of Crete. But then a mighty wind, called the Euroclydon, sprang up. The ship was caught in the wind and ran with it, out of control.

The storm battered the ship, and they were in danger of running aground. To lighten the ship, they threw their cargo overboard. The storm continued, and on the third day, the crew threw the sails and the ropes into the sea.

For many days, they did not see the sun during the day or the stars at night. The ship rose and fell in the raging sea. Every man feared for his life. They had not eaten for days. All hope was gone. Then Paul walked into the group of men, who were huddled together, and said, "Men, you should have listened to me. But do not be afraid. No man will die, but the ship will be lost. Tonight an angel of the God I serve came to me and told me not to fear the storm. And God will also save your lives. I believe my God, and everything will be as He has said. We will run aground on an island."

At midnight on the fourteenth night of their tossing at sea, the sailors thought they could see land. They tested the depth of the water and found that it was twenty fathoms. The ship was driven further in, and they sounded fifteen fathoms. Then, fearing that they would crash upon rocks, they threw four anchors over the stern and waited anxiously for daylight.

The sailors were still afraid and wanted to abandon ship. But Paul went to the centurion and the soldiers, and said, "If you wish to be saved, you must stay in the ship."

The lifeboat was cut loose, because they now believed Paul's words. When day broke, Paul said, "We have eaten nothing for fourteen days. It is now time to eat. You must take food for your health. Do not be afraid; no harm will come to you."

After these words, Paul took some bread, gave thanks to God in front of the sailors and soldiers, broke the bread, and began to eat. When the crew saw this, their spirits rose, and they also ate. There were two hundred and seventy-six men on board.

PHILIPPIANS 4
"*Brothers, whatever is true, honest, just, pure, lovely, of good standing, virtuous and worthy of praise, all these must be the object of your thoughts.*

"*Whatever you have learnt, received, and heard from me, whatever you have seen in me, practise it.*

"*And the God of peace be with you.*"

COLOSSIANS 3
"*If you have risen with Christ, seek those things which are on high, where Christ sits on the right hand of God. Think of things on high, not on things on the earth.*"

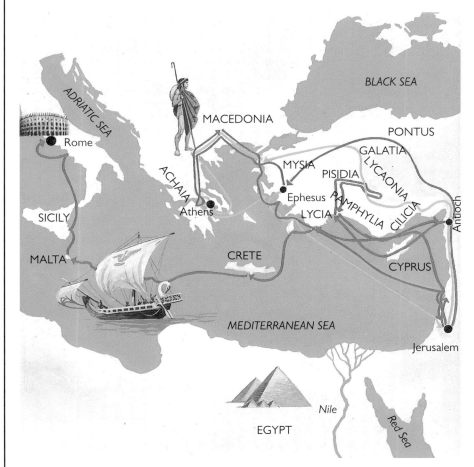

The map shows the three voyages of Paul, the places where he stayed, and his journey to Rome. Paul was the first to bring the gospel of Jesus Christ to foreign countries.

Each of the journeys by land followed the roads built by the Romans. By land and sea he travelled a total of more than 932 miles.

Paul had understood that it was possible to bring Christianity to different cultures with different approaches to life.

The book of the Acts of the Apostles gives us a record of Paul's travels.

When they had eaten enough, they made the ship lighter by throwing the rest of the food into the sea.

By this time it was day. They did not recognise the land that lay before them. But they saw a possible place to run the ship aground, so they pulled up anchor.

The ship ran with the wind. When it hit the shore, the bow stayed firm while the stern broke under the strength of the waves. The soldiers shouted that the prisoners should be killed in case they escaped into the sea. But the centurion did not agree and wanted to save Paul. He gave the order that those who could swim should jump into the water at once and swim to shore. Others reached land by holding onto planks of wood from the ship.

All reached dry land safely, and not a man was lost.

WINTER IN MALTA

After they all had escaped the storm, they learnt that the island was called Malta.

The people were kind, and they built fires to warm the men and to protect them from the cold and the rain. Then, when Paul picked up a bundle of sticks to put on the fire, a snake came out of the sticks and sank its mouth into his hand. Seeing this, the people of the island said, "This man must be a murderer. He may have escaped the sea, but obviously he does not deserve to live, and so he will die."

But Paul shook the snake off his hand into the fire.

The people stared at Paul, waiting for his hand to swell or for him to drop dead. But when nothing happened, the people changed their minds and decided that Paul must be a god.

In that part of the island, there was a man named Publius, who was a Roman. For three days, he took care of all the men in a generous and kind way.

Publius's father was sick with a high fever. Paul went to see this man, and he put his hands on him and cured him. When others heard what Paul had done, they brought their sick to him, and Paul healed them all.

When it was time for the travellers to leave, they were given everything they needed for their voyage.

Three months later, they left in a ship from Alexandria that had spent the winter in that port. They reached Syracuse and stayed there for three days. Then they went on to Rhegium and Puteoli. Finally, they reached Rome, and their sea voyage was over.

THE LAST YEARS OF PAUL'S LIFE

When the followers of Paul learnt of his arrival in Rome, they rushed to meet him. And when Paul saw them, he was overjoyed. He gave thanks to God and felt encouraged.

In Rome, the centurion delivered his prisoners to the captain of the guard. Paul, however, was given a house by himself with a soldier to guard him.

Three days after his arrival in Rome, Paul called a meeting of the chief Jews in the area and said to them, "My brothers, I have committed no sin against the people or the customs of our ancestors, but I was

Acts 28

II TIMOTHY 4
"My blood will soon be shed, and the moment of my departure approaches. I have fought a good fight, I have finished my course, I have kept the faith. There remains a crown of righteousness, which the Lord, the righteous judge, shall give me on that day. But not only to me but to all who love his coming.

"Try to visit me as soon as possible. The others have abandoned me. Only Luke is with me. Bring Mark with you, for I can use him in the ministry. When you come, bring me the cloak I left at Troas with Carpus; especially bring the books and parchments.

"The Lord Jesus Christ be with your spirit. Grace be with you. Amen."

Acts 28

Opposite: The ship ran with the wind. When it hit the shore, the bow stayed firm while the stern broke under the strength of the waves.

put in prison in Jerusalem and then brought here and kept under guard by the Romans.

"The Romans questioned me and would have let me go, because they found no reason to kill me. Then the Jews said bad things about me, and I was forced to appeal to Caesar, even though I had done nothing to offend my people.

"This is why I have called you here today. I have hopes for the nation of Israel, but that is why I am bound in chains."

The Jews replied, "We received no news of you from Judea. Our brothers who came from that region did not speak badly of you. But we do want to hear your opinions, for everywhere we go Christianity is condemned."

So they arranged a day when they would meet at Paul's house. And on that day a large crowd arrived, and Paul spoke to them. He told them about the kingdom of God. He spoke of Jesus, drawing from the law of Moses and the prophets. And Paul spoke from morning until evening.

Some believed what Paul said, but others did not. They could not all agree on what to believe, and still arguing, they left.

Paul stayed for two years in his house under Roman guard. Anyone who visited him was made welcome. And Paul always spoke about the kingdom of God. He spoke from his heart about the Lord Jesus Christ. He spoke openly and not at all like a prisoner.

He said that all men, Jews and Gentiles, could be saved by God. And he spoke of the mercy of Jesus Christ.

THE LETTERS OF PETER

The apostle Peter wrote letters to the followers of Jesus Christ. This is part of what he wrote:

Who can say anything bad about you, if what you say is fair and true? Besides, when you suffer for justice, you will be happy! Do not be afraid. Do not let your hearts be troubled. Worship Christ the Lord.

It is better to suffer in the name of God and to do good than to do evil. Christ also suffered for your sins. He wants you to meet God. The flesh will die, but the spirit lives on.

When you speak with people, be humble, not proud. God has no time for pride, but He values those who are simple and honest in what they say.

Be humble beneath the powerful hand of God, so that when the time comes, He will make you powerful. Give your cares to God, and He will take care of you.

Be careful. The devil is like a roaring lion. He is everywhere and can eat anyone up at any time.

Resist evil with a firm and steady faith, and know that your fellow human beings suffer in the same way you do.

But, my beloved, be aware of this: To the Lord, one day is like a thousand years, and a thousand years is like a single day.

The Lord is not slow to keep His promise, as some men might say. On the contrary, He is long-suffering. He does not want our souls to perish. He wants us to repent, so that we can be saved.

The day of the Lord will come like a thief in the night. Then the heavens will disappear with huge crashing noises. The elements will melt in fire, and the earth will be destroyed. Knowing that this will happen, should we not behave in a godlike way? According to the promise of the Lord, we wait for new heavens and a new earth, where justice lives and continues for ever. That is why, my beloved, while we wait for these things to happen, we must free ourselves from sin. We must wait for the Lord as we keep our souls clean.

Believe that the Lord is generous and that He will save you. Your beloved brother Paul also wrote this in the wisdom that was given to him. You may find Paul's wisdom in his letters.

Grow in grace and in the knowledge of our Lord and Saviour, Jesus Christ.

A LITTLE BIT OF HISTORY
The last pages of the New Testament were written at a time of terrible persecution of the Christians by the Romans. They promise glory in heaven for Christians suffering on this earth, and they teach Christians how to conquer human weakness. These pages follow the Letters of Paul and include the Letters of four other leaders of the newborn Church. They are Peter, John, James, and Jude.

Peter, the apostle of Christ, was crucified in Rome. He was a victim of Nero's persecutions.

THE VISION OF JOHN

I am John, your brother and friend in times of despair. I am your companion in the kingdom and patience of Jesus Christ. God sent me to the Greek island of Patmos to preach about Jesus Christ.

On the day of the Lord, I was overcome with joy. Hearing a mighty voice behind me, I turned round and the voice spoke to me, saying, "Whatever you see, write it down in a book, and send it to the churches."

Then I saw an angel coming down from the sky. And the angel had great power, and the earth was lit up with his brilliance. In a mighty voice, he cried, "The great Babylon has fallen! Only devils live there now. Every filthy spirit seeks to hide in that place. It is like a cage that houses an unclean bird."

And I heard another voice in heaven, which said, "Stay far away from Babylon, my people. You must not become infected with those sins and that evil. For God knows all about the sins of Babylon and remembers the evil done in the past.

"The rulers of the earth, when they see Babylon in flames, will keep far away for fear of its anguish. They will say, 'Bad fortune! Evil fortune! A huge city reduced to nothing in one hour!'"

A NEW WORLD

I saw a new heaven and a new earth. The first heaven and the first earth had disappeared, and the sea no longer existed. I also saw, coming out of the heavens and close to God, the holy city, the new Jerusalem. She was dressed like a bride waiting to meet her husband.

I heard a powerful voice, which said, "Look, and you will see that the tabernacle of God is with men. And God will live with them, and they will be His people. And God Himself will be their God. And then God will wipe the tears from their eyes. There will be no more death, no more sorrow, no more crying or pain. Such things will no longer be with us."

The angel carried my spirit away to a high mountain. From there he showed me the holy city of Jerusalem descending from God in heaven. Because the city contained the glory of God, its light shone like a precious stone. And that stone was a jasper, clear as crystal.

The city was surrounded by a great, high wall, and within the wall there were twelve gates. At the gates were twelve angels, and the names of the twelve tribes of Israel were inscribed on the gates. There were three gates on the north, three on the south, three on the east, and three on the west.

The wall of the city was constructed on twelve foundations, and these foundations contained the names of the twelve apostles of the Lamb.

I saw no temple in the city. The Lord God Almighty and the Lamb were themselves the Temple!

And the city did not need a sun or a moon to give it light. The glory of God lit the city, and the Lamb was its lantern.

The nations that are saved will walk in the light of this city. Kings of the earth will bring their glory and honour to it. The gates of this city will never shut by day, because night will no longer exist.

And I, John, saw and heard all these things. I fell down at the feet of

A LITTLE BIT OF HISTORY
The last book of the Bible, the Revelation or Apocalypse, begins in the present and looks with hope to the future. The theme develops as a vision played out in several acts and scenes. There are two main designs: the heavenly and the earthly.

A number of the prophecies that it contains are veiled attacks on Rome, the great power of the first century after Jesus Christ. That is why reference is made to Babylon. Babylon was the ancient capital of paganism, and in the eyes of the first Christians equivalent to Rome.

the angel who had taken me to the holy city, and I heard a voice say to me, "I am the first and the last, the beginning and the end. I, Jesus, have sent my angel to show you these things so that you will speak of them in the churches. I am the root and the offspring of David. I am the bright and shining star of morning."

The Spirit and the church welcome you. They say, "Enter! And let whoever is thirsty for the love of Jesus Christ enter! That person will drink freely from the water of life!" And whoever enters the church of the Lord Jesus will find him swiftly.

The grace of our Lord Jesus Christ be with you all. Amen.

"I saw a new heaven and a new earth. The first heaven and the first earth had disappeared, and the sea no longer existed. I also saw, coming out of the heavens and close to God, the holy city, the new Jerusalem. She was dressed like a bride waiting to meet her husband."

GLOSSARY

The glossary is to facilitate the reading of the biblical text.

A

AARON Moses' eldest brother. He belonged to the Levi tribe. Moses made Aaron the first Jewish high priest. In this role, he helped Moses guide the Hebrews towards the Promised Land.

ABEL Adam and Eve's second son. He was a shepherd. He often made sacrifices to God, who loved him dearly. He was killed by his brother Cain, who was jealous of him.

ABIATHAR Which means "the father is respected". A priest and a descendant of Eli. After escaping a massacre ordered by Saul, he became a follower of David.

ABNER Saul's cousin and chief of his army. After Saul's death Abner had his son, Ishbosheth, elected king and supported him against David. After a disagreement with Ishbosheth, he joined David.

ABRAHAM First and greatest head of the Hebrew families. Shem's descendant, son of Terah. God promised him a glorious lineage and the land of Canaan. It was God's will that his name, *Abram*, which means "very high father", be changed to *Abraham*, which means "father of a large multitude". His wife Sarah was very old when she gave birth to Isaac with God's help. Abraham had an older son called Ishmael, whose mother was Abraham's slave, Hagar.

ABSALOM Third son of David. He was talented and very ambitious. He killed his brother Ammon, and after being forgiven by David, he became king in Hebron. Later, he was defeated in battle. In his flight, Absalom was caught in the low branches of an oak tree, where he was killed by Joab.

ACHAIA At first, a Greek state in the northern Peloponnese. However, at the time of the New Testament, it was a Roman province, with a much wider territory than the earlier state. Corinth was its capital, and its main towns included Athens and Cenchreae. During Paul's time it was governed by Gallio, the proconsul. Paul travelled through Achaia during his second and third voyages.

ACTS OF THE APOSTLES The second of Luke's works in the New Testament. It is dedicated, just as the Gospel is, to the "ex-cellent" Theophilus. The story is about the apostles Paul and Peter and their good acts. The book gives us a history of the first years of the Church of Jesus.

ADAM Which means "made of earth". The first man. God placed him in Eden and gave him Eve for companionship. He was banished from Eden for having disobeyed God's order. He was the father of Cain, Abel, and Seth.

AHAB King of Israel (reigned 864-853 B.C.). He married Jezebel, daughter of the king of Sidon. Jezebel persuaded Ahab to give up his religion. This made Elijah very angry.

AHAZ King of Judah (reigned 737-716 B.C.). Because he did not join forces with Rekahiah, king of Israel, and Rezin, king of Syria, against Assyria, these kings attacked Jerusalem.

AHIMELECH High priest of the Nob sanctuary. Ahimelech welcomed and looked after David, who had fled from Saul's anger. Because he helped David, Saul ordered that Ahimelech be put to death.

AI Second town to fall into the hands of Joshua and the Israelites after they invaded Canaan. When they attacked Ai the first time, the Israelites were defeated as a punishment from God. After making peace with God, they captured the town.

ALEXANDRIA City founded by Alexander the Great in 331 B.C. It is situated in the western part of the Nile delta. Because of its location, it was a meeting point between the East and West. The city's library, founded by Ptolemy, contained about 700,000 books. The library was destroyed by the Saracens in A.D. 642. The city's famous lighthouse was 498 feet high.

AMALEK Esau's grandson and chief of the Amalekites.

AMALEKITES A tribe that lived in the northern part of the Sinai Peninsula. In exchange for money they would often fight battles for foreign armies. While the Hebrews were on their way to the Promised Land, the Amalekites attacked them but were defeated.

AMMONITES Ammon's descendants. The Ammonites were related to the Hebrews and originally lived northwest of the Dead Sea. They were later pushed farther east. They often fought against the Hebrews but were nearly always defeated by them.

AMON Name of an Egyptian god and of three historical figures, of whom the most famous was the fourteenth king of Judah. This king, the son of Manasseh, was killed after a two-year reign (642-640 B.C.). The pious Josiah was king after Amon.

AMORITES The name comes from the ancient Babylonian and means "land to the west of the Euphrates". The Amorites were Semitic and did not have a permanent home.

AMOS The third of the lesser-known prophets. Amos lived at the same time as Hosea, a Jewish prophet in Israel during the reign of Jeroboam the Second.

ANANIAS Common name used fifteen times in the Bible. One Ananias was a Christian from Jerusalem who, with his wife Sapphira, failed the young Christian community and therefore the Holy Spirit. He and his wife paid for their mistake with their deaths.

ANDREW Which means in Greek "virile". An apostle, Peter's brother. He was born in Bethsaida and lived in Capernaum. A fisherman, he was a disciple of John the Baptist and later turned to Jesus. According to some ancient writers, he may have preached in southern Russia and the Balkans, and then died a martyr in Patras on a cross in the shape of an X. This kind of cross is still called a Saint Andrew's cross.

ANGELS Which means "messengers". Pure spirits created by God. Traditionally they are presented as belonging to nine orders: the seraphim, the cherubim, the thrones, the dominations, the virtues, the powers, the principalities, the archangels, and the angels. In the Bible, angels appear as messengers or representatives of God to carry out His will. The Old Testament mentions a few names of angels: Raphael, Michael, and Gabriel.

APOCALYPSE Means "revelation" and refers to books popular among Jews from the second century B.C. to the second century A.D. These books were full of visions and symbols. By predicting ultimate Jewish victory, they strengthened the courage of the Jews under the persecutions they were then enduring.

ARAM A region in western Asia that is today northern Iraq. Its centre was Haran, which Abraham left to begin his wanderings. Later, the name was used to refer to what is now Syria.

ARARAT Noah's ark came to rest on this mountain after the Great Flood.

ARK OF THE COVENANT At the time when the Hebrew people were still without a homeland, they used this golden ark as a container for the Ten Commandments, given by God to Moses.

ARTAXERXES Name of several Persian kings. The Bible tells us of an Artaxerxes who allowed Nehemiah's return to Jerusalem. The same king may have allowed the return of Ezra. He may have been Artaxerxes the First (reigned 465-424 B.C.).

ASIA MINOR In the New Testament, a Roman province comprised of Mysia, Lydia, Carie, and Phrygia. It dates back to 133 B.C. Its capital was Ephesus.

ASSYRIA The story of this ancient empire is little known. It appears to have been an independent power that defended itself against the Akkadian kingdom. Its second powerful king was Shamshi-Adad the First (reigned 1750-1718 B.C.), who was eventually conquered by his Babylonian rival Hammurabi. After this defeat Assyria disappears from the map as one of the great powers of Asia Minor. Only later, as the Middle Assyrian empire, does it again acquire importance.

ASSYRIANS People who lived near the Euphrates. The Assyrians were named after Assur. They were very important in ancient history because they managed to create a large and powerful state. They are famous for being cruel warriors—the terror of the ancient Orient.

ATHENS, ATHENIANS The cultural capital of Greece and of the ancient world. 125,000 people lived there at the peak of its splendor. People in Athens were very religious, but they liked to investigate new ideas. There were about three thousand temples and places to worship. Paul mentions the altar for an "unknown god" in his

famous speech given during a visit to Athens. Paul's mission to Athens was not very successful because only a few people converted to the Church of Jesus.

B

BAAL Which means "lord". The name was used by the Canaanites and the Phoenicians to mean a god (also known under other names) adored by nearly all the people in the ancient Orient, as well as a few in Africa. Baal was thought to be the giver of fertility and the symbol of masculinity, and the bull was his holy animal. He was in command of nature, and he spoke through thunder. He would send lightning, ride on top of clouds, and make it rain. He is represented as holding weapons in his hand. His head was crowned with a circle of rays.

BABEL The Hebrew name for Babylon, an important Asian city on the Euphrates River.

BABYLON Which means "God's door". The word is used to mean both a region and its capital city. The region is in the area of the lower Tigris and Euphrates, near the Persian Gulf. The city was founded by the Sumerians and is mentioned for the first time in about the year 2700 B.C. In 539 B.C., Cyrus conquered Babylon, which then became a province of the Persian Empire. It disappears from history in the year 127 B.C., after its conquest by the Parthians.

BALAAM A priest and a prophet, son of Beor. He came from the city of Pethor on the right bank of the Euphrates in Mesopotamia.

BALAK King of Moab and son of Zippor. During his lifetime the Hebrews were about to take control of Palestine. He is thought by some to have been the first king of Moab.

BARABBAS Which means "son of the father". His full name may have been "Jesus Barabbas". He was a thief and was arrested for murder. The Jews demanded that he be released instead of Jesus, who was then crucified.

BARNABAS Which means "the son of consolation" or "the son of prophecy". Nickname given by the apostles to their follower Joseph. A Levite from Cyprus, well known for his generosity and good works. He was the cousin of Mark the Evangelist. He accompanied Paul and was at the Jerusalem Council. Then he was with Mark, who had refused to follow Paul to Cyprus.

BARTHOLOMEW One of the twelve apostles. Jesus appeared to him after his resurrection.

BEELZEBUB The prince of the devils. The Pharisees accused Jesus of using his help to chase less important devils away.

BELSHAZZAR King of Babylon and the son of that Nebuchadnezzar who is referred to in the Book of Daniel. During the conquest of Babylon by the Persians, Belshazzar was killed by a Babylonian lieutenant. The Bible describes his death as a punishment for using the holy vessels.

BENJAMIN Which means "son on the right". He was Jacob and Rachel's last son. One of the twelve tribes of Israel was named after him.

BETHANY Which means "house of the indigent" or "house of the date trees" or "house of Ananias". A small city on the eastern part of the Mount of Olives, a little over one-and-one-half miles from Jerusalem. It was the home of Lazarus and his two sisters, Martha and Mary. Jesus liked to stay with them. It was also the city of Simon the Leper, the host who asked Jesus to lunch.

BETHLEHEM Which means "city of the bread" or "city of (the goddess) Lachama". Jesus' place of birth. A town in Judea, between Hebron and Jerusalem. It was where Rachel was buried. Bethlehem was Isaiah's and David's hometown.

BETHSAIDA Which means "the fishing house". A place on the Sea of Tiberias, close to the Jordan, homeland of the apostles Peter, Andrew, and Philip. Jesus healed a blind woman there, and then she was cursed because she could not believe Jesus had such power. Jesus also performed the miracle of the multiplication of the loaves in this neighbourhood.

BULLOCK A steer or a young bull.

C

CAESAR The family name of the first dynasty of Roman emperors. In the New Testament the following Caesars are mentioned: Augustus, who reigned from 29 B.C. to A.D. 14, and under whom Jesus was born; Tiberius (reigned A.D. 14-37), under whom Jesus' public ministry took place (the phrase "render unto Caesar what is Caesar's" referred to him); Claudius (reigned A.D 37-54), who chased the Jews away from Rome (as is reported in the Book of Acts); and Nero (reigned A.D. 54-68), to whom Paul appealed.

CAESAREA Name of two towns in the New Testament: 1) Maritime Caesarea, a port on the Mediterranean between Joppa and Dor. Herod the Great named the port after Caesar Augustus. Caesarea later came under the control of the Roman procurators. The deacon Philip introduced Christianity there. Cornelius, a centurion from Caesarea, was the first converted pagan. 2) Caesarea Philippi, also known as "Panias Philippi", which was built at the source of the river Jordan in 3 B.C. According to the first three gospels, this is where Peter recognised the Messiah. Today, it is a village called Banis.

CAIAPHAS The last name of Joseph, the high priest from A.D. 18 to 36.

CAIN Adam and Eve's first son. He was a farmer. He killed his brother Abel because he was jealous of him. Then he fled. He founded the very first city, which he named after his son, Enoch.

CANA Which means "bulrush". In the New Testament, Cana refers to a village in Galilee, where Jesus performed his first miracle by turning water into wine. The location of Cana is much debated.

CANAAN A country first occupied by the Canaanites and promised to the Hebrews by God.

CAPERNAUM Which means "city of Nahum". City on the right bank of the Sea of Tiberias. It was a border town with a customs checkpoint and a Roman garrison. It was the centre of most of Jesus' life, and he called it "my city". The people of Capernaum did not believe in Jesus. It was destroyed by an earthquake in A.D. 666.

CARMEL The name of a city in Judah, but above all the name of a range of mountains about fifteen miles long, between the Mediterranean Sea and the plain of Israel. Its peak is 525 metres high. A very ancient religious place where part of the Elijah story took place and also where Elisha liked to take shelter. The cave of Elijah is open to visitors.

CHERUBIM, see ANGELS

CHRISTIANS Christ's followers. The word appears three times in the New Testament and was first used in Antioch in Syria in A.D. 43. The Christians called themselves "saints" (blessed), "the chosen ones", "brothers", and "the ones who follow the new path". Christianity is the religion founded by Jesus Christ.

CHURCH The word comes from Greek. It means the gathering of the people of Israel as a religious community. In the New Testament, it means the followers of Jesus.

CILICIA A region in the south of Asia Minor. The main town is Tarsus, Paul's hometown. The people are of Hittite origin.

CITY OF DAVID Refers to Zion, a city conquered by David.

CLEOPAS One of the two disciples to whom Jesus appeared at Emmaus. A man called Cleophas was the husband or relative of a Mary present by the cross of Jesus when he died. This Cleophas may have been the brother of Joseph and uncle of Jesus.

COLOSSIANS People who lived in Colossae, a city in Phrygia. Even though he had never visited this city, Paul wrote a letter to the Colossians, in which he praised the kindness of the Christian faith.

COMMANDMENTS God gave Moses the Ten Commandments on Mount Sinai. They are the basis of the moral law, not only for the Hebrews but for all the people influenced by them.

CORINTH One of the most famous Greek cities. It was the capital of Achaia. The city was both wealthy and extremely poor since two thirds of the population were slaves. It was also famous for having a lot of crime—so much, in fact, that the verb "to corinthize" meant to lead a bad life. One reason for this state of affairs lay in the worship of Aphrodite, the goddess of love. Pagan life as described in the first chapter of the Letter to the Romans is very similar to life in Corinth. Every four years the Isthmian games were held there. Paul went there twice and even possibly went back a third time after being held a captive in Rome. He wrote four letters there, of which we still have two.

CRETE An island in the eastern Mediterranean. It was a Roman province where many Jews lived. Paul went there during his last trip to Rome. Later, Titus, Paul's companion, was established there as a bishop.

CUBIT A unit of measurement based on the length of the forearm from the tip of the middle finger to the elbow, which usually equals about 50 centimetres.

CYPRUS An island in the Mediterranean. Its shape is triangular. Cyprus has very rich soil and was known for its metals (*cuprum*=copper). The Bible calls its inhabitants the "Kittims". Colonized by the Phoenicians, it finally became a Roman province. First Paul and Barnabas, then Barnabas and Mark visited it.

CYRUS Founder of the Persian empire, who reigned from 550 to 529 B.C. He was a politician without extreme views. In 538 B.C. he freed the Hebrews so that they could return to their homeland.

D

DAMASCUS A city in southern Syria, in the southeast of Lebanon.

DANIEL Which means "God is my judge". A prophet who was sent to Babylon in 605 B.C. God gave him exceptional wisdom. He turned out to be remarkably good at telling what dreams and visions meant.

DAVID A Hebrew shepherd. On God's orders, he was secretly made king of Israel by the prophet Samuel. He was introduced to the court of Saul as a harp player. He was known for his bravery. He killed the giant Goliath, ending the war between the Hebrews and the Philistines. After becoming king after Saul's death, he conquered Jerusalem and made it the capital of the Kingdom of Israel. After he died, his son Solomon became king.

DECAPOLIS A cluster of cities to the east of the Jordan River.

DELILAH Delilah means "thin" or "delicate". She was Samson's mistress. No one knows if she was Hebrew or Philistine. She was probably Philistine. She caused Samson's capture.

E

EDEN Paradise on earth in which God placed Adam and Eve after the creation, and from which he banished them after they ate fruit from the forbidden tree. It may have been in Mesopotamia.

EDOM A mountainous region to the south of the Dead Sea, close to Mount Seir.

ELI Second to last of the Hebrew judges. Although his career lasted over forty years, we do not know anything about it. He was descended from Ithamar.

ELIJAH [ELIAS] One of the greatest of Israel's prophets. He lived in the ninth or tenth century B.C.

ELISABETH Which means "God has sworn". Wife to the priest Zacharias, she was the mother of John the Baptist and a relative of the Virgin Mary.

ELISHA Elijah's disciple, a prophet known for kindness and mercy.

EMMAUS A village about eight miles from Jerusalem.

EPHESUS, EPHESIANS A city in Lydia in Asia Minor at the mouth of the river Cayster through which passed the Roman route to the East. The temple of Artemis in Ephesus was one of the seven wonders of the world. Paul visited Ephesus during his second and third missionary journeys, stopping over for three years. He was chased away by the revolt started by the silversmith Demetrius. The apostle John was the chief of the Christian community there. According to tradition, the Virgin Mary, mother of Jesus, died there.

ESAU Isaac and Rebekah's firstborn son, nicknamed Edom because of his red hair. He sold his birthright to his brother Jacob in exchange for a dish of lentils.

EUCHARIST Communion. A sacrament originated by Jesus Christ at the Last Supper, in which bread and wine are consecrated and consumed.

EUPHRATES A river in Asia Minor. Its course defines the plain of Mesopotamia.

EUTYCHUS Which means "fortunate". Young man from Troas. He fell asleep during a long speech of Paul's, fell out of a window, and died. Paul revived him.

EVE Which means "mother of the living". The first woman, created by God from Adam's rib. The serpent persuaded her to taste the fruit of the forbidden tree.

EZEKIEL Which means "power of God". A priest and a prophet. He was the son of Buzi. He wrote a book that he named after himself. He was exiled in 597 B.C. to Babylon, where he died, possibly by murder.

EZRA Which means "God is assistance". A priest, "rather knowledgeable in law", and a councillor representing the Hebrews in the Persian government. He was later sent to Palestine to organise the Jews after their return to their homeland. He fought against mixed marriages. At a later point he may have been called back to Persia. He wrote a book about his activities. He is thought to have founded the Great Synagogue.

F

FATHOM A unit of measurement equal to 1.8 metres and most commonly used for measuring the depth of water.

FELIX· Marc Antony Felix was procurator of Judea from A.D. 54 to 60. He was favoured by the emperor Claudius. He married Drusilla, the youngest daughter of King Agrippa the Second. Paul appeared at his tribunal and made a speech on justice, abstinence, and the judgement to come, which impressed Felix very much. Festus became procurator after Felix died.

FURLONG A unit of measurement equal to 201 metres; a measurement of distance.

G

GABRIEL Which means "man of God" or "God has proved to be strong". Name of an angel. He announced the birth of John the Baptist to Zachariah. He also told Mary that she would bear the son of God, Jesus.

GALATIA, THE GALATIANS Name of a region that was made up of different territories in different periods. Originally, it was the area now known as northern Turkey, and Ancira was its capital (modern Ankara). In about 25 B.C., it became a Roman province that reached to the south of Asia Minor. The Galatian people were of Celtic descent. Originally, after leaving Asia, they moved to Europe and settled mostly in Gaul. They then moved to Greece, and some went as far as central Asia Minor. Paul visited the cities of southern Galatia during his first and second missionary journeys. However, he addressed the Letter to the Galatians to the churches of the old Galatia (in the north). This church was possibly founded at the time of his second missionary journey, and he visited it again on his third missionary journey.

GALILEE The Palestinian high plateau.

GAMALIEL Which means "God has done good things for me". He was a high rabbi, Paul's master. When the apostles Peter and John were jailed, he freed them. He is said to have died a Christian, after leaving the Hebrew faith. However, this is uncertain.

GAZA Canaanite city in the southwest corner of Palestine, on the only route that led from Egypt to Syria.

GENTILES Comes from the Latin *gentes*, which means "men". The Hebrews used the word *gentiles* to refer to people who were not Hebrew.

GETHSEMANE Which means "oil press". Garden on the western slopes of the Mount of Olives.

GILBOA A group of hills that divide the waters between the Jordan Valley and the Mediterranean coast. The battle of the Israelites against the Philistines, during which Saul and his three sons died, took place on the "mounts of Gilboa".

GILGAL Which means "the circle". First campsite of the Israelites after they crossed the Jordan.

GOLGOTHA Which means "place of the skull". Place where Jesus was crucified. It is situated away from Jerusalem, near a garden. Its Latin name was "Calvary". The name is linked to the round shape of the rock, which makes it look like a skull. According to an old tradition, the skull of Adam was buried there.

GOLIATH Philistine hero. He was a giant defeated and killed by David. He was from Gath.

GREECE Region in the Balkan peninsula in southern Europe. Greece only made contact with Judah at the time of Alexander the Great. It later became a Roman province. Christianity adopted the Greek language, then an international language. Paul preached widely in Greece.

GREEKS Originally, this word meant women and men of the Greek race. Later, after Alexander the Great's conquests, it meant all people whose lifestyle or language was Greek. In the Bible, it also refers to the pagans.

H

HAM Noah's son, founder of the Semitic race.

HANNAH Which means "grace" or "mercy". Elkana's favourite wife. Even though she could not have children, God gave her a son. In Shiloh, she dedicated this son, Samuel, to the Lord.

HEBREWS (or **ISRAELITES**) A people of Semitic race. The Hebrews had no homeland, but came from the steppe regions of

Mesopotamia. Moses organised the people into tribes, and led by him, they finally managed to settle in Canaan. Their kingdom had glorious moments under King David and King Solomon. Later, it split into two countries: the Kingdom of Israel in the north and that of Judah in the south. The Hebrews were ruled by other peoples several times. In A.D. 70, the Roman emperor Titus destroyed the holy city of the Hebrews, Jerusalem.

HEBRON A city in southern Palestine, south of Jerusalem. Abraham, Sarah, Isaac, Rebekah, Leah, and Jacob are buried there. David lived there.

HEROD Several characters in the Bible bear this name. The first one referred to in the New Testament is Herod the Great. He succeeded in becoming king of all Palestine. His reign (37-34 B.C.) was associated with his activity as a builder and his cruelty. In the New Testament, he appears as the king who tried to kill the baby Jesus by having every baby in Palestine killed.

HEROD AGRIPPA THE FIRST He aappears in the Book of the Acts, where he is called Herod. He was proclaimed king of Palestine, by the emperor Caligula first and then by Claudius. He supported the Jews and persecuted the Christians. He had the apostle James the Greater, brother of the evangelist John, killed, and he also jailed Peter. He died accidentally in Caesarea.

HEROD ANTIPAS Son of Herod the Great and of his fourth wife. He married Herodias, his niece and sister-in-law, for which he was criticised by John the Baptist. Pressed by Herodias, he had John the Baptist jailed and later had him killed.

HERODIAS Daughter of Aristobulus and Berenice, she was first married to Herod Philip, son of Herod the Great, with whom she had her daughter Salome. Then she lived as the wife of Herod Antipas, her uncle. She was the one who told her daughter to ask for John the Baptist's head. John had blamed her for her guilty relationship with Herod Antipas. Her daughter Salome then married the tetrarch Philip, who must not be confused with Herodias's first husband, Herod Philip. When Antipas fell out of the emperor's favour, Herodias refused the imperial grace and followed him into exile.

HOSEA Israelite prophet whose book is among the best of the minor prophetic books.

HOUSE OF DAVID Refers to the descendants of King David and the kingdom of Judah. Similarly, expressions such as House of Jacob, House of Isaac, and House of Israel (Israel was Jacob's other name) refer either to the kingdom in the north or to the Hebrew people as a whole.

I

ICONIUM In the Greco-Roman age, it was the capital of Lycaonia. A wealthy city in an enchanting location, it was visited by Barnabas and Paul during their first missionary journey.

IMMANUEL Which means "God is with us". The symbolic name of the Saviour expected by the Jews. Christians think of the word as referring to Jesus.

ISAAC The head of a large Hebrew family. Son of Abraham and Sarah. He married Rebekah and had two sons, Esau and Jacob.

ISAIAH A descendant of David and the first and greatest of the four major prophets.

ISHBOSHETH Son of Saul. After Saul's death, Abner made Ishbosheth king of Israel. To escape the Philistines, he lived in Mahanaim. After losing Abner's help, he was not able to stay in power and was killed by his people. His followers joined David, who was then king of Hebron.

J

JACOB The head of a large Hebrew family. Son of Isaac. He bought his brother's birthright. After a fight with an angel, he was nicknamed "Israel", which means "fight against God". He married Leah and Rachel, daughters of Laban. The twelve tribes of Israel were descended from his twelve sons.

JAMES Son of Zebedee and brother of the apostle and evangelist John. He became a martyr in A.D. 44 under Herod Agrippa the First.

JAPHETH Son of Noah and founder of the Japhethic or Indo-European race.

JEHOVAH Which means "I am". God wished Moses and the Hebrew people to call him by this name.

JEHU Tenth king of Israel, who reigned from 842 to 815 B.C. Founder of the fifth dynasty. With the help of Elijah and Elisha, he fought against the cult of Baal.

JEREMIAH [JEREMIAS] Lived during the seventh century B.C. The second of the older prophets. The prophet of suffering and comfort. He predicted the destruction of Jerusalem, the seventy years of slavery in Babylon, and the banishments.

JERICHO Palestinian city. It was the first city that the Israelites came upon in the land of Canaan after crossing the Jordan. Thanks to God's help, the Israelites conquered Jericho and destroyed it.

JEROBOAM Which means "may the people multiply". Name of two kings of Israel. Jeroboam the First (reigned 929-909 B.C.) was the founder of the first dynasty. He belonged to Ephraim's tribe and was the chief of Solomon's workers. Solomon forced him into exile. He was responsible for founding the holy places of Bethel and Dan. He continually fought against the Kingdom of Judah. Jeroboam the Second (reigned 783-740 B.C.) was the thirteenth king of Israel. He was a member of the Jehu dynasty. He was the greatest king of Israel—as great as Solomon. He enlarged his kingdom to include Philistia, Edom, Moab, and Ammon. His kingdom was known for being luxurious and sinful and was criticised by the prophets Amos and Hosea. Jonah prophesied in favour of Jeroboam. This prophecy is contained in the Book of Jonah.

JERUSALEM Originally a Canaanite city, it was conquered by King David in the eleventh century B.C. It became the capital of the Kingdom of Judah and the seat of the temple (see **ZION**).

JESSE Which means "man of Yahweh". Father of King David and ancestor of Jesus. The Messiah is often called the "offspring of Jesse's tree".

JESUS Which means "the Lord is salvation". Born in Bethlehem, possibly in 6 B.C. He lived in Nazareth and preached the gospel in Galilee and in Judea. He was sentenced to die on the cross in A.D. 30 by the Roman procurator Pontius Pilate. He is at the centre of the New Testament, where he appears as the son of God and Saviour (see **MESSIAH**).

JEWS In the Bible, the inhabitants of the Kingdom of Judah or the province of Judea are called Jews. Generally, the word refers to the members of the Hebrew race and to all followers of the Jewish faith.

JEZEBEL Wife of Ahab, king of Israel. She followed the pagan cult of Baal and attacked

Elijah. Jehu had her thrown out of a window. In the Apocalypse her name becomes the symbol of sin.

JOAB David's military chief. He was one of the strongest supporters of David's kingdom. He could have been king himself, but he preferred the post of military dictator under the king.

JOASH King of Israel between 836 and 797 B.C. Son of Ahaziah. Joash escaped death when Athaliah had his family killed. He was made king at the age of seven.

JOHN Which means "favourite of God". Many characters in the Bible are called John. John the Apostle, son of Zebedee and Salome, was first a disciple of John the Baptist, then a disciple of Jesus. He was also a friend of Peter. Paul calls him the "pillar" of the Church. Jesus asked John to look after his mother, the Virgin Mary. John was the only apostle present at Jesus' crucifixion. Later, he settled in Ephesus, where he governed the churches of Asia Minor until his death. Under the Emperor Domitian, he was exiled to the little island of Patmos. He wrote a gospel, three letters, and the Apocalypse. His symbol is the eagle, because of the loftiness of his teachings.

JOHN THE BAPTIST Son of Zacharias and Elisabeth, who were told in their old age by the angel Gabriel that they would have this very special son. He was born about six months before his relative, Jesus. He advised sinners to repent and baptised them, which was how he acquired his nickname "the Baptist". Jesus insisted on being baptised by him. After he persistently criticised Herod Antipas for marrying his own niece, Herod jailed him. He was killed because he was hated by Herod's wife, Herodias. Jesus praised John highly, calling him the greatest of all prophets and saying that he was the Elijah the Jews had been waiting for.

JONAH Which means "dove". One of the less important prophets, usually identified with the prophet Jonah, son of Amittai, who appeared under Jeroboam the Second.

JONATHAN Which means "God has given". One of the Bible's greatest heroes. The eldest son of Saul. He was a little older than David. He knew immediately that he would befriend David. His friendship with David made Saul extremely angry.

JORDAN A river in Palestine that flows into the Dead Sea.

JOSEPH Eleventh son of Jacob and Rachel's firstborn. He was his father's favourite child. His jealous brothers sold him to the Ishmaelites, who took him to Egypt. His master's wife, offended by a refusal he made to her, had her husband imprison him. After he was freed, the pharaoh began to like him for his wisdom and ability to predict events to come. Made vice-king of Egypt, Joseph not only forgave his brothers but also welcomed his old father in Goshen. He married Asenath, daughter of Potiphar, and had two sons: Ephraim and Manasseh.

JOSEPH, MARY'S SPOUSE Which means "may God grow". Husband of the Holy Virgin, Jesus' father. He was a descendant of David. He probably died before Jesus started his public life, since the Gospels do not mention him and since the Virgin Mary was entrusted to the apostle John and not her husband.

JOSEPH OF ARIMATHEA A wealthy man from Jerusalem and a disciple of Jesus. He had Jesus' body delivered to him by Pilate. With Nicodemus's help, he then had Jesus buried in his own new tomb.

JOSHUA He replaced Moses as the guide of the chosen people and led them into the Promised Land.

JOSIAS Which means "God heals". Sixteenth king of Judah. He reigned between 640 and 609 B.C. He became king at the age of eight and ruled for thirty years. He was one of the most pious kings. He made important religious changes. He found the Book of Deuteronomy. Jeremiah preached during the time of Josias.

JUBILEE In Moses' books and also in those of the prophets, the year of the jubilee was celebrated every fifty years. Debts would be settled and slaves freed. In the Catholic faith, the word was used with a purely spiritual meaning to suggest the forgiveness of sins.

JUDAH Jacob and Leah's son. Founder of the most powerful of the twelve tribes of Israel, which occupied the southern part of the Hebraic territory.

JUDEA Name used from the time following the death of Alexander the Great to mean the western region of the Jordan, made up chiefly of the territories of the old tribes of Judah, Benjamin, and Dan.

JUDAS ISCARIOT One of the twelve apostles. Son of Simon. He always appears last on the list of apostles: He was the traitor. After Jesus was put to death, Judas felt guilty for betraying Jesus for money and killed himself.

JUDGES Chiefs of the people of Israel from a period after Joshua's death until the time of Samuel.

L

LABAN Son of Nahor, he was Rebekah's brother and therefore Jacob's uncle. He had two daughters, Leah and Rachel.

LAZARUS OF BETHANY Brother of Martha and Mary and friend of Jesus, who raised Lazarus from the dead. Six days before Jesus' last Passover, Lazarus and his sisters made him their guest for supper. Lazarus is only mentioned in the Fourth Gospel.

LEAH Laban's first daughter, Rachel's sister. Laban cunningly married her to Jacob, who had asked for Rachel's hand.

LEBANON Mountainous range in Syria famous for its cedar forests, which have now nearly disappeared.

LETTERS OF THE APOSTLES In the New Testament, there are fourteen letters or epistles written by Paul and by four other apostles.

LEVI Father of a large Hebrew family. Jacob and Leah's son. His descendants were the first Levite priestly race, dedicated to serving the temple. The Levi tribe was not given a part of the Promised Land but lived all over Israel. This was a divine chastisement to punish Levi for having joined with Simeon in some cruel murders.

LUKE A doctor from Antioch. He died in A.D. 83. He was a disciple and friend of Paul. A very skilled writer in Greek, he was the author of the Third Gospel and of the Acts of the Apostles. His writing gives us a clear understanding of Paul's ideas.

LYCIA Region and Roman province of Asia Minor.

M

MACEDONIA Region on the north coast of the Aegean Sea. It was inhabited by the Macedonians, who were originally Greek. It was made famous by King Philip and much more so by his son, Alexander the

Great. At the time of the early Christians, it was a Roman province, with Thessalonica as its capital. It was the first European area that Paul tried to convert to Christianity.

MAGI Wise men who came from the Orient to Bethlehem to worship the infant Jesus. Their homeland may have been Arabia, Mesopotamia, or Persia. Because their gifts were all Arabian products, perhaps they were Arabs. The New Testament does not say that they were kings. There were probably three of them because there were three gifts: gold, frankincense, and myrrh. Their names are not mentioned before the eighth century A.D. Traditionally, they represent Europe, Asia, and Africa.

MALTA Island in the Mediterranean, fifty-five miles south of Sicily. It belonged first to the Phoenicians, then to the Greeks, later to the Carthaginians, and finally to the Romans. The language spoken there was Phoenician, which Paul could understand. He stopped in Malta because the ship that was taking him to Rome was wrecked.

MARA A place on the east bank of the Red Sea. The Hebrews went through Mara during the Exodus. The water there tasted bitter, but Moses made it sweet by hitting it with his rod.

MARK A Hebrew from Jerusalem. He was the evangelist who wrote the Second Gospel. He was known by two names: a Hebrew name (John) and a Latin one (Mark). Converted to Christianity, he was Paul's friend and assistant and accompanied him to Rome. On this trip, which occured between A.D. 50 and 60, he may have written his gospel. Later, he prophesied in Egypt and died a martyr in Alexandria in A.D. 68. According to tradition, his body was transported to Venice in 828. He is the patron saint of Venice.

MARY In Hebrew, "Miriam". A very common name at Jesus' time. In the Old Testament it only appears as Moses' sister's name. She was a prophetess. She accompanied her brothers on the journey to the Promised Land and was with them at the happiest times.

MARY MAGDALEN Probably so called because she was from the town of Magdala on the western bank of the Sea of Tiberias. Jesus healed her of diseases and evil spirits. She was one of the devoted women who stood by the cross and visited the sepulchre of Jesus. She was the first person to see Jesus after the Resurrection.

MARY, MOTHER OF JAMES AND JOSEPH She was another of the women who stood by the cross and who visited Jesus' sepulchre. She may have been Cleophas's wife.

MARY, MOTHER OF JESUS Nearly all the known details of the Blessed Virgin's life are to be found in Luke's chapters on Jesus' childhood. She probably was from Nazareth and like her husband Joseph descended from David. She was a relative of Zacharias and Elisabeth. At the time of the Annunciation, she was engaged. The angel Gabriel hails her as "full of grace" and tells her that she will be the mother of the Messiah by the Holy Spirit, even though she will remain a virgin. At the beginning of Jesus' public activity, Mary asked her son to work the miracle of Cana. After this episode she keeps a low profile. She is present at the cross, and the dying Jesus entrusts her to the apostle John. We do not know if Mary died in Jerusalem, or in Ephesus.

MARY, MOTHER OF MARK A well-off woman from Jerusalem, she had a house with a hall and a servant. The first Christians gathered for a meeting in her house, and this was where Peter went after coming out of prison.

MARY OF BETHANY Sister of Lazarus and Martha. She was praised by Jesus for being very thoughtful. She was devoted to Jesus. Six days before Jesus' last Passover, she anointed his feet with a precious ointment.

MATTHEW Tax gatherer in Capernaum. He followed Jesus and became one of his twelve apostles. After the Ascension, he may have stayed in Palestine to preach there. According to legend he died a martyr in Ethiopia. He wrote his gospel in the Aramaic language between A.D. 42 and 50.

MEGGIDO A powerful Palestinian town. Meggido was the popular stopping place of travellers on their way from Egypt to Mesopotamia. It was conquered by the Egyptians. It later belonged to the Hebrews and finally to the Assyrians. The city lost its importance over time.

MEPHIBOSHETH Son of Jonathan and grandson of Saul. He was lame from birth. David, wishing to honour the memory of Jonathan, treated Mephibosheth with great generosity.

MESOPOTAMIA Region between the Tigris and the Euphrates.

MESSIAH A word of Hebrew origin that means the same as the Greek word *Christ*. It referred to a person blessed with divine power to accomplish a mission from God. The prophets used this word for the Saviour who was to free humanity from sin. For Christians, Jesus was the Messiah.

MICHAL Daughter of Saul and wife to David. She helped David to avoid her father's deadly tricks.

MITE A small coin or a small amount of money.

MOSES A descendant of Levi, he was born in Egypt. In order to save him from the massacre of all Hebrew babies ordered by the pharaoh, the baby Moses was placed in a cradle that was put on the river Nile. The pharaoh's daughter found him and took care of him. God revealed to him that he was chosen to free the Israelites from their slavery in Egypt and to lead them in their escape to Canaan, the land God had promised them. God gave him the Ten Commandments on Mount Sinai. He was not allowed to enter the Promised Land and died after appointing Joshua to take his place.

MOUNT OF OLIVES A hill to the west of Jerusalem, separated from it by the Cedron Valley. It is about 812 metres high and has three peaks. At its feet is the Garden of Gethsemane, where Jesus suffered agony while awaiting arrest.

N

NAPHTALI Son of Jacob and founder of an Israelite tribe. Both his tribe and the region where it settled were named after him.

NAZARETH A small village in Galilee. It is only mentioned in the New Testament. It was the village where Mary, Joseph, and the young Jesus lived.

NEBO Mount in the Abarim mountain range, situated to the east of the Dead Sea. From its peak it is possible to see the whole of Palestine. Moses climbed to this peak before he died.

NEBUCHADNEZZAR Which means "God [Nebu] protects the son". Son of Nabopolassar and ruler of the Neo-Babylonian empire between 605 and 562 B.C., he conquered Jerusalem three times and on the third occasion destroyed it. He is a character in the Book of Daniel as well as in that of Judith. He was the worst of Jerusalem's many enemies.

NEBUZARADAN The captain of Nebuchadnezzar's guard. He treated Jeremiah kindly. Five years after destroying Jerusalem, he sent the Jews into Babylon, where they were forced to remain.

NEGEB A desert area in the far south of Palestine.

NEHEMIAH Which means "God is comfort". Jewish cupbearer to King Artarxerxes the First of Persia. He reorganised the Jewish people with great energy. In the Book of Nehemiah, he tells his own story.

NERO The fifth Roman Emperor. He was in power after Claudius. Nero was famous for his cruelty. In A.D. 64 he started attacking the Christians. The best-known victims were Peter and Paul.

NINEVEH A city on the western bank of the river Tigris, opposite what is now Mosul. Genesis says that this city was founded by Nimrod. Thanks to Senna-cherib, it became the capital of the Assyrian kingdom. Ashurbanipal gathered many written tablets in his library there, which was discovered in 1850. The city was destroyed by a coalition of the Medes and the Neo-Babylonians. In the Bible, Jonah was sent to save Nineveh.

NOAH Founder of a large Hebrew family, son of Lamech and a descendant of Seth. Noah was a good man at a time of great evil and violence. God decided to send a terrible flood to destroy humanity, and to save only Noah and his family. He had three sons: Shem, Ham, and Japheth.

NOAH'S ARK A boat built by Noah according to God's orders. Noah used it for shelter at the time of the Great Flood, together with his family and two of every kind of animal.

O

OMER A unit of dry measure equal to a bit less than four litres.

P

PAMPHYLIA A region in Asia Minor, between Lycia and Cilicia on the Mediterranean. Its capital was Perga. Its name, which means "everybody's lover", comes from the fact that it had been colonised by many nations. Paul visited Perga during his first missionary journey.

PARABLE A story that illustrates a moral or religious principle.

PASSOVER Its origin can be traced back to the story in which Moses ordered the Hebrews to smear lamb's blood on the lintels and frames of their doors so that God's angel would spare their lives. Every year Jews celebrate Passover in memory of this event with a feast known as Seder.

PAUL "Saul" in Hebrew. He was born in the early first century A.D. He took part in the first persecutions against the Christians. He later became Christian and devoted his life to preaching. He accomplished several missionary journeys. He was arrested, and after spending two years in prison, he was sent to Rome. In the year 67 he was beheaded. Fourteen of his letters (the Epistles) are among the writings of the New Testament.

PENTECOST A holy day celebrated fifty days after Easter. Originally, it was a Jewish farming celebration. It then became a day to remember the Ten Commandments. During the first celebration of Pentecost after Jesus' death, the Holy Spirit descended on the apostles in the shape of tongues of fire and gave them the ability to speak many languages. They then used this ability to courageously preach Jesus' message. The Christian Pentecost is now celebrated as the birth of the Church.

PERSIA Modern Iran. As early as the age of Cyrus the Second, it was the centre of an empire that dominated the whole of the ancient orient.

PETER Simon bar Jonah. When Jesus called Simon bar Jonah to be a disciple, he changed his name to Peter, which means "rock". He was to be the rock on which Jesus was going to found his church. Originally he was a man who fished in the Sea of Tiberias. He was the brother of Andrew. He was born in Bethsaida and lived in Capernaum. He was always present during the crucial moments of Jesus' career. Jesus promised him that he would be important. He is always mentioned first in the lists of the apostles. After the Ascension he became the leader of the first Christian community, as is shown in the Book of Acts. He led the first Council of Jerusalem. According to tradition, he was crucified by the emperor Nero in A.D. 67.

PHARAOH Title given to the kings of ancient Egypt. An Egyptian pharaoh, possibly Rameses the Second, plays an important role in the Book of Exodus.

PHARISEES A Jewish sect of the period between the Old and New Testaments, it was noted for its strict observances of the rites and ceremonies of the Mosaic Law.

PHILIP Which means "friend of the horses". The name of many characters in both the Old and the New Testaments. In particular, Philip the Apostle. He was from Bethsaida and followed Jesus from the beginning. He is mentioned in the story of the multiplication of the loaves and the story of the Last Supper.

PHILIPPI A city on the coast of Macedonia. It was named after Alexander the Great's father, Philip, who turned it into a fortress. In 42 B.C. it was the site of an important battle in which Brutus and Cassius were defeated by Antony and Octavius (Augustus). Some years later Octavius defeated Antony and made Philippi a Roman colony, thereby giving its people the same rights and privileges as Romans. Paul visited Philippi on his second missionary journey.

PHILISTINES Inhabitants of Philistia (Hebrew name for Palestine).

PILATE Pontius Pilate was governor of Judea from A.D. 26 to 36. The historians Tacitus and Josephus say that he was cruel and unpopular. In the Gospels he is mostly mentioned in relation to Jesus' trial.

PISIDIA Mountainous region in the north of Pamphilia. It is cut across by the Taurus mountain range. Its main city was Antioch.

PONTUS Eastern coast of the Black Sea. Some Hebrews from Pontus were in Jerusalem on Pentecost Day when the apostles preached to the crowds. Peter's first letter was addressed to the persecuted Christians from Pontus.

POTIPHAR Egyptian official in the pharaoh's court who bought Joseph, Jacob's son, as a slave.

POZZUOLLI or **PUTEOLI** Which means "little well". A port in Italy north of Naples, founded in 528 B.C. and well known for its sulphurous thermal springs. It was a boarding point for passengers to and from Rome. Paul stopped here and was made welcome by the Christians of the town.

PRIESTS Aaron was the first Hebrew priest. The priests had to teach, offer sacrifices, and—after the temple was built—administer its belongings and look after it. They had to wear a particular suit and avoid impure acts. They were divided into twenty-four classes and at their head was the high priest, the holiest sacrificer.

PRODIGAL Carelessly extravagant.

PROPHETS Prophets were messengers. They were called by God to hear His plans and His messages. Then they were sent by him to bring his message to the people or to accomplish particular missions.

PSALM From the Greek "psalterion", meaning stringed instrument. The word in its original sense meant a song accompanied by a stringed instrument. The Hebrews referred to the psalms in the Bible as prayers.

PUBLICANS Tax collectors.

R

RACHEL Daughter of Laban, wife of Jacob, sister of Leah. She was the mother of Joseph and Benjamin.

RAMESES (also **RAMSES**) Egyptian city in the country of Goshen. Rameses the Second named it after himself. The departure of the Israelites to the Promised Land started from this city.

REBEKAH Sister of Laban, wife of Isaac. She was the mother of Esau and Jacob.

REPHIDIM Area close to Sinai where the Israelites stopped during their exodus to the Promised Land. A dry and parched region, where Moses struck a rock with his rod to produce water.

REHOBOAM Son of Solomon and Naamah and first king of Judah after the division of the kingdom. He reigned from 931 to 913 B.C.

ROMANS People who lived in or came from Rome or enjoyed the rights of Roman citizens. When the Jews heard about the conquests of the Romans (see the Book of Maccabees), they were so impressed that they considered joining forces with them. Rome became first the guardian of the Jews and then their master.

S

SADDUCEES One of the two great parties of Judaism from the second century B.C. until A.D. 70. They exercised a strong political influence, but most of their members were priests. Their name comes from Zadok, the high priest during Solomon's reign. They only recognised the Law. They did not believe that the dead could be resurrected or in the existence of spirits. They rejected all oral traditions. They are frequently mentioned in the Gospels and are described in the works of Josephus.

SAMARIA, SAMARITANS Name of both a district and its capital city. In the time of the Maccabees and of Jesus Christ, the district included the central part of Palestine, between Galilee and Judea. The city occupied a good position for defence, on a mountain 473 metres above sea level.

SAMSON Which means "the sun". Son of Manoah, born in Zorah, fifteen miles west of Jerusalem. He was a man of great strength. He fought against the Philistines and died in an act of vengeance against them.

SAMUEL Last of the line of judges. He lived in the eleventh century B.C. His birth was prophesied to Hannah. The monarchy began when he anointed Saul king of Israel. After Saul betrayed his trust, he made David the king.

SARAH Wife of Abraham.

SATAN Which means "the enemy". Originally, the word meant any kind of opponent. In the Book of Chronicles it means specifically the fallen angel who tempts Man to oppose God. The character of Satan is clearly defined in the New Testament.

SAUL Hebrew king chosen by Samuel. He died in battle against the Philistines.

SAUL, see **PAUL**

SCRIBES Those who served as copyists, editors, and teachers of the Scriptures in ancient Israel during New Testament times.

SERAPHIM, see **ANGELS**

SHECHEM Town in the centre of Palestine.

SHEKEL A unit of weight equal to 14 grams, and a coin of this weight.

SHEM Son of Noah, ancestor of Abraham.

SHILOH Ancient place in Palestine, within the borders of the tribe of Ephraim and about twenty-five miles to the north of Jerusalem. Here the first Jewish assemblies took place. It was also a place to which people made pilgrimages. It was here that the Ark of the Covenant and the Tabernacle were kept.

SIDON One of the oldest and most important maritime towns in Phoenicia.

SILAS A Jewish Christian from Jerusalem and a Roman citizen, he went with Paul on his second voyage to Corinth. He stopped in Berea with Timotheus. He is linked with Paul and Timotheus in sending the two letters to the Thessalonians. He is also the Silas who carried the first of the Letters of Paul to its destination.

SIMEON Which means "God has granted my prayer". In the Old Testament, son of Jacob and Leah. In the New Testament, he is the aged witness who, seeing Christ brought into the temple, speaks the prayer later known as the "Nunc Dimittis", and a prophetic blessing of the Holy Virgin.

SIMON BAR JONAH, see **PETER**

SIMON OF CYRENE Father of Alexander and Rufus. He was forced by the soldiers to carry the cross of Christ.

SIMON THE CANAANITE He was an apostle. In the Book of the Acts, he is called Simon the Zealot. We do not know for sure if he really was a member of the party of the Zealots, which wanted to free Palestine from Roman rule by force.

SIN Desert region in the southern part of the Sinai peninsula.

SINAI, MOUNT On Mount Sinai, 245 metres high, Moses received from God the tablets with the Ten Commandments.

SOLOMON Which means "the wise". Son of David and Bathsheba. He ascended the throne of Israel after David.

STEPHEN Which means "crowned". One of the seven deacons of the early Church. Of Greek origin, he is presented as "a man full of faith and the Holy Spirit". He had a strong influence on the Christian community because of his miracles and his predictions. The Jews loathed him and condemned him to be stoned. Saul approved of his murder. Stephen became the first Christian martyr.

SYRACUSE Town on the south coast of Sicily, founded in 735 B.C. and colonised first by the Corinthians, then by other Greeks.

SYRIA Refers to the lands to the east of the Mediterranean that lie between the sea and the desert. After Alexander the Great, it was governed by the Seleucid dynasty. Later it became a Roman province.